Fodor's InFocus

SANTA FE

14 TOP EXPERIENCES

Santa Fe offers terrific experiences that should be on every traveler's list. Here are Fodor's top picks for a memorable trip.

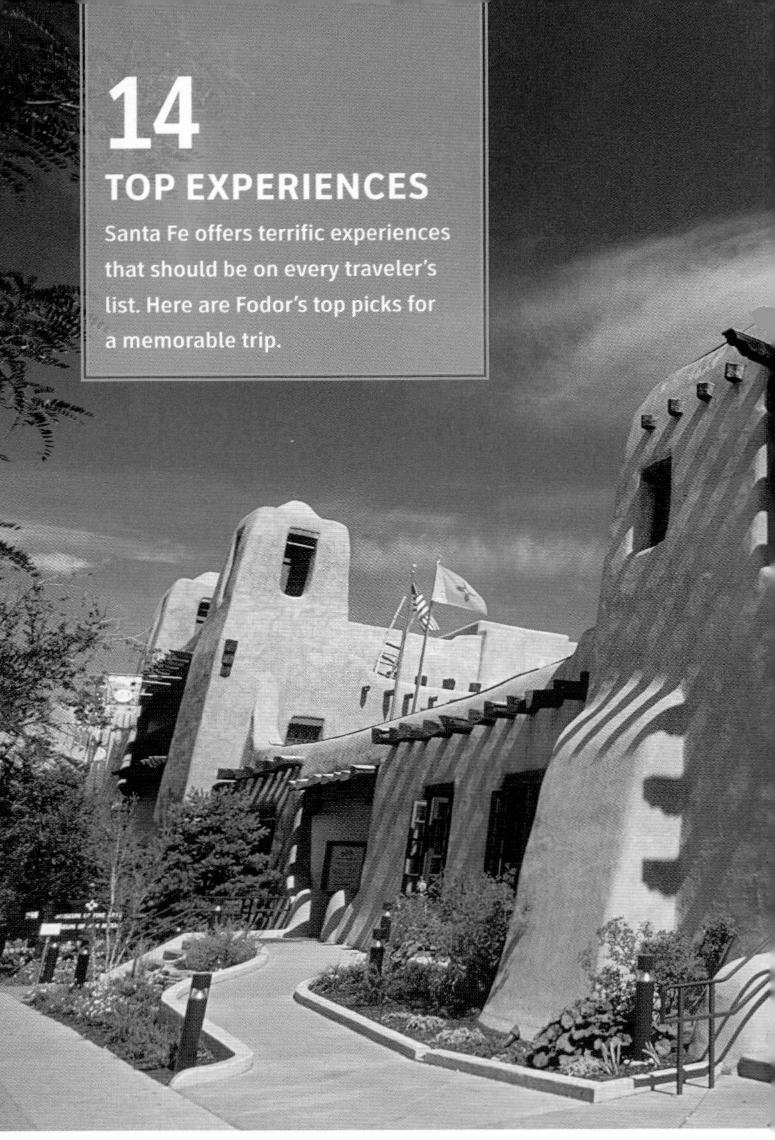

1 Museums

Learn about local and regional culture at the excellent institutions on Santa Fe's Museum Hill. The Museum of Indian Arts and Culture (pictured) presents interactive exhibits in its adobe-style building. *(Ch. 2)*

2 Dining

A rising national culinary destination, the city has superb restaurants that offer both traditional New Mexican fare and more eclectic global cuisine. *(Ch. 3)*

3 Railyard District

The popular indoor-outdoor farmers' market, a fun urban park, and hip restaurants, galleries, and indie shops keep things bustling in this redeveloped area. *(Ch. 2)*

4 Turquoise Trail

A fabled, 70-mile-long mountain drive between Santa Fe and Albuquerque, scenic NM 14 weaves past rustic houses, churches, and old mining towns such as Madrid. *(Ch. 8)*

5 Santa Fe Opera

Simply stunning, the opera's indoor-outdoor amphitheater is carved into a hillside. A noted summer festival presents five works every June through August. *(Ch. 5)*

6 Galleries

Gallery hopping is a prime activity in Santa Fe, including First Friday night Art Walks. The city's nearly 200 galleries tempt with ceramics, paintings, photography, and sculptures for all budgets. *(Ch. 6)*

7 Santa Fe Plaza

Join the fun in this lively square, the city's historic heart and gathering spot. Events such as September's Fiestas de Santa Fe are good times to explore galleries and restaurants—or browse in tourist shops. *(Ch. 2)*

8 Intimate Inns

Unwind in a southwestern-style abode like the captivating Inn of the Anasazi. Traditional artwork, handcrafted furnishings, and authentic woven rugs capture the city's unique ambience. *(Ch. 4)*

9 Georgia O'Keeffe

Connect with the work of this prominent American Modernist artist, who drew inspiration from the area's landscape, at the exceptional Georgia O'Keeffe Museum. You can also visit her house in Abiquiu. *(Ch. 2, 8)*

10 Holiday Season

Ancient buildings aglow in lights, Christmas Eve strolls, and elaborate celebrations make the city's most festive season a truly magical experience. *(Ch. 2)*

11 Kasha Katuwe Tent Rocks National Monument

Known for bizarre sandstone rock formations that look like stacked tepees, this box canyon is a memorable hiking getaway about 40 miles west of Santa Fe. *(Ch. 8)*

12 Bandelier National Monument

See the cave dwellings and ceremonial kivas of ancestral Puebloans in this 33,000-acre natural wonder with abundant wildlife, waterfalls, cliffs, and mesas. *(Ch. 8)*

13 Spas

Indulge yourself in a day (or two) of relaxation at a tranquil retreat such as Bishop's Lodge's ShāNah Spa, set against the striking Sangre de Cristo mountains. *(Ch. 4)*

14 Native American Culture

Santa Fe celebrates Native culture at historic monuments and museums throughout the city. During the summer, Museum Hill's Milner Plaza hosts Native American dances and jewelry-making demonstrations *(Ch. 2)*

CONTENTS

About this Guide. 10

1 EXPERIENCE SANTA FE. . 11

What's Where 12

Santa Fe Planner 14

What's New in New Mexico. . . 15

If You Like 16

Great Itineraries 18

Glossary of Terms 21

2 EXPLORING SANTA FE . . 25

3 WHERE TO EAT 47

4 WHERE TO STAY 73

5 NIGHTLIFE AND THE ARTS 87

Nightlife 88

The Arts 90

6 SHOPS, GALLERIES, AND SPAS. 95

Art Galleries 96

Shops. 101

Spas 110

7 SPORTS AND THE OUTDOORS. 115

8 DAY TRIPS FROM SANTA FE 123

The Turquoise Trail. 124

Kasha-Katuwe Tent Rocks National Monument. 127

The Santa Fe Trail 127

Bandelier and Los Alamos . . .131

Georgia O'Keeffe Country. . . .134

The High Road to Taos 136

9 ALBUQUERQUE. 141

Orientation and Planning. . . .143

Exploring. 149

Where to Eat. 163

Where to Stay 175

Nightlife and the Arts. 183

Shopping. 187

Sports and the Outdoors 191

10 TAOS 195

Orientation and Planning. . . .197

Exploring. 201

Where to Eat. 209

Where to Stay 216

Nightlife and the Arts. 220

Shopping. 222

Sports and the Outdoors 225

TRAVEL SMART SANTA FE 229

INDEX 243

ABOUT OUR WRITERS . . 256

MAPS

Downtown Santa Fe 35

Where to Eat in Downtown Santa Fe 50

Where to Eat in Greater Santa Fe 66–67

Where to Stay in Downtown Santa Fe. 78

Where to Stay in Greater Santa Fe 82–83

Day Trips from Santa Fe 129

Albuquerque. 150–151

Albuquerque Old Town. 155

Where to Eat in Albuquerque. 168–169

Where to Stay in Albuquerque. 178–179

Taos 204

Where to Eat in Taos 210

Where to Stay in Taos 217

ABOUT THIS GUIDE

Fodor's Recommendations

Everything in this guide is worth doing—we don't cover what isn't—but exceptional sights, hotels, and restaurants are recognized with additional accolades. Fodor's Choice★ indicates our top recommendations; and **Best Bets** call attention to notable hotels and restaurants in various categories. Care to nominate a new place? Visit Fodors.com/contact-us.

Trip Costs

We list prices wherever possible to help you budget well. Hotel and restaurant price categories from **$** to **$$$$** are noted alongside each recommendation. For hotels, we include the lowest cost of a standard double room in high season. For restaurants, we cite the average price of a main course at dinner or, if dinner isn't served, at lunch. For attractions, we always list adult admission fees; discounts are usually available for children, students, and senior citizens.

Hotels

Our local writers vet every hotel to recommend the best overnights in each price category, from budget to expensive. Unless otherwise specified, you can expect private bath, phone, and TV in your room. For expanded hotel reviews, facilities, and deals visit Fodors.com.

Restaurants

Unless we state otherwise, restaurants are open for lunch and dinner daily. We mention dress code only when there's a specific requirement and reservations only when they're essential or not accepted. To make restaurant reservations, visit Fodors.com.

Credit Cards

The hotels and restaurants in this guide typically accept credit cards. If not, we'll say so.

Top Picks

★ Fodor's Choice

Listings

- ✉ Address
- Branch address
- Mailing address
- ☎ Telephone
- Fax
- Website
- E-mail
- Admission fee
- Open/closed times
- Ⓜ Subway
- Directions or Map coordinates

Hotels & Restaurants

- Hotel
- Number of rooms
- Meal plans
- ✕ Restaurant
- Reservations
- Dress code
- No credit cards
- $ Price

Other

- ⇨ See also
- ☞ Take note
- Golf facilities

EXPERIENCE SANTA FE

WHAT'S WHERE

1 The Plaza. The heart of historic Santa Fe.

2 Old Santa Fe Trail and South Capitol. A historic section that joins the plaza after passing the state capitol and some of the area's oldest neighborhoods.

3 East Side and Canyon Road. One of the city's oldest streets lined with galleries, shops, and restaurants housed in adobe compounds.

4 Museum Hill. Camino Lejo, aka Museum Hill, has four museums, the new Santa Fe Botanical Garden, a café, and superb views of the Jeméz and Sangre de Cristo mountains.

5 The Railyard District. Formerly known as the Guadalupe District, this area is home to the vibrant farmers' market, hip restaurants, shops, and contemporary art galleries.

6 West of the Plaza. This mostly residential neighborhood contains one main commercial thoroughfare, Guadalupe Street, which has several notable restaurants and shops.

7 North Side. This scenic expanse of Sangre de Cristo foothills is home to the charming village of Tesuque, the Santa Fe Opera House, and some fine resorts (Ten Thousand Waves, the Four Seasons).

8 South Side. A sprawling tract of residential and commercial development with affordable chain lodgings (mostly along Cerrillos Road) that extends from south of the Railyard District to Interstate 25.

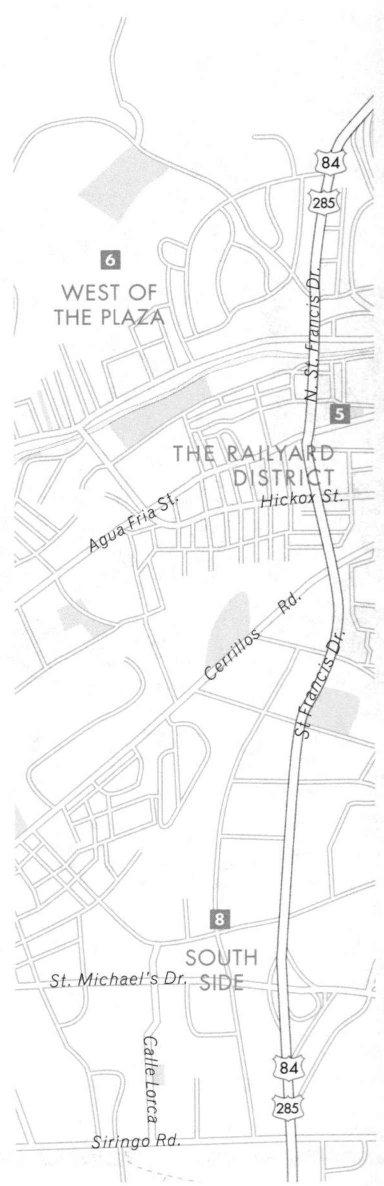

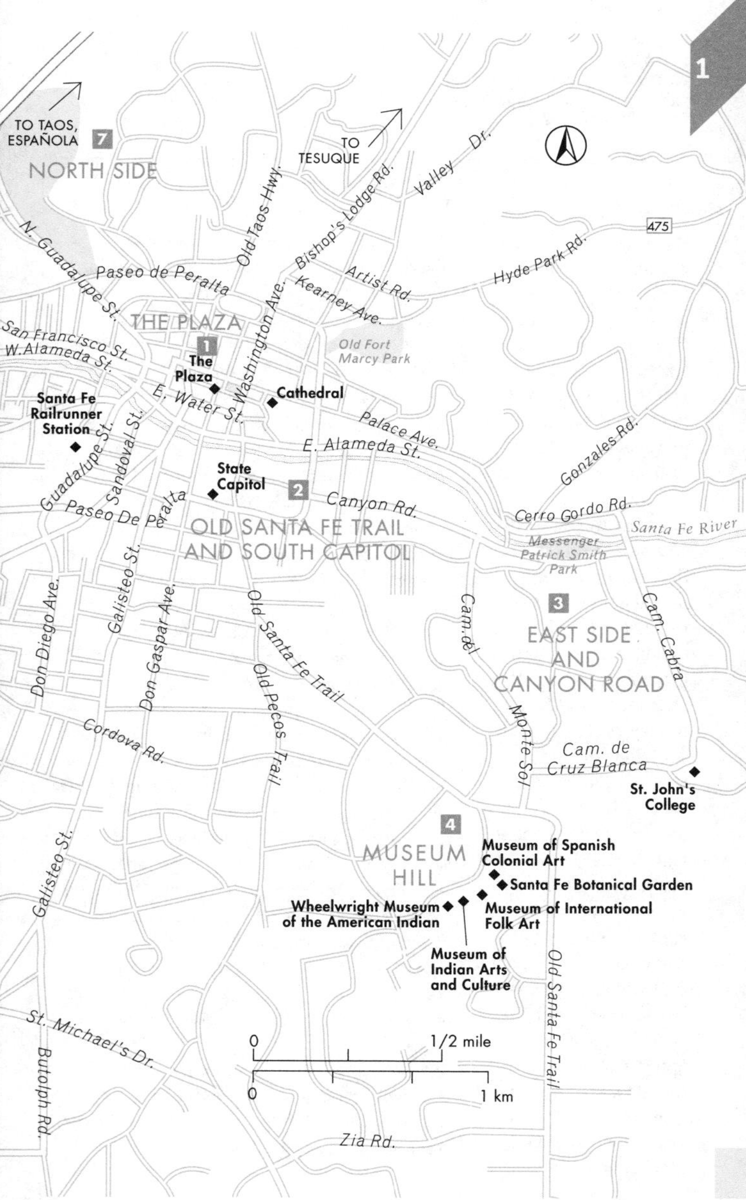
1
TO TAOS, ESPAÑOLA
7
NORTH SIDE
TO TESUQUE
Valley Dr.
475
Old Taos Hwy.
Bishop's Lodge Rd.
Hyde Park Rd.
N. Guadalupe St.
Paseo de Peralta
Artist Rd.
Kearney Ave.
Washington Ave.
THE PLAZA
San Francisco St.
W. Alameda St.
1
The Plaza
Old Fort Marcy Park
Cathedral
Santa Fe Railrunner Station
E. Water St.
Palace Ave.
E. Alameda St.
Gonzales Rd.
Guadalupe St.
Sandoval St.
State Capitol
2
Canyon Rd.
Paseo De Peralta
Cerro Gordo Rd.
Santa Fe River
OLD SANTA FE TRAIL AND SOUTH CAPITOL
Messenger Patrick Smith Park
Galisteo St.
Don Diego Ave.
Don Gaspar Ave.
Old Santa Fe Trail
Old Pecos Trail
Cam. del Monte Sol
3
EAST SIDE AND CANYON ROAD
Cam. Cabra
Cordova Rd.
Cam. de Cruz Blanca
St. John's College
4
MUSEUM HILL
Museum of Spanish Colonial Art
Santa Fe Botanical Garden
Wheelwright Museum of the American Indian
Museum of International Folk Art
Museum of Indian Arts and Culture
Galisteo St.
Old Santa Fe Trail
St. Michael's Dr.
0
1/2 mile
0
1 km
Butolph Rd.
Zia Rd.

SANTA FE PLANNER

When to Go

Hotel rates are highest in summer. Between September and November and in April and May they're lower, and (except for the major holidays) from December to March they're the lowest. Santa Fe has four distinct seasons, and the sun shines brightly during all of them (about 320 days a year). June through August temperatures typically hit the high 80s to low 90s during the day and the low 50s at night, with afternoon rain showers usually cooling the air. The often sudden rain showers can come unexpectedly and quickly drench you. September and October bring beautiful weather and a marked reduction in crowds. Temperatures—and prices—drop significantly after Halloween. December through March is ski season. Spring comes late at this elevation. April and May are blustery, with warmer weather finally arriving in May.

Getting Here and Around

Santa Fe is easy to reach by plane but a full day's drive from major metro areas in the neighboring states. Unless you're a big fan of long road trips (the scenery en route is spectacular, especially coming from Arizona, Utah, and Colorado), it generally makes the most sense to fly here.

Most visitors to Santa Fe and north-central New Mexico fly into the state's main air gateway, Albuquerque International Sunport (ABQ), which is served by all of the nation's major domestic airlines as well as some smaller regional ones; there are direct flights from all major West Coast and Midwest cities and a number of big East Coast cities. From here it's an easy 60-minute drive to Santa Fe, or a 2½-hour drive to Taos (shuttle services are available). Santa Fe Municipal Airport (SAF) has ramped up commercial service in recent years and is increasingly a viable option, as it now has direct flights on American Airlines from Dallas and Los Angeles, Great Lakes Airline from Denver and Phoenix, and United from Denver. A car is your best way to get around the region. You can see much of Downtown Santa Fe and Taos on foot, but a car is handy for exploring farther afield. In Albuquerque a car is really a necessity for any serious touring and exploring. Note that it's easy to get from Albuquerque to Santa Fe either by regularly scheduled shuttle bus or on the scenic Rail Runner commuter train. *For more flight information and ground transportation options, see the Travel Smart section at the back of this book.*

WHAT'S NEW IN NEW MEXICO

Garden Party

In summer 2013, the much-awaited Santa Fe Botanical Garden opened on Museum Hill, joining that neighborhood's clutch of superb museums and taking advantage of the great mountain and mesa views afforded from this area of town. The 12-acre garden has four distinct sections laced by easy, well-marked trails. This is one of the newest attractions in the region, joining the small but excellent Pablita Velarde Museum of Women in the Arts, which occupies a historic adobe building near downtown's Cathedral Basilica.

Hotel Happenings

Santa Fe's glamorous and still relatively young Rancho Encantado resort became an even lovelier place to stay in 2012 when the venerable Four Seasons brand took over the property—for a special-occasion getaway, it's hard to beat this intimate compound on a secluded hillside in the foothills northeast of Santa Fe. The Four Seasons is one of several spa-oriented resorts in the region that have upped their game, including the historic and tranquil Ojo Caliente Mineral Springs Resort & Spa, about an hour north of Santa Fe, which has added luxury casitas and suites and undergone an ambitious makeover that balances modern elegance with this laid-back property's friendly vibe and vintage aesthetic. On the horizon, with an anticipated opening of summer 2014, the historic (and huge) 1950s former St. Vincent Hospital building—just a few blocks east of the Plaza in Santa Fe—will become the 182-room Drury Plaza Hotel. A restaurant, meeting center, and parking garage are part of the plans for this ambitious hotel project from the mid-priced, Missouri-based Drury Hotels chain.

New Trails to Santa Fe

Well, contrails anyway. After years of little or no commercial air service, Santa Fe Municipal Airport (SAF) ushered in daily service from two of the nation's busiest airports, DFW in Dallas and LAX in Los Angeles, on American Eagle (the regional carrier of American Airlines). The service has been highly popular, which helped spur Great Lakes Airline to add service to SAF from Denver and Phoenix, and United to add its own Denver flight in 2013. It's now easier to reach Santa Fe as well as points north, such as Las Vegas and Taos, as Santa Fe's small, convenient airport is an hour closer to these areas than Albuquerque, which also has added new service in 2013: JetBlue now flies to the Duke City directly from New York City's JFK Airport, providing one of the few direct routes from the East Coast to New Mexico.

IF YOU LIKE

Historic Sites

There's no state in the Union with a richer historical heritage than New Mexico, which contains not only buildings constructed by Europeans well before the Pilgrims set foot in Massachusetts but also still-inhabited pueblos that date back more than a millennium. Santa Fe and the surrounding region are particularly rife with ancient sites, including mystical Native American ruins and weathered adobe buildings. Stately plazas laid out as fortifications by the Spanish in the 17th century still anchor many communities in this part of the state, including Albuquerque, Las Vegas, Santa Fe, and Taos. Side trips from these cities lead to ghost towns and deserted pueblos that have been carefully preserved by historians. Here are some of the top draws for history buffs.

Santa Fe's **San Miguel Mission** is a simple, earth-hue adobe structure built in about 1625—it's the oldest church still in use in the continental United States.

A United Nations World Heritage Site, the 1,000-year-old **Taos Pueblo** has the largest collection of multistory pueblo dwellings in the United States.

The oldest public building in the United States, the Pueblo-style **Palace of the Governors** anchors Santa Fe's historic Plaza and has served as the residence for 100 Spanish, Native American, Mexican, and American governors; it's now the state history museum.

A scenic hour-long side trip from Santa Fe, the small town of Las Vegas, which was developed as a major stop on the Old Santa Fe Trail, has one of the most picturesque plazas in New Mexico and is also home to several historic districts and more than 900 buildings on the National Register of Historic Places.

Hiking Adventures

At just about every turn in northern New Mexico, whether you're high in the mountains or low in a dramatic river canyon, hiking opportunities abound. Five national forests cover many thousands of acres around New Mexico, as do 40 state parks and a number of other national and state monuments and recreation areas. Ski areas from Albuquerque north to Taos make for great mountaineering during the warmer months, and the state's many Native American ruins are also laced with trails.

Hiking is a year-round activity in Santa Fe and the surrounding area, as you can virtually always find temperate weather somewhere in the state. Consider the following areas for an engaging ramble.

About midway between Santa Fe and Albuquerque, **Kasha-Katuwe Tent Rocks National Monument** is so named because its bizarre rock formations look like tepees rising over a narrow box canyon. The hike here is relatively short and only moderately challenging, offering plenty of bang for the buck.

On the main road to Santa Fe's ski area, the Aspen Vista Trail takes in breathtaking fall-foliage scenery but makes for an enjoyable trek in spring and summer, too—in winter, it's a popular spot for snowshoeing.

One of the more strenuous hiking challenges in the state is **Wheeler Peak**. The 8-mile trek to New Mexico's highest point (elevation 13,161 feet) rewards visitors with stunning views of the Taos Ski Valley.

From the northeastern fringes of Albuquerque, **La Luz Trail** winds 9 miles (with an elevation gain of more than 3,000 feet) to Sandia Crest.

Dramatic Photo Ops

Northern New Mexico's spectacular landscapes and crystal clear atmosphere can help just about any amateur with a decent camera produce professional-quality photos. Many of the common scenes around the state seem tailor-made for photography sessions: terra-cotta-hued adobe buildings against azure blue skies, souped-up lowrider automobiles cruising along wide-open highways, and rustic fruit and chile stands by the side of the road. In summer, dramatic rain clouds contrast with vermilion sunsets to create memorable images. Come fall, shoot the foliage of cottonwood and aspen trees, and in winter, snap the state's snowcapped mountains.

The **High Road to Taos,** a stunning drive from Santa Fe with a rugged alpine backdrop, encompasses rolling hillsides studded with orchards and tiny villages.

More than 500 balloons lift off from the **Albuquerque International Balloon Fiesta,** affording shutterbugs countless opportunities for great photos—whether from the ground or the air. And there are year-round opportunities to soar above the city.

The dizzyingly high **Rio Grande Gorge Bridge,** near Taos, stands 650 feet above the Rio Grande—the reddish rocks dotted with green scrub contrast brilliantly against the blue sky.

GREAT ITINERARIES

ALBUQUERQUE TO TAOS: NEW MEXICO MOUNTAIN HIGH

Day 1: Albuquerque

Start out by strolling through the shops of Old Town Plaza, then visit the New Mexico Museum of Natural History and Science. Also check out the Albuquerque Museum of Art and History and then make your way over to the Albuquerque Biological Park, which contains the aquarium, zoo, and botanic park. For lunch, try Church Street Café in Old Town.

Later in the afternoon, you'll need a car to head east a couple of miles along Central to reach the University of New Mexico's main campus and the nearby Nob Hill District. Start with a stroll around campus with its many historic adobe buildings; if you have time, pop inside either the Maxwell Museum of Anthropology or the University Art Museum. Afterwards, walk east along Central into Nob Hill and check out the dozens of offbeat shops. If it's summer, meaning that you still have some time before the sun sets, it's worth detouring from Old Town to Far Northeast Heights (a 15-minute drive), where you can take the Sandia Peak Aerial Tramway 2.7 miles up to Sandia Peak for spectacular sunset views of the city. Have dinner back in Nob Hill at Zinc or Zacatecas. If you're up for more fun, head back Downtown for a bit of late-night barhopping.

Days 2 and 3: Santa Fe

On Day 2, head to Santa Fe early in the morning by driving up the scenic Turquoise Trail; when you arive, explore the adobe charms of the Downtown central Plaza. Visit the Palace of the Governors and check out the adjacent New Mexico History Museum. At the nearby Museum of Indian Arts and Culture you can see works by Southwestern artists, and a short drive away at the Museum of International Folk Art you can see how different cultures in New Mexico and elsewhere in the world have expressed themselves artistically. Give yourself time to stroll the narrow, adobe-lined streets and treat yourself to some authentic New Mexican cuisine in the evening, perhaps with a meal at The Shed or Cafe Pasqual's.

On your second day in town, plan to walk a bit. Head east from the Plaza up to Canyon Road and peruse the galleries. Have lunch at one of the restaurants midway uphill, such as the Teahouse or El Farol. If you're up for some exercise, hike the foothills—there are trails within beginning at the Randall Davey Audubon Center and also from the free parking area (off Cerro Gordo Road) leading into

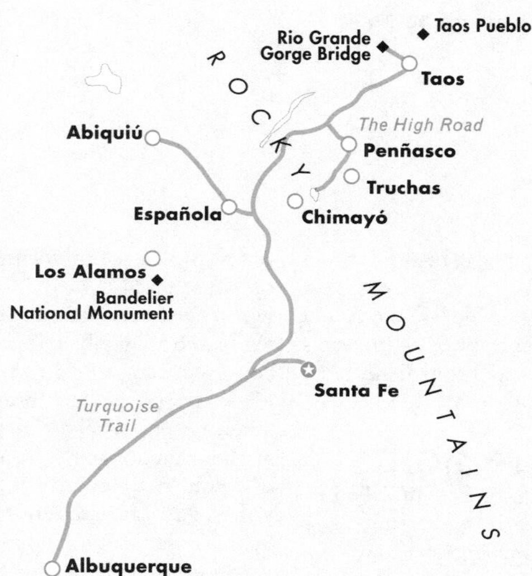

the Dale Ball Trail Network, both a short drive from the Plaza. You might want to try one of Santa Fe's truly stellar, upscale restaurants your final night in town, either La Boca or the French bistro Bouche.

Day 4: Abiquiú

From Santa Fe, drive north up U.S. 285/84 through Española, and then take U.S. 84 from Española up to Abiquiú, the fabled community where Georgia O'Keeffe lived and painted for much of the final five decades of her life. On your way up, make the detour toward Los Alamos and spend the morning visiting Bandelier National Monument. In Abiquiú, plan to tour Georgia O'Keeffe's home (open mid-March–late November).

Days 5 and 6: Taos

Begin by strolling around Taos Plaza, taking in the galleries and crafts shops. Head south two blocks to visit the Harwood Museum. Then walk north on Paseo del Pueblo to the Taos Art Museum and Fechin House. In the afternoon, drive out to the Rio Grande Gorge Bridge. On your way back to town see the Millicent Rogers Museum. In the evening, stop in at the Adobe Bar at the Taos Inn and plan for dinner at Love Apple or Antonio's. On the second day, drive out to Taos Pueblo in the morning and tour the ancient village. Return to town and go to the Blumenschein Home and Museum, lunching afterward at the Dragonfly Café. After, drive out to La Hacienda de los Martinez for a look at early life in Taos and then to Ranchos de Taos to see the San Francisco de Asís Church.

Day 7: The High Road

On your final day, drive back down toward Albuquerque and Santa Fe via the famed High Road, which twists through a series of tiny, historic villages—including Peñasco, Truchas, and Chimayó.

In the latter village, be sure to stop by El Santuario de Chimayó. Have lunch at Rancho de Chimayó, and do a little shopping at Ortega's Weaving Shop. From here, it's a 30-minute drive to Santa Fe.

SANTA FE SIGHTS

It's best to explore Santa Fe one neighborhood at a time and arrange your activities within each. If you've got more than two days, be sure to explore the northern Rio Grande Valley. For the best tour, combine your adventures in Santa Fe with some from the Side Trips section, which highlights several trips within a 30- to 90-minute drive of town.

Plan on spending a full day wandering around Santa Fe Plaza, strolling down narrow lanes, under portals, and across ancient cobbled streets. Sip coffee on the Plaza, take in a museum or two (or three) and marvel at the cathedral. The **New Mexico History Museum** and **Palace of the Governors** are great places to start to gain a sense of the history and cultures that influence this area. ■ TIP→ **Take one of the docent-led tours offered by the museums.** Almost without exception the docents are engaging and passionate about their subjects. You gain invaluable insight into the collections and their context by taking these free tours. Inquire at the front desk of the museums for more information.

A few miles south of the Plaza on Museum Hill, you'll find four world-class museums, all quite different and all highly relevant to the culture of Santa Fe and northern New Mexico, plus the brand-new Santa Fe Botanical Garden. Start at the intimate gem, the **Museum of Spanish Colonial Art,** where you'll gain a real sense of the Spanish empire's influence on the world beyond Spain. The **Museum of International Folk Art** is thoroughly engaging for both young and old. If you have the stamina to keep going, have a tasty lunch at the Museum Hill Café and then visit the **Museum of Indian Arts and Culture** before moving on to the **Wheelwright Museum of the American Indian.** There is a path linking all these museums together, and the walk is easy. The museum shops are all outstanding—if you're a shopper, you could easily spend an entire day in the shops alone.

A short walk from any of the Downtown lodgings, Canyon Road should definitely be explored on foot. Take any of the side streets and stroll among historical homes and ancient *acequias* (irrigation ditches). If you really enjoy walking, keep going up the road past Cristo Rey Church, where the street gets even narrower and is lined with residential compounds. At the top is the **Randall Davey Audubon Center**, where bird-watching abounds.

GLOSSARY OF TERMS

Perhaps more than any other region in the United States, New Mexico has its own distinctive cuisine and architectural style, both heavily influenced by Native American, Spanish-colonial, Mexican, and American frontier traditions. The brief glossary that follows explains terms used frequently in this book.

Menu Guide

Aguacate: Spanish for avocado, the key ingredient of guacamole.

Albóndigas: Meatballs, usually cooked with rice in a meat broth.

Bizcochitos: Buttery cookies flavored with cinnamon and anise seeds and served typically at Christmas but available throughout the year.

Burrito: A warm flour tortilla wrapped around meat, beans, and vegetables and smothered in chiles and cheese; many New Mexicans also love breakfast burritos (filled with any combination of the above, along with eggs and, typically, bacon or sausage and potatoes).

Calabacitas: Summer squash, usually served with corn, chiles, and other vegetables.

Carne adovada: Red-chile-marinated pork (or, occasionally, chicken).

Chalupa: A corn tortilla deep-fried in the shape of a bowl, filled with pinto beans (sometimes meat), and topped with cheese, guacamole, sour cream, lettuce, tomatoes, and salsa.

Chicharrones: Fried pork rinds.

Chilaquiles: Often served at breakfast, this casserole-like dish consists of small pieces of fried tortillas baked with red or green chiles, bits of chicken or cheese, and sometimes eggs.

Chile relleno: A poblano pepper peeled, stuffed with cheese or a special mixture of spicy ingredients, dipped in batter, and fried.

Chile: A stewlike dish with Texas origins that typically contains beans, beef, and red chile.

Chiles: New Mexico's infamous hot peppers, which come in an endless variety of sizes and in various degrees of hotness, from the thumb-size jalapeño to the smaller and often hotter serrano. They can be canned or fresh, dried or cut up into salsa. Most traditional New Mexican dishes are served either with green, red, or both types of chiles (ask for "Christmas" when indicating to your server that you'd like both red and green). Famous regional uses for green chile include green-chile stew (usually made with shredded pork), green-chile cheeseburgers, and green-chile-and-cheese tamales.

Chimichanga: The same as a burrito, only deep-fried and topped with a dab of sour cream or salsa. (The chimichanga was allegedly invented in Tucson, Arizona.)

Chipotle: A dried smoked jalapeño with a smoky, almost sweet, chocolaty flavor.

Chorizo: Well-spiced Spanish sausage, made with pork and red chiles.

Enchilada: A rolled or flat corn tortilla filled with meat, chicken, seafood, or cheese, an enchilada is covered with chile and baked. The ultimate enchilada is made with blue Native American corn tortillas. New Mexicans order them flat, sometimes topped with a fried egg.

Fajitas: A Tex-Mex dish of grilled beef, chicken, fish, or roasted vegetables and served with peppers, onions, and pico de gallo, served with tortillas; traditionally known as *arracheras*.

Flauta: A tortilla filled with cheese or meat and rolled into a flutelike shape ("flauta" means flute) and lightly fried.

Frijoles refritos: Refried beans, often seasoned with lard or cheese.

Frito Pie: Originally from Texas but extremely popular in New Mexican diners and short-order restaurants, this savory, humble casserole consists of Fritos snack chips layered with chile, cheese, green onions, and pinto beans.

Guacamole: Mashed avocado, mixed with tomatoes, garlic, onions, lemon juice, and chiles, used as a dip, a side dish, or a topping.

Hatch: A small southern New Mexico town in the Mesilla Valley, known for its outstanding production and quality of both green and red chiles. The "Hatch" name often is found on canned chile food products.

Huevos rancheros: New Mexico's answer to eggs Benedict—eggs doused with chile and sometimes melted cheese, served on top of a corn tortilla (they're best with a side order of chorizo).

Nopalitos: The pads of the prickly pear cactus, typically cut up and served uncooked in salads or baked or stir-fried as a vegetable side dish. (The tangy-sweet, purplish-red fruit of the prickly pear is often used to make juice drinks and margaritas.)

Posole: Resembling popcorn soup, this is a sublime marriage of lime, hominy, pork, chiles, garlic, and spices.

Quesadilla: A folded flour tortilla filled with cheese and meat or vegetables and warmed or lightly fried so the cheese melts.

Queso: Cheese; an ingredient in many Mexican and Southwestern recipes (cheddar or Jack is used most commonly in New Mexican dishes).

Ristra: String of dried red chile peppers, often used as decoration.

Salsa: Finely chopped concoction of green and red chile peppers, mixed with onion, garlic, and other spices.

Sopaipilla: Puffy deep-fried bread that's similar to Navajo fry bread (found in Arizona and western New Mexico); it's served either as a dessert with honey drizzled over it or savory as a meal stuffed with pinto beans or meat.

Taco: A corn or flour tortilla served either soft, or baked or fried and served in a hard shell; it's then stuffed with vegetables or spicy meat and garnished with shredded lettuce, chopped tomatoes, onions, and grated cheese.

Tacos al carbón: Shredded pork cooked in a mole sauce and folded into corn tortillas.

Tamale: Ground corn made into a dough, often filled with finely ground pork and red chiles; it's steamed in a corn husk.

Tortilla: A thin pancake made of corn or wheat flour, a tortilla is used as bread, as an edible "spoon," and as a container for other foods. Locals place butter in the center of a hot tortilla, roll it up, and eat it as a scroll.

Trucha en terra-cotta: Fresh trout wrapped in corn husks and baked in clay.

Verde: Spanish for "green," as in chile verde (a green chile sauce).

Art and Architecture

Adobe: A brick of sun-dried earth and clay, usually stabilized with straw; a structure made of adobe.

Banco: A small bench, or banquette, often upholstered with handwoven textiles, that gracefully emerges from adobe walls.

Bulto: Folk-art figures of a santo (saint), usually carved from wood.

Camposanto: A graveyard.

Capilla: A chapel.

Casita: Literally "small house," this term is generally used to describe a separate guesthouse.

Cerquita: A spiked, wrought-iron, rectangular fence, often marking grave sites.

Coyote fence: A type of wooden fence that surrounds many New Mexico homes; it comprises branches, usually from cedar or aspen trees, arranged vertically and wired tightly together.

Farolito: Small votive candles set in paper-bag lanterns, farolitos are popular at Christmastime. The term is used in northern New Mexico only. People in Albuquerque and points south call the lanterns *luminarias,* which in the north is the term for the bonfires of Christmas Eve.

Heishi: Technically the word means "shell necklace," but the common usage refers to necklaces made with rounded, thin, disc-shaped beads in various materials, such as turquoise or jet.

Hornos: Domed outdoor ovens made of plastered adobe or concrete blocks.

Kiva: A circular ceremonial room, built at least partially underground, used by Pueblo Indians of the Southwest. Entrance is gained from the roof.

Kiva fireplace: A corner fireplace whose round form resembles that of a kiva.

Nicho: A built-in shelf cut into an adobe or stucco wall.

Placita: A small plaza.

Portal: A porch or large covered area adjacent to a house.

Pueblo Revival (also informally called Pueblo style): Most homes in this style, modeled after the traditional dwellings of the Southwest Pueblo Indians, are cube or rectangle shaped. Other characteristics are flat roofs, thick adobe or stucco walls, small windows, rounded corners, and viga beams.

Retablo: Holy image painted on wood or tin.

Santero: Maker of religious images.

Terrones adobes: Adobe cut from the ground rather than formed from mud.

Viga: Horizontal roof beam made of logs, usually protruding from the side of the house.

2

EXPLORING SANTA FE

Updated by Andrew Collins

On a plateau at the base of the Sangre de Cristo Mountains—at an elevation of 7,000 feet—Santa Fe is brimming with reminders of nearly four centuries of Spanish and Mexican rule, and of the Pueblo cultures that have been here for hundreds more.

The town's placid central Plaza has been the site of bullfights, gunfights, political rallies, promenades, and public markets since the early 17th century. A one-of-a-kind destination, Santa Fe is fabled for its chic art galleries, superb restaurants, and diverse shops selling everything from Southwestern furnishings and cowboy gear to Tibetan textiles and Moroccan jewelry. If Santa Fe had a somewhat provincial, regional vibe at one time, the scene has changed considerably of late, with more and more retail and dining mixing local with international, often cutting-edge, styles.

La Villa Real de la Santa Fe de San Francisco de Asísi (the Royal City of the Holy Faith of St. Francis of Assisi) was founded in the early 1600s by Don Pedro de Peralta, who planted his banner in the name of Spain. During its formative years, Santa Fe was maintained primarily for the purpose of bringing the Catholic faith to New Mexico's Pueblo Indians. In 1680, however, the Indians rose in revolt and the Spanish colonists were driven out of New Mexico. The tide turned 12 years later, when General Don Diego de Vargas returned with a new army from El Paso and recaptured Santa Fe. To commemorate de Vargas's recapture of the town in 1692, Las Fiestas de Santa Fe have been held annually since 1712. The nation's oldest community celebration takes place on the weekend after Labor Day, with parades, mariachi bands, pageants, and the burning of Zozóbra—a must-see extravaganza held in Fort Marcy Park just blocks north of the Plaza.

Following de Vargas's defeat of the Pueblos, the then-grand Camino Real (Royal Road), stretching from Mexico City to Santa Fe, brought an army of conquistadors, clergymen, and settlers to the northernmost reaches of Spain's New World conquests. In 1820 the Santa Fe Trail—a prime artery of U.S. westward expansion—spilled a flood of covered wagons from Missouri onto the Plaza. A booming trade with the United States was born. After Mexico achieved independence from Spain in 1821, its subsequent rule of New Mexico further increased this commerce.

The Santa Fe Trail's heyday ended with the arrival of the Atchison, Topeka & Santa Fe Railway in 1880. The trains, and later the nation's first highways, brought a new type of settler to Santa Fe—artists who fell in love with its cultural diversity, history, and magical color and light. They were especially drawn to the area because eccentricity was embraced, not discouraged, as it often was in the social confines of the East Coast. Their presence attracted tourists, who quickly became a primary source of income for the proud, but largely poor, populace.

Santa Fe is renowned for its arts (both visual and, increasingly, performing), vibrant tricultural (Native American, Hispanic, and Anglo) heritage, and adobe architecture. The Pueblo people built their homes using a "puddled-mud" method (liquid mud poured between upright wooden frames), which melded well with the adobe brick construction introduced to the Spanish by the Moors. The Hispanic culture, still deeply rooted in its ancient ties to Spain and Catholicism, remains a strong influence on the easier pace of this city.

Cosmopolitan visitors from around the world are consistently surprised by the city's rich and varied cultural offerings despite its relatively small size. Often referred to as the "City Different," Santa Fe became the first American city to be designated a UNESCO Creative City, acknowledging its place in the global community as a leader in art, crafts, design, and lifestyle.

Orientation and Planning Humorist Will Rogers said on his first visit to Santa Fe, "Whoever designed this town did so while riding on a jackass, backwards, and drunk." The maze of narrow streets and alleyways confounds motorists; however, pedestrians delight in the vast array of shops, restaurants, flowered courtyards, and eye-catching galleries at nearly every turn. Park your car, grab a map, and explore the town on foot.

Interstate 25 cuts just south of Santa Fe, which is 62 miles northeast of Albuquerque. U.S. 285/84 runs north–south through the city. The NM 599 bypass, also called the Santa Fe Relief Route, cuts around the west side of the city from Interstate 25's Exit 276 to U.S. 285/84; it's a great shortcut if you're heading from Albuquerque to Abiquiú, Taos, or other points north of Santa Fe. The modest flow of water called the Santa Fe River runs west, parallel to Alameda Street, from the Sangre de Cristo Mountains to the open prairie southwest of town, where it disappears into a narrow canyon before joining the Rio Grande. There's a *dicho,* or saying, in New Mexico: "*agua es vida*"—water is life—and every little trickle counts.

EXPLORING SANTA FE

THE PLAZA

Much of the history of Santa Fe, New Mexico, the Southwest, and even the West has some association with Santa Fe's central Plaza, which New Mexico governor Don Pedro de Peralta laid out in 1610. The Plaza was already well established by the time of the Pueblo revolt in 1680. Freight wagons unloaded here after completing their arduous journey across the Santa Fe Trail. The American flag was raised over the Plaza in 1846, during the Mexican War, which resulted in Mexico's loss of all its territories in the present southwestern United States. For a time the Plaza was a tree-shaded park with a white picket fence. In the 1890s it was an expanse of lawn where uniformed bands played in an ornate gazebo. Particularly festive times on the Plaza are the weekend after Labor Day, during Las Fiestas de Santa Fe, and at Christmas, when all the trees are filled with lights, and rooftops are outlined with *farolitos,* votive candles lit within paper-bag lanterns.

TOP ATTRACTIONS

Georgia O'Keeffe Museum. One of many East Coast artists who visited New Mexico in the first half of the 20th century, O'Keeffe returned to live and paint here, eventually emerging as the demigoddess of Southwestern art. O'Keeffe's innovative view of the landscape is captured in *From the Plains,* inspired by her memory of the Texas plains, and *Jimson Weed,* a study of one of her favorite plants. Special exhibitions with O'Keeffe's modernist peers are on view throughout the year—many of these are exceptional, sometimes even more interesting than the permanent collection. The museum is also your point of contact for booking guided tours of O'Keeffe's historic home and studio an hour north in Abiquiú. ✉ *217 Johnson St., The Plaza* ☎ *505/946–1000* 🌐 *www.okeeffemuseum.org* 🎟 *$12* ⏲ *Mon.–Thurs. and weekends 10–5, Fri. 10–7.*

★ Fodor's Choice **The New Mexico History Museum.** This impressive
FAMILY museum, opened in 2009, is the anchor of a campus that encompasses the **Palace of the Governors,** the **Museum of New Mexico Press,** the **Fray Angélico Chávez History Library,** and **Photo Archives** (an assemblage of more than 1 million images dating from the 1850s). Behind the palace on Lincoln Avenue, the museum thoroughly encompasses the early history of indigenous people, Spanish colonization, the Mexican Period, and travel and commerce on the

TOP REASONS TO GO

A winter stroll on Canyon Road. There are few experiences to match walking this ancient street on Christmas Eve when it's covered with snow, scented by piñon fires burning in luminarias along the road, and echoing with the voices of carolers and happy families.

A culinary adventure. Start with blue-corn pancakes for breakfast and try Spanish tapas or farm-to-table regional Southwestern fare for dinner. Enjoy some strawberry-habanero gelato at Ecco or sip an Aztec Warrior Chocolate Elixir at Kakawa Chocolate. Take a cooking lesson. Santa Fe is an exceptional dining town, the perfect place to push the frontiers of your palate.

Into the wild. Follow the lead of locals and take any one of the many easy-access points into the incredible, and surprisingly lush, mountains that rise out of Santa Fe. Raft the Rio Grande, snowboard, snowshoe, or try mountain biking.

Market mashup. Summer offers the phenomenal International Folk Art Market, the famed Indian Market, and the two-for-one weekend of Traditional Spanish Market and Contemporary Hispanic Market. Plus there's an outstanding farmers' market on Saturday mornings. The offerings are breathtaking and the community involvement is yet another aspect of Santa Fe to fall in love with.

legendary Santa Fe Trail. Inside are changing and permanent exhibits. From 1 until 5, Tuesday–Friday, visitors have access (call ahead to make arrangements) to the comprehensive Fray Angélico Chávez Library and its rare maps, manuscripts, and photographs (more than 120,000 prints and negatives). The Palace Print Shop & Bindery, which prints books, pamphlets, and cards on antique presses, also hosts bookbinding demonstrations, lectures, and slide shows. The Palace of the Governors is a humble one-story neo-Pueblo adobe on the north side of the Plaza, and is the oldest public building in the United States. Its rooms contain period furnishings and exhibits illustrating the building's many functions over the past four centuries. Built at the same time as the Plaza, circa 1610 (scholars debate the exact year), it was the seat of four regional governments—those of Spain, Mexico, the Confederacy, and the U.S. territory that preceded New Mexico's statehood, which was achieved in 1912. The building was abandoned

NEW MEXICO CULTURE PASS

With a New Mexico Culture Pass (🌐 www.newmexicoculture.org), which you can purchase for $25 online or at any participating museum, you gain admission to each of the 14 state museums and monuments once over a 12-month period. These include a number of attractions elsewhere in the state (Albuquerque's National Hispanic Center and New Mexico Museum of Natural History and Science, the state monuments in Jèmez, Coronado, and several other places) as well as the following Santa Fe museums: New Mexico History Museum/Palace of the Governors, Museum of Fine Arts, Museum of Indian Arts and Culture, and Museum of International Folk Art. For $20, you can also buy a pass good for unlimited admission over a four-day period to these four museums.

in 1680, following the Pueblo Revolt, but resumed its role as government headquarters when Don Diego de Vargas successfully returned in 1692. It served as the residence for 100 Spanish, Mexican, and American governors, including Governor Lew Wallace, who wrote his epic *Ben Hur* in its then drafty rooms, all the while complaining of the dust and mud that fell from its earthen ceiling.

Dozens of Native American vendors gather daily under the portal of the Palace of the Governors to display and sell pottery, jewelry, bread, and other goods. With few exceptions, the more than 500 artists and craftspeople registered to sell here are Pueblo or Navajo Indians. The merchandise for sale is required to meet strict standards: all items are handmade or hand-strung in Native American households; silver jewelry is either sterling (92.5% pure) or coin (90% pure) silver; all metal jewelry bears the maker's mark, which is registered with the Museum of New Mexico. Prices tend to reflect the high quality of the merchandise but are often significantly less that what you'd pay in a shop. Please remember not to take photographs without permission.

There's an outstanding gift shop and bookstore with many high-quality, New Mexico–produced items. ✉ *Palace Ave., north side of Plaza, Lincoln Ave., west of the Palace, The Plaza* ☎ *505/476–5100* 🌐 *www.nmhistorymuseum.org* 🎟 *$9, 4-day pass $20 (good at all 4 state museums), free Fri. 5–8* ⏲ *Tues.–Sun. 10–5 (also Mon. 10–5 and Fri. until 8 late May–early Oct.).*

★ Fodor's Choice **New Mexico Museum of Art.** Designed by Isaac Hamilton Rapp in 1917, the museum (formerly known as the Museum of Fine Arts) contains one of America's finest regional collections. It's also one of Santa Fe's earliest Pueblo Revival structures, inspired by the adobe structures at Acoma Pueblo. Split-cedar *latillas* (branches set in a crosshatch pattern) and hand-hewn vigas form the ceilings. The 20,000-piece permanent collection, of which only a fraction is exhibited at any given time, emphasizes the work of regional and nationally renowned artists, including the early modernist Georgia O'Keeffe; realist Robert Henri; the Cinco Pintores (five painters) of Santa Fe (including Fremont Elis and Will Shuster, the creative mind behind Zozóbra); members of the Taos Society of Artists (Ernest L. Blumenschein, Bert G. Phillips, Joseph H. Sharp, and E. Irving Couse, among others); and the works of noted 20th-century photographers of the Southwest, including Laura Gilpin, Ansel Adams, and Dorothea Lange. Rotating exhibits are staged throughout the year. Many excellent examples of Spanish-colonial-style furniture are on display. An interior *placita* (small plaza) with fountains, WPA murals, and sculpture, and the St. Francis Auditorium, where concerts and lectures are often held, are other highlights. ✉ *107 W. Palace Ave., The Plaza* ☎ *505/476–5072* 🌐 *www.nmartmuseum.org* 🎟 *$9, 4-day pass $20 (good at all 4 state museums), free Fri. 5–8* ⏲ *Tues.–Sun. 10–5 (also Mon. 10–5 and Fri. until 8 late May–early Oct.).*

St. Francis Cathedral Basilica. The iconic cathedral, a block east of the Plaza, is one of the rare significant departures from the city's nearly ubiquitous Pueblo architecture. Construction was begun in 1869 by Jean Baptiste Lamy, Santa Fe's first archbishop, who worked with French architects and Italian stonemasons. The Romanesque style was popular in Lamy's native home in southwest France. The circuit-riding cleric was sent by the Catholic Church to the Southwest to change the religious practices of its native population (to "civilize" them, as one period document puts it) and is buried in the crypt beneath the church's high altar. He was the inspiration behind Willa Cather's novel *Death Comes for the Archbishop* (1927). In 2005 Pope Benedict XVI declared St. Francis the "cradle of Catholicism" in the Southwestern United States, and upgraded the status of the building from mere cathedral to cathedral basilica—it's one of just 36 in the country.

A small adobe chapel on the northeast side of the cathedral, the remnant of an earlier church, embodies the Hispanic architectural influence so conspicuously absent from the cathedral itself. The chapel's *Nuestra Señora de la Paz* (Our Lady of Peace), popularly known as *La Conquistadora,* the oldest Madonna statue in the United States, accompanied Don Diego de Vargas on his reconquest of Santa Fe in 1692, a feat attributed to the statue's spiritual intervention. Every Friday the faithful adorn the statue with a new dress. Take a close look at the keystone in the main doorway arch: it has a Hebrew tetragrammaton on it. It's widely speculated that Bishop Lamy had this carved and placed to honor the Jewish merchants of Santa Fe who helped provide necessary funds for the construction of the church. ✉ *231 Cathedral Pl., The Plaza* ☎ *505/982–5619* 🌐 *www.cbsfa.org* 🕑 *Mon.–Sat. 6–6, Sun. 7–7, except during Mass. Mass Mon.–Sat. at 7 am and 5:15 pm and Sun. at 8 am, 10 am, noon, and 5:15 pm. Visitor hours: weekdays 8:30–4:30.*

WORTH NOTING

La Fonda. A *fonda* (inn) has stood on this site, southeast of the Plaza, for centuries. Architect Isaac Hamilton Rapp, who put Santa Fe style on the map, built this area landmark in 1922. Remodeled in the early 20th century by architects John Gaw Meem and Mary Elizabeth Jane Colter, the hotel was sold to the Santa Fe Railway in 1926 and remained a Harvey House hotel until 1968. The property completed its latest major renovation in 2013, its guest rooms receiving a smart but still classic makeover, but the historic public areas retain their original design elements. Because of its proximity to the Plaza and its history as a gathering place for everyone from cowboys to movie stars (Errol Flynn stayed here), it's referred to as "The Inn at the End of the Trail." Step inside to browse the shops on the main floor or to eat at one of the restaurants (La Plazuela or the French Bakery). The dark, cozy bar draws both locals and tourists and has live music many nights. For a real treat: Have a drink at the fifth-floor Bell Tower Bar (open late spring–early fall), which offers tremendous sunset views. ✉ *E. San Francisco St., at Old Santa Fe Trail, The Plaza* ☎ *505/982–5511* 🌐 *www.lafondasantafe.com.*

Museum of Contemporary Native Arts (MoCNA). This fascinating museum that's part of the esteemed Institute of American Indian Arts (IAIA) is just a block from the Plaza and contains the largest collection—some 7,500 works—of contemporary Native American art in the United States.

A GOOD WALK: THE PLAZA

Begin your walk on the Plaza. You can get an overview of the history of Santa Fe and New Mexico at the **Palace of the Governors** on the campus of the **New Mexico History Museum,** which borders the northern side of the Plaza on Palace Avenue. Outside, under the palace portal, dozens of Native American artisans sell handcrafted wares. From the palace, walk across the street to the **New Mexico Museum of Art,** where the works of regional masters are on display. The **Georgia O'Keeffe Museum,** on nearby Johnson Street, exhibits the works of its namesake, New Mexico's best-known painter.

From the O'Keeffe Museum, return to the Plaza and cut across to its southeast corner to Old Santa Fe Trail, where you can find the town's oldest hotel, **La Fonda,** a good place to soak up a little of bygone Santa Fe. One block east on Cathedral Place looms the imposing facade of **St. Francis Cathedral Basilica.** Across from the cathedral is the **Museum of Contemporary Native Arts (part of the Institute of American Indian Arts)**. A stone's throw from the museum is cool, quiet Sena Plaza, accessible through two doorways on Palace Avenue.

TIMING

It's possible to zoom through this compact area in about five hours—two hours exploring the Plaza and the Palace of the Governors, one hour seeing the Museum of Fine Arts, and two hours visiting the other sites.

The collection of paintings, photography, sculptures, prints, and traditional crafts was created by past and present students and teachers. In the 1960s and 1970s it blossomed into the nation's premier center for Native American arts and its alumni represent almost 600 tribes around the country. The museum continues to showcase the cultural and artistic vibrancy of indigenous people and expands what is still an often limited public perception of what "Indian" art is and can be. Be sure to step out back to the beautiful sculpture garden. Artist Fritz Scholder taught here, as did sculptor Allan Houser. Among their disciples was the painter T. C. Cannon and sculptor and painter Dan Namingha. ✉ *108 Cathedral Pl., The Plaza* ☎ *505/983–1777, 888/922–4242* 🌐 *www.iaia.edu* 🎟 *$10* ⏲ *Mon. and Wed.–Sat. 10–5, Sun. noon–5.*

NEED A BREAK? **Ecco Gelato and Espresso.** **This airy, contemporary café across from the Downtown public library has large plate-glass windows, and brushed-metal tables inside and out on the sidewalk under the portal. Try the delicious and creative gelato flavors (strawberry-habanero, saffron-honey, minty white grape, chocolate-banana) or some of the espressos and coffees, pastries, and sandwiches (roast beef and blue cheese, tuna with dill, cucumber, and sprouts).** ✉ ***105 E. Marcy St., The Plaza*** ☎ ***505/986–9778*** 🌐 ***www.eccogelato.com.***

Pablita Velarde Museum of Indian Women in the Arts. This small, new museum near the Cathedral Basilica has an important and relevant mission for this part of the world: to celebrate and showcase the extensive accomplishments of the country's indigenous female artists, beginning with the museum's namesake, Pablita Velarde (1918–2006), who was born at Santa Clara Pueblo (near Española) and went on to paint for the WPA and then to exhibit her vibrant watercolors and "earth paintings" (using pigments she created from local minerals) nationally and internationally. Exhibits here focus on not just visual artists but also musicians, poets, filmmakers, and other creative talents who have contributed to the growing body of art by Native women. ✉ *213 Cathedral Pl., The Plaza* ☎ *505/988–8900* 🌐 *www.pvmiwa.org* 🎟 *$10* ⏲ *Tues.–Sun. 10–5.*

Sena Plaza. Two-story buildings enclose this courtyard, which can be entered only through two small doorways on Palace Avenue or the shops facing Palace Avenue. Surrounding the oasis of flowering fruit trees, a fountain, and inviting benches are a variety of locally owned shops. The quiet courtyard is a good place for repose or to have lunch at La Casa Sena. The buildings, erected in the 1700s as a single-family residence, had quarters for blacksmiths, bakers, farmers, and all manner of help. ✉ *125 E. Palace Ave., The Plaza.*

OLD SANTA FE TRAIL AND SOUTH CAPITOL

It was along the Old Santa Fe Trail that wagon trains from Missouri rolled into town in the 1820s, forever changing Santa Fe's destiny. This street, off the south corner of the Plaza, is one of Santa Fe's most historic and is dotted with houses, shops, markets and the (relatively modern) state capitol several blocks down.

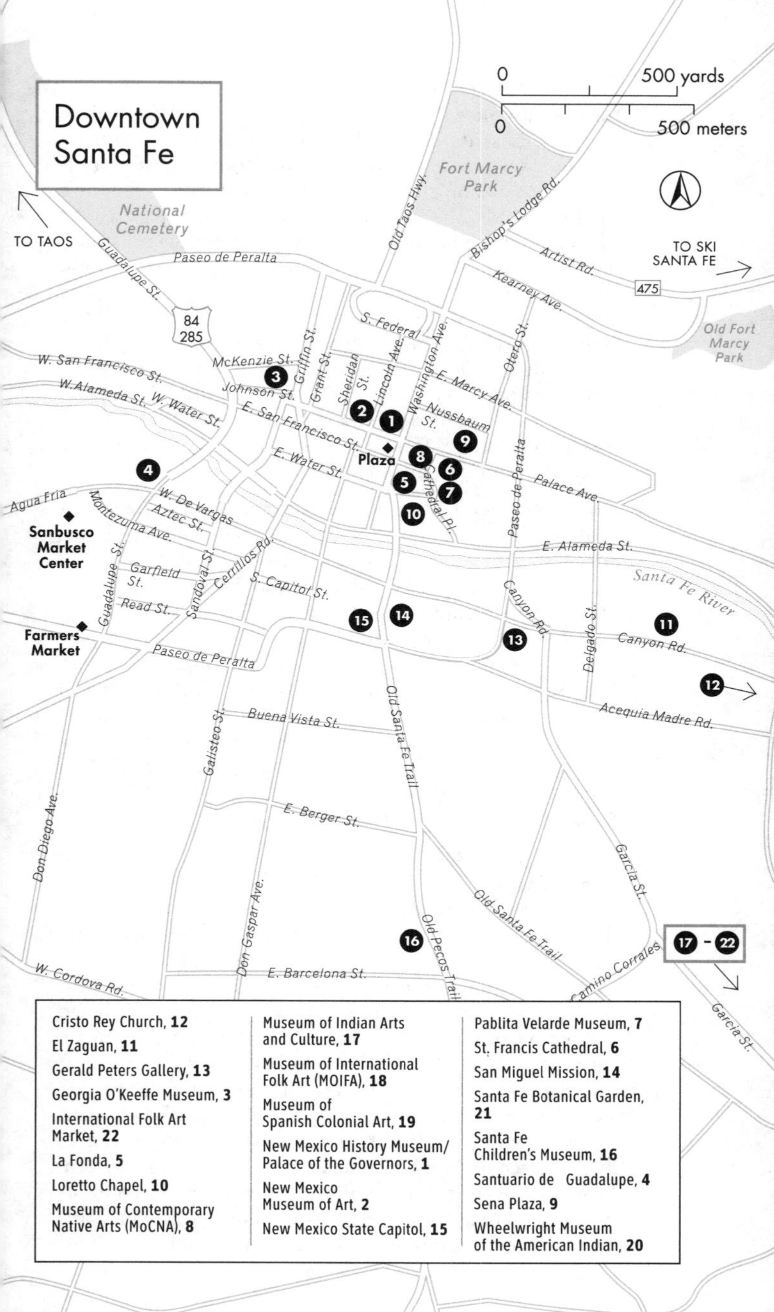

Downtown Santa Fe
0
500 yards
0
500 meters
TO TAOS
National Cemetery
Fort Marcy Park
Old Fort Marcy Park
TO SKI SANTA FE
475
84
285
Paseo de Peralta
Guadalupe St.
Old Taos Hwy.
Bishop's Lodge Rd.
Artist Rd.
Kearney Ave.
S. Federal
Lincoln Ave.
Washington Ave.
Otero St.
E. Marcy Ave.
Nussbaum St.
Griffin St.
Grant St.
Sheridan St.
McKenzie St.
Johnson St.
W. San Francisco St.
W. Alameda St.
W. Water St.
E. San Francisco St.
E. Water St.
Plaza
Cathedral Pl.
Palace Ave.
Paseo de Peralta
Agua Fria
W. De Vargas
Aztec St.
Montezuma Ave.
Sanbusco Market Center
Garfield St.
Read St.
Sandoval St.
Cerrillos Rd.
S. Capitol St.
E. Alameda St.
Santa Fe River
Canyon Rd.
Delgado St.
Farmers Market
Acequia Madre Rd.
Old Santa Fe Trail
Buena Vista St.
Galisteo St.
E. Berger St.
Don Diego Ave.
Don Gaspar Ave.
Old Pecos Trail
Garcia St.
Camino Corrales
W. Cordova Rd.
E. Barcelona St.
Cristo Rey Church, 12
El Zaguan, 11
Gerald Peters Gallery, 13
Georgia O'Keeffe Museum, 3
International Folk Art Market, 22
La Fonda, 5
Loretto Chapel, 10
Museum of Contemporary Native Arts (MoCNA), 8
Museum of Indian Arts and Culture, 17
Museum of International Folk Art (MOIFA), 18
Museum of Spanish Colonial Art, 19
New Mexico History Museum/ Palace of the Governors, 1
New Mexico Museum of Art, 2
New Mexico State Capitol, 15
Pablita Velarde Museum, 7
St. Francis Cathedral, 6
San Miguel Mission, 14
Santa Fe Botanical Garden, 21
Santa Fe Children's Museum, 16
Santuario de Guadalupe, 4
Sena Plaza, 9
Wheelwright Museum of the American Indian, 20

TOP ATTRACTIONS

New Mexico State Capitol. The symbol of the Zía Pueblo, which represents the Circle of Life, was the inspiration for the capitol, also known as the Roundhouse. Doorways at opposing sides of this 1966 structure symbolize the four winds, the four directions, and the four seasons. Throughout the building are artworks from the outstanding collection of the Capitol Art Foundation, historical and cultural displays, and handcrafted furniture—it's a superb and somewhat overlooked array of fine art. The **Governor's Gallery** hosts temporary exhibits. Six acres of imaginatively landscaped gardens shelter outstanding sculptures. ✉ *Old Santa Fe Trail at Paseo de Peralta, Old Santa Fe Trail and South Capitol* ☎ *505/986–4589* 🌐 *www.nmlegis.gov/lcs/visitors.aspx* 🎟 *Free* ⏲ *Weekdays 7–6 (also Sat. late May–late Aug., 9–5); guided tours by appt.*

★ Fodor's Choice **San Miguel Mission.** Believed to be the oldest church still in use in the United States, this simple earth-hue adobe structure was built in the 1610s by the Tlaxcalan Indians of Mexico, who came to New Mexico as servants of the Spanish. Badly damaged in the 1680 Pueblo Revolt, the structure was restored and enlarged in 1710. On display in the chapel are priceless statues and paintings and the San José Bell, weighing nearly 800 pounds, which is believed to have been cast in Spain in 1356. In winter the church sometimes closes before its official closing hour. Mass is held on Sunday at 5 pm. ✉ *401 Old Santa Fe Trail, Old Santa Fe Trail and South Capitol* ☎ *505/983–3974* 🎟 *$1* ⏲ *Mon.–Sat. 9–5, Sun. 10–4.*

WORTH NOTING

Loretto Chapel. A delicate Gothic church modeled after Sainte-Chapelle in Paris, Loretto was built in 1878 by the same French architects and Italian stonemasons who built St. Francis Cathedral. The chapel is known for the "Miraculous Staircase" that leads to the choir loft. Legend has it that the chapel was almost complete when it became obvious that there wasn't room to build a staircase to the choir loft. In answer to the prayers of the cathedral's nuns, a mysterious carpenter arrived on a donkey, built a 20-foot staircase—using only a square, a saw, and a tub of water to season the wood—and then disappeared as quickly as he came. Many of the faithful believed it was St. Joseph himself. The staircase contains two complete 360-degree turns with no central support; no nails were used in its construction. The chapel closes for services and special events. Adjoining the chapel are a small museum and gift shop. ✉ *207 Old Santa Fe Trail, Old Santa Fe Trail and South Capitol* ☎ *505/982–0092* 🌐 *www.lorettochapel.com* 🎫 *Donations accepted* 🕒 *Mon.–Sat. 9–6, Sun. 10:30–5.*

EAST SIDE AND CANYON ROAD

Once a trail used by indigenous people to access water and the lush forest in the foothills east of town, then a route for Hispanic woodcutters and their burros, and for most of the 20th century a prosaic residential street with only a gas station and a general store, Canyon Road is now lined with upscale art galleries, shops, and restaurants. The narrow road begins at the eastern curve of Paseo de Peralta and stretches for about 2 miles at a moderate incline toward the base of the mountains. Lower Canyon Road is where you'll find the galleries, shops, and a few restaurants. Upper Canyon Road (above East Alameda) is narrow and residential, with access to hiking and biking trails along the way, and the Randall Davey Audubon Center at the very top. Elsewhere on neighboring streets in the East Side, you'll find several noteworthy B&Bs as well as the beautifully situated campus of St. John's College, but this part of town is mostly residential. Still, it's pretty to stroll through, with its narrow lanes and many old adobe homes with thick, undulating walls that appear to have been carved out of the earth.

In Canyon Road galleries, you'll find art ranging from cutting-edge contemporary to traditional and even ancient works. Some artists are internationally renowned, like Fernando Botero, others' identities have been lost with time, like the weavers of magnificent Navajo rugs.

There are few places as festive as Canyon Road on Christmas Eve, when thousands of farolitos illuminate walkways, walls, roofs, and even trees. In May the scent of lilacs wafts over the adobe walls, and in August red hollyhocks enhance the surreal color of the blue sky on a dry summer day.

WORTH NOTING

Cristo Rey Church. Built in 1940 and designed by legendary Santa Fe architect John Gaw Meem to commemorate the 400th anniversary of Francisco Vásquez de Coronado's exploration of the Southwest, this church is the largest Spanish adobe structure in the United States and is considered by many the finest example of Pueblo-style architecture

A GOOD WALK: CANYON ROAD

Begin on Paseo de Peralta at the **Gerald Peters Gallery,** which has an enormous, museum-quality collection. Continue a half block north to Canyon Road. Turn right (east) and follow the road, which unfolds in shadows of undulating adobe walls. Street parking is at a premium, but there's a city-owned pay lot at the corner of Camino del Monte Sol, a few blocks up, and you can often find free parking on nearby residential streets (just read signs carefully to be sure you don't park in a section zoned for residents). Between visits to galleries and shops, take a break at one of the courtyards or grab a bite in one of the excellent restaurants. Be sure to stop by the beautiful gardens outside **El Zaguan.** At the intersection of Upper Canyon and Cristo Rey, you'll find the massive **Cristo Rey Church.** Wear good walking shoes and watch out for the irregular sidewalks, which can get icy in winter.

TIMING

A tour of Canyon Road could take a whole day or as little as a few hours. If art is more than a curiosity to you, you may want to view the Gerald Peters Gallery apart from your Canyon Road tour. There's so much to see there that visual overload could hit before you get halfway up the road. Even on a cold day the walk is a pleasure, with massive, glistening icicles hanging off roofs and a silence shrouding the side streets.

anywhere. The church was constructed in the old-fashioned way by parishioners, who mixed the more than 200,000 mud-and-straw adobe bricks and hauled them into place. The 225-ton stone reredos (altar screen) is magnificent. ✉ *1120 Canyon Rd., at Cristo Rey, East Side and Canyon Road* ☎ *505/983–8528* ⏲ *Daily 8–5.*

El Zaguan. Headquarters of the **Historic Santa Fe Foundation (HSFF),** this 19th-century Territorial-style house has a small exhibit on Santa Fe architecture and preservation, but the real draw is the small but stunning garden abundant with lavender, roses, and 160-year-old trees. You can relax on a wrought-iron bench and take in the fine views of the hills northeast of town. Tours are available of many of the foundation's properties on Mother's Day. ✉ *545 Canyon Rd., East Side and Canyon Road* ☎ *505/983–2567* 🌐 *www.historicsantafe.org* 🎟 *Free* ⏲ *Foundation office weekdays 9–noon and 1:30–5; gardens Mon.–Sat. 9–5.*

2

Gerald Peters Gallery. While under construction, this 32,000-square-foot building was dubbed the "ninth northern pueblo," its scale supposedly rivaling that of the eight northern pueblos around Santa Fe. The suavely designed Pueblo-style gallery is Santa Fe's premier showcase for American and European art from the 19th century to the present. It feels like a museum, but all the works are for sale. Pablo Picasso, Georgia O'Keeffe, Charles M. Russell, Winslow Homer, Grant Wood, and members of the Taos Society are among the artists represented, along with nationally renowned contemporary ones. ✉ *1011 Paseo de Peralta, East Side and Canyon Road* ☎ *505/954–5700* 🌐 *www.gpgallery.com* 🎟 *Free* ⏲ *Mon.–Sat. 10–5.*

NEED A BREAK? **Downtown Subscription. Locals congregate in the courtyard or on the front portal of Downtown Subscription, a block east of Canyon Road. A great, friendly spot to people-watch, this café-newsstand sells coffees, snacks, and pastries, plus one of the largest assortments of newspapers and magazines in town. It has lovely outdoor spaces to sit and sip during warm weather.** ✉ ***376 Garcia St., East Side and Canyon Road*** ☎ ***505/983–3085.***

MUSEUM HILL

What used to be the outskirts of town became the site of gracious, neo-Pueblo style homes in the mid-20th century, many of them designed by the famed architect John Gaw Meem. Old Santa Fe Trail takes you to Camino Lejo, aka Museum Hill, where you'll find four excellent museums, a botanical garden opened in summer 2013, and a café.

TOP ATTRACTIONS

Museum of Indian Arts and Culture. An interactive, multimedia exhibition tells the story of Native American history in the Southwest, merging contemporary Native American experience with historical accounts and artifacts. The collection has some of New Mexico's oldest works of art: pottery vessels, fine stone and silver jewelry, intricate textiles, and other arts and crafts created by Pueblo, Navajo, and Apache artisans. Changing exhibitions feature arts and traditions of historic and contemporary Native Americans. You can also see art demonstrations and a video about the life and work of Pueblo potter Maria Martinez. ✉ *710 Camino Lejo, Museum Hill* ☎ *505/476–1250* 🌐 *www.indianartsandculture.org* 🎟 *$9, 4-day pass $20 (good at all 4*

A GOOD TOUR: MUSEUM HILL

This tour begins 2 miles southeast of the Plaza, an area known as Museum Hill that's best reached by car or via one of the city buses that leaves hourly from near the Plaza. Begin at the **Museum of Indian Arts and Culture,** which is set around Milner Plaza, an attractively landscaped courtyard and gardens with outdoor art installations. On some summer days the Plaza hosts Native American dances, jewelry-making demonstrations, kids' activities, and other interactive events; there's also the Museum Hill Café, which is open for lunch (daily except Mondays) and serves delicious and reasonably priced salads, quiche, burgers, sandwiches and wraps, ice cream, and other light fare. To get here from Downtown, drive uphill on Old Santa Fe Trail to Camino Lejo. Across Milner Plaza is the **Museum of International Folk Art (MOIFA).** From Milner Plaza, a landscaped pedestrian path leads a short way to the **Museum of Spanish Colonial Art.** Return to Milner Plaza, from which a different pedestrian path leads west a short way to the **Wheelwright Museum of the American Indian.** Across the street from the parking lot below Milner Plaza, you can visit the new Santa Fe Botanical Garden. To reach the **Santa Fe Children's Museum,** you need to drive back down the hill or ask the bus driver to let you off near it.

TIMING

Set aside a full day to see all the museums on Old Santa Fe Trail and Museum Hill. Kids usually have to be dragged from the Children's Museum, even after an hour or two.

state museums), free Fri. 5–8 ⏲ Tues.–Sun. 10–5 (also Mon. 10–5 and Fri. until 8 late May–early Oct.).

★ FodorsChoice **Museum of International Folk Art (MOIFA).** A delight FAMILY for adults and children alike, this museum is the premier institution of its kind in the world, with a permanent collection of more than 130,000 objects from about 100 countries. In the Girard Wing you'll find thousands of amazingly inventive handmade objects—a tin Madonna, a devil made from bread dough, dolls from around the world, and miniature village scenes galore. The Hispanic Heritage Wing contains art dating from the Spanish-colonial period (in New Mexico, 1598–1821) to the present. The 3,000-piece exhibit includes religious works—particularly *bultos* (carved wooden statues of saints) and retablos, as well as textiles and furniture. The exhibits in the Neutrogena Wing rotate, showing subjects ranging from outsider art to the magnificent quilts of Gee's Bend. Lloyd's Treasure Chest, the wing's innovative basement section, provides a behind-the-scenes look at this collection. You can rummage through storage drawers, peer into microscopes, and, on occasion, speak with conservators and other museum personnel. Allow time to visit the incredible gift shop and bookstore. ✉ *706 Camino Lejo, Museum Hill* ☎ *505/476–1200* 🌐 *www.moifa.org* 🎫 *$9, 4-day pass $20 (good at all 4 state museums), free Fri. 5–8* ⏲ *Tues.–Sun. 10–5 (also Mon. 10–5 and Fri. until 8 late May–early Oct.).*

★ Fodor's Choice **Museum of Spanish Colonial Art.** This 5,000-square-foot adobe museum occupies a classically Southwestern former home designed in 1930 by acclaimed regional architect John Gaw Meem. The Spanish Colonial Art Society formed in Santa Fe in 1925 to preserve traditional Spanish-colonial art and culture, and the museum, which sits next to the Museum of International Folk Art and the Museum of Indian Arts and Culture complex, displays the fruits of the society's labor—one of the most comprehensive collections of Spanish-colonial art in the world. Objects here, dating from the 16th century to the present, include *retablos* (holy images painted on wood or tin), elaborate santos, tinwork, straw appliqué, furniture, ceramics, and ironwork. The contemporary collection of works by New Mexico Hispanic artists of the 20th century helps put all this history into regional context. On the grounds outside, you can also view the exterior of a 1780s Mexican Colonial house and visit the small but colorful Artist's Garden. ✉ *750 Camino Lejo, Museum Hill* ☎ *505/982–2226* 🌐 *www.spanishcolonial.org* 🎫 *$5* ⏲ *Tues.–Sun. 10–5 (also Mon. 10–5 June–Sept.).*

★ Fodor's Choice **Santa Fe Botanical Garden.** With the beautiful landscaped paths and lovely Milner Plaza, Museum Hill has always been about much more than the collections inside its four world-class museums. The summer 2013 opening of this 12-acre garden across the street from Milner Plaza's parking lot has added another great reason for exploring this neighborhood situated on a bluff with fantastic views of the surrounding mountains. The facility is divided into four sections that emphasize distinct elements of New Mexico's flora and terrain: the Orchard Gardens, the Naturalistic Gardens, the Courtyard Gardens, and the Arroyo Trails. You can gain a much fuller sense of what's planted and why by embarking on one of the free guided tours, offered each day at 10 am and 2 pm. The organization also operates Leonora Curtin Wetland Preserve (entrance at 27283 I–25 W. Frontage Rd. next to El Rancho de las Golondrinas), which is open spring through fall; and the Ortiz Mountains Educational Preserve, which is near Cerillos (off NM 14, the Turquoise Trail) and open only by appointment for docent-led hikes—check the SFBG website for more on these other properties. ✉ *715 Camino Lejo, Museum Hill* ☎ *505/471–9103* 🌐 *www.santafebotanicalgarden.org* 🎫 *$5* ⏲ *Apr.–Oct., daily 9–5; Nov.–Mar., Tues.–Sun. 10–4.*

WORTH NOTING

International Folk Art Market. Held the second full weekend in July on Milner Plaza, this market is *a truly remarkable* art gathering. Master folk artists from every corner of the planet come together to sell their work amidst a festive array of huge tents, colorful banners, music, food, and delighted crowds. There is a feeling of fellowship and celebration here that enhances the satisfaction of buying wonderful folk art. ✉ *706 Camino Lejo, Museum Hill* ☎ *505/476–1197* 🌐 *www.folkartmarket.org.*

FAMILY **Santa Fe Children's Museum.** Stimulating hands-on exhibits, a solar greenhouse, oversize geometric forms, and an 18-foot indoor rock-climbing wall all contribute to this museum's popularity with kids. Outdoor gardens with climbing structures, forts, and hands-on activities are great for whiling away the time in the shade of big trees. Puppeteers and storytellers perform often. ✉ *1050 Old Pecos Trail, Old Santa Fe Trail and South Capitol* ☎ *505/989–8359* 🌐 *www.santafechildrensmuseum.org* 🎫 *$9* ⏲ *Sept.–May, Wed. and Fri.–Sat. 10–5, Thurs. 10–7, Sun. noon–5; June–Aug., Tues.–Sat. 10–6, Sun. noon–5.*

Wheelwright Museum of the American Indian. A private institution in a building shaped like a traditional octagonal Navajo hogan, the Wheelwright opened in 1937. Founded by Boston scholar Mary Cabot Wheelwright and Navajo medicine man Hastiin Klah, the museum originated as a place to house ceremonial materials. Those items were returned to the Navajo in 1977, but what remains is an incredible collection of 19th- and 20th-century baskets, pottery, sculpture, weavings, metalwork, photography, paintings, including contemporary works by Native American artists, and typically fascinating changing exhibits. The Case Trading Post on the lower level is modeled after the trading posts that dotted the southwestern frontier more than 100 years ago. It carries an outstanding selection of books and contemporary Native American jewelry, kachina dolls, weaving, and pottery. ✉ *704 Camino Lejo, Museum Hill* ☎ *505/982–4636* 🌐 *www.wheelwright.org* 🎫 *Free* ⏲ *Daily 10–5; guided gallery tours daily (call for schedule).*

RAILYARD DISTRICT

The most significant development in Santa Fe in recent years has taken place in the Railyard District, a neighborhood just south of the Plaza that was for years called the Guadalupe District (and is occasionally still known as that). Comprising a few easily walked blocks along Guadalupe Street between Agua Fria and Paseo de Peralta, the district has been revitalized with a snazzy park and outdoor performance space, a permanent indoor-outdoor home for the farmers' market, and quite a few notable restaurants, shops, and galleries.

This historic warehouse and rail district endured several decades of neglect after the demise of the train route through town. But rather than tearing the buildings down (this is a city where 200-year-old mud-brick buildings sell at a premium, after all), developers gradually converted the low-lying warehouses into artists' studios, antiques shops, bookstores, indie shops, and restaurants. The Rail Runner commuter train to Albuquerque has put the rail tracks as well as the vintage mission-style depot back into use; the restored scenic train to Lamy canceled service in 2013 due to financial challenges, but as of this writing, its operators were planning to resume service in 2014.

A central feature of the district's redevelopment is the Railyard Park, at the corner of Cerrillos Road and Guadalupe Street, which was designed to highlight native plants and provide citizens with a lush, urban space. The buildings just north, in the direction of the Plaza, contain the vibrant Santa Fe Farmers' Market, the teen-oriented community art center Warehouse21, SITE Santa Fe museum, art galleries, shops, restaurants, and live-work spaces for artists. This dramatic development reveals the fascinating way Santa Feans have worked to meet the needs of an expanding city while paying strict attention to the city's historic relevance.

WORTH NOTING

Santuario de Guadalupe. A massive-walled adobe structure built by Franciscan missionaries between 1776 and 1795, this is the oldest shrine in the United States to Our Lady of Guadalupe, Mexico's patron saint. The church's adobe walls are nearly 3 feet thick, and among the sanctuary's religious art and artifacts is a beloved image of Nuestra Virgen de Guadalupe, painted by Mexican master José de Alcíbar in 1783. Highlights are the traditional New Mexican carved and painted altar screen called a reredo, an authentic 19th-century sacristy, a pictorial-history archive, a library devoted to Archbishop Jean-Baptiste Lamy that is furnished with many of his belongings, and a garden with plants from the Holy Land. ✉ *100 Guadalupe St., Railyard District* ☎ *505/988–2027* 🎫 *Donations accepted* ⏲ *May–Oct., Mon.–Sat. 9–4; Nov.–Apr., weekdays 9–4.*

NEED A BREAK? **Whoo's Donuts. Begun by Jeff and Kari Keenan, the talents behind the terrific artisan shop ChocolateSmith, which is next door and also well worth investigating for a sweet snack, Whoo's has developed a near-fanatical following for its traditional as well as creative doughnuts (maple-bacon with dark chocolate glaze and chile–brown sugar, blueberry jelly with cherry glaze, white chocolate–pistachio), which are prepared daily from scratch, sourcing organically as much as possible. Get here early—Whoo's is open daily from 7 until 3 (or until that day's doughtnuts have sold out).** ✉ ***851 Cerrillos Rd., Railyard District*** ☎ ***505/629–1678*** 🌐 ***www.whoosdonuts.com.***

WEST OF THE PLAZA

Although most of downtown's commercial activity beyond the Plaza extends south and east, a handful of notable restaurants, shops, and inns do lie to the west, especially along Guadalupe Street between Alameda Street and Paseo de Peralta and the historic blocks just west. At the intersection with of Paseo de Peralta and Guadalupe, you'll find the expansive DeVargas shopping center, which has a few notable shops and eateries, a movie theater, and some larger grocery and big-box stores—handy if you just need basic supplies (and still within walking distance of the Plaza).

A GOOD TOUR: RAILYARD DISTRICT

From the Plaza, head west on San Francisco Street, take a left onto Galisteo Street, then a right onto Alameda Street, and continue two blocks to Guadalupe Street, where you'll see the **Santuario de Guadalupe** just across the Santa Fe River. After you visit the Santuario, take your time browsing through the shops and eating lunch in one of the restaurants lining Guadalupe Street or around the corner, to the right on Montezuma Street, at the Sanbusco Market Center, a massive, converted warehouse that's home to a few fine boutiques. Back on Guadalupe, head south to the historic Gross Kelly Warehouse, one of the earliest Santa Fe–style buildings. Note Santa Fe's two train depots—one is now the site of popular, but touristy, Tomasita's Restaurant; the other, set farther back, is the Santa Fe Depot, where New Mexico Rail Runner departs. Continue a short distance south on Guadalupe until you reach **SITE Santa Fe** gallery and performance space, set inside a former bottling warehouse. Across the street, spend some time wandering the aisles, or picking up picnic supplies, at the friendly, bustling **Santa Fe Farmers' Market**. It's amazing both the amount of produce and goods coming from this high desert region and the huge crowds that pack the grounds on market days. Just beyond the Farmers' Market is the Railyard Park (at Paseo de Peralta and Guadalupe Street) where you can stroll, or lounge and enjoy your edible goodies amidst green grass, lovely trees, and great stonework. Catercorner from SITE Santa Fe, **El Museo Cultural de Santa Fe** is one of the state's more unusual museums, a combination performance space, classroom, gallery, and event venue that promotes Hispanic culture and education in the City Different. In the gallery at Santa Fe Clay, next door to El Museo, you'll find world-class ceramic sculpture and working studios.

TIMING

A visit to the Santuario de Guadalupe can take 15 minutes to an hour, depending on whether or not there's an art show in progress. If you like shopping and visiting art galleries, and decide to eat in this area, you might spend hours in this diverse and exciting neighborhood. At a minimum, allow yourself two hours to stroll from the Plaza through the neighborhood as far south as Railyard Park.

NORTH SIDE

You'll find some of Santa Fe's prettiest scenery on the hilly north side of town, which extends from the Sangre de Cristo foothills (home to some distinctive accommodations, including Ten Thousand Waves and the Four Seasons) west through the historic and artsy village of Tesuque, and then across rolling, sagebrush-dotted mesas that contain the city's famed opera house and one of the popular Marty Sanchez golf courses.

SOUTH SIDE

The majority of Santa Feans live in the South Side, which encompasses a vast stretch of relatively level mesa land. What this largely middle-class and in some places sprawly part of town lacks in scenic beauty—especially along traffic-choked and strip-mall-lined Cerrillos Road—it makes up for in convenient services. It's also where you're going to find most of the area's mid-range and budget chain accommodations and fast-food restaurants, along with an increasing number of genuinely notable eateries, from down-home neighborhood favorites like Horseman's Haven and Tecolote Café to inspired contemporary spots like Harry's Roadhouse, Midtown Bistro, and Dr. Field Goods Kitchen.

3

WHERE TO EAT

Eating out is a major pastime in Santa Fe and it's well worth coming here with a mind to join in on the fun. Restaurants with high-profile chefs stand beside low-key joints, many offering unique and intriguing variations on regional and international cuisine. You'll find restaurants full of locals and tourists alike all over the Downtown and surrounding areas. Although Santa Fe does have some high-end restaurants where dinner for two can exceed $200, the city also has plenty of reasonably priced dining options.

Waits for tables are very common during the busy summer season, so it's a good idea to call ahead even when reservations aren't accepted, if only to get a sense of the waiting time. Reservations for dinner at the better restaurants are a must in summer and on weekends the rest of the year.

So-called Santa Fe–style cuisine has so many influences that the term has become virtually meaningless, especially with many of the city's top eateries embracing a more international approach to cuisine, albeit all the while sourcing more and more from local farms and ranches. At many top spots in town, you'll detect Latin American, Mediterranean, and East Asian influences. Yet plenty of traditional, old-style Santa Fe restaurants still serve authentic New Mexican fare, which combines both Native American and Hispanic traditions and is quite different from Americanized as well as regional Mexican cooking.

Santa Fe's culinary reputation continues to grow not just in terms of restaurants but also in businesses that produce or sell specialty foods and beverages, from fine chocolates and local honeys and jams to increasingly acclaimed New Mexico wines, beers, and spirits. *See Shopping, Chapter 6, for a list of these purveyors.* Don't miss Saturday morning's Santa Fe Farmers' Market, one of the best in the Southwest.

Prices in the restaurant reviews are the average cost of a main course at dinner or, if dinner is not served, at lunch; taxes and service charges are generally included.

WHERE TO EAT

THE PLAZA

★ Fodor'sChoice ✕ **Cafe Pasqual's.** *Eclectic.* A perennial favor-
$$$ ite, this cheerful cubbyhole dishes up Nuevo Latino and occasional Asian specialties for breakfast, lunch, and dinner. Don't be discouraged by lines out front—it's worth

BEST BETS FOR SANTA FE DINING

Fodor's Choice★
Cafe Pasqual's, Clafoutis, The Compound, Galisteo Bistro, Geronimo, Harry's Roadhouse, Il Piatto, Inn of the Anasazi, La Boca and Taberna, La Choza, The Shed

BEST BURGERS
The Compound, Santa Fe Bite, Tune-Up Cafe

BEST CAFÉS
Chocolate Maven, Clafoutis

BEST ASIAN
Mu Du Noodles, Shohko

BEST CONTEMPORARY
315 Restaurant & Wine Bar, Cafe Pasqual's, Restaurant Martin

BEST ITALIAN
Andiamo, Il Piatto

BEST NEW MEXICAN
Atrisco's Café & Bar, La Choza, Tia Sophia's

BEST BAR MENU
El Farol, El Mesón & Chispa Tapas Bar, Zia Diner

BEST BREAKFAST
Cafe Pasqual's, Harry's Roadhouse, Tecolote Café, Tia Sophia's

the wait (reservations are available—and strongly recommended—for dinner only). The culinary muse behind it all is Katharine Kagel, who champions organic, local ingredients, and whose expert kitchen staff produces mouthwatering breakfast and lunch specialties like the breakfast relleno (a big, cheese-stuffed chile with eggs and a smoky tomato salsa served with beans and tortillas), huevos motuleños (eggs in a tangy tomatillo salsa with black beans and fried bananas), and the sublime grilled free-range chicken sandwich. Dinner is a more formal, though still friendly and easygoing, affair: the double lamb chop with pomegranate-molasses glaze is a pleasure; the starter of Vietnamese flash-sautéed scallops on a salad of jicame, grapefruit, and purple cabbage is a revelation. Mexican folk art, colorful tiles, and murals by Oaxacan artist Leovigildo Martinez create a festive atmosphere. Try the chummy communal table, or go late morning or after 1:30 pm to (hopefully) avoid the crush. *Average main: $30 ✉ 121 Don Gaspar Ave., The Plaza ☎ 505/983–9340 🌐 www.pasquals.com.*

$$$$ ✕ **Coyote Cafe.** *Southwestern.* Noted chef Eric DiStefano operates this long-running pioneer of contemporary Southwestern cuisine, although results here have always been a bit more uneven than at his other restaurant, Geronimo. Coyote Cafe is reliable for taste variations on the beloved green chile, but the menu has evolved to include the flavors

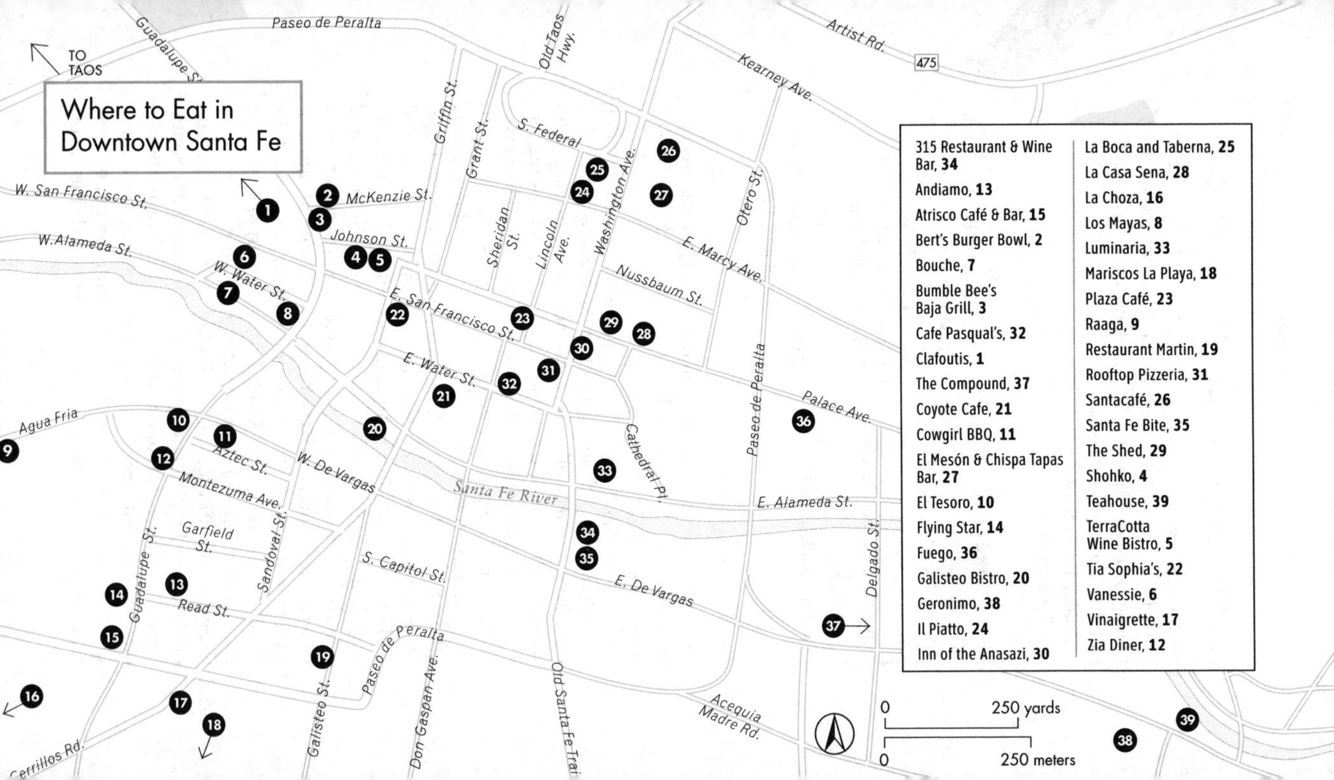
Where to Eat in Downtown Santa Fe
TO TAOS
315 Restaurant & Wine Bar, 34
Andiamo, 13
Atrisco Café & Bar, 15
Bert's Burger Bowl, 2
Bouche, 7
Bumble Bee's Baja Grill, 3
Cafe Pasqual's, 32
Clafoutis, 1
The Compound, 37
Coyote Cafe, 21
Cowgirl BBQ, 11
El Mesón & Chispa Tapas Bar, 27
El Tesoro, 10
Flying Star, 14
Fuego, 36
Galisteo Bistro, 20
Geronimo, 38
Il Piatto, 24
Inn of the Anasazi, 30
La Boca and Taberna, 25
La Casa Sena, 28
La Choza, 16
Los Mayas, 8
Luminaria, 33
Mariscos La Playa, 18
Plaza Café, 23
Raaga, 9
Restaurant Martin, 19
Rooftop Pizzeria, 31
Santacafé, 26
Santa Fe Bite, 35
The Shed, 29
Shohko, 4
Teahouse, 39
TerraCotta Wine Bistro, 5
Tia Sophia's, 22
Vanessie, 6
Vinaigrette, 17
Zia Diner, 12
Paseo de Peralta
Guadalupe St.
Artist Rd.
475
Kearney Ave.
Old Taos Hwy.
Griffin St.
Grant St.
S. Federal
W. San Francisco St.
McKenzie St.
Johnson St.
W.Alameda St.
W. Water St.
Sheridan St.
Lincoln Ave.
Washington Ave.
Otero St.
E. Marcy Ave.
Nussbaum St.
E. San Francisco St.
E. Water St.
Palace Ave.
Agua Fria
Aztec St.
W. De Vargas
Montezuma Ave.
Santa Fe River
Cathedral Pl.
E. Alameda St.
Garfield St.
Sandoval St.
S. Capitol St.
Delgado St.
E. De Vargas
Read St.
Galisteo St.
Don Gaspan Ave.
Old Santa Fe Trai
Acequia Madre Rd.
Cerrillos Rd.
0
250 yards
0
250 meters

of French and Asian cuisine. Menu offerings include fiery hot-and-sweet Mexican white prawns with crisp almond rice cakes; a peppery elk tenderloin; and the rotisserie rock hen with herbs de Provence. Service and food quality vary widely—not an encouraging trend considering the high cost of dining here. Your best bet may be to head to the adjacent Rooftop Cantina (open April through October), a fun outdoor gathering spot with a loud and lively social scene where you can enjoy cool cocktails and flavorful under-$15 fare like burgers and Mexico-inspired fish tacos. On the ground floor, a lounge called the Den serves first-rate craft cocktails, but the overly slick vibe feels out of place in laid-back Santa Fe. *Average main: $36* *132 W. Water St., The Plaza* *505/983–1615* *www.coyotecafe.com* *No lunch at Coyote Cafe (Rooftop Cantina only).*

$$$ × **El Mesón & Chispa Tapas Bar.** *Spanish.* This place is as fun for having drinks and late-night tapas or catching live music (from tango nights to Sephardic music) as for enjoying a full meal. The dining room has an old-world feel with simple dark-wood tables and chairs, creamy plastered walls, and a wood-beam ceiling—unpretentious yet elegant. The Chispa bar is livelier and feels like a Spanish *taberna*. The delicious tapas menu includes dishes like Serrano ham and fried artichoke hearts stuffed with Spanish goat cheese over *romesco* sauce. Among the more substantial entrées are a stellar paella as well as veal roulade stuffed with Serrano ham and Manchego and served over a light, sweet tomato sauce. *Average main: $27* *213 Washington Ave., The Plaza* *505/983–6756* *www.elmeson-santafe.com* *Closed Sun. and Mon. No lunch.*

$$$ × **Fuego.** *Southwestern.* An elegant yet comfortable dining room inside the oasis of La Posada resort, Fuego has become a local favorite for reliably good Latin-inspired American and New Mexican food and flawless service. Once known for sky-high prices and more elaborate fare, Fuego has become both more accessible and wallet-friendly, turning out a good mix of well-prepared lighter bites (lamb burgers, prosciutto and lobster salad, Korean tacos) and heartier entrées, including a commendable steak frites with green-chile aioli and pan-blackened salmon. The wine list is impressive and the helpful sommelier is always on hand to advise. The expansive, shady patio is a lovely spot for breakfast or lunch; there's live entertainment in the evenings. *Average main: $25* *La Posada de Santa Fe Resort and Spa, 330 E. Palace Ave., East Side and Canyon Road* *505/986–0000* *www.laposadadesantafe.com.*

★ Fodor'sChoice ✕ **Galisteo Bistro.** *Eclectic.* Walk into this inviting
$$ space a few blocks from the Plaza—with its open kitchen, stacked stone walls, and high ceiling—and you'll likely hope that the food tastes as good as the room feels. Thankfully, it does. The crab cakes are stellar; leading entrées include "farmhouse" meatloaf (beef, veal, and pork with a marsala-mushroom demi-glace), and slow-braised lamb shank in maple-barbecue sauce, and there's also a noteworthy cheese list and a menu of lighter, international tapas selections. The beautiful desserts often favor chocolate. There's a nice selection of wines, plus a limited offering of locally brewed beers. *Average main: $23 ✉ 227 Galisteo St., The Plaza ☎ 505/982–3700 ⊕ www.galisteobistro.com ⊗ Closed Mon. and Tues. No lunch.*

★ Fodor'sChoice ✕ **Il Piatto.** *Italian.* Chef Matt Yohalem contin-
$$ ues to charm the legions of local fans and lucky visitors who dine at his place with creative pasta dishes like *pappardelle* with braised duckling, caramelized onions, sun-dried tomatoes, and mascarpone-duck au jus or homemade pumpkin ravioli with pine nuts and sage brown butter. Entrées include rabbit leg panée with purple potatoes and mustard gravy, and a superb pancetta-wrapped trout with rosemary, wild mushrooms, and polenta. The menu, which usually features several creative specials, emphasizes locally sourced ingredients. It's a crowded but enjoyable trattoria with informal ambience, reasonable prices, and a snug bar. For about $33, the prix-fixe dinner, with an appetizer, main dish, and dessert, is a steal, as is the late-night happy hour (served from 9 pm until close). Add a glass of wine from the reputable list of Italians and both your stomach and your wallet will leave happy. *Average main: $20 ✉ 95 W. Marcy St., The Plaza ☎ 505/984–1091 ⊕ www.ilpiattosantafe.com ⊗ No lunch Sun.*

★ Fodor'sChoice ✕ **Inn of the Anasazi.** *American.* Argentine chef
$$$$ Juan Bochenski balances a Latin and European sensibility in his approach to the kitchen at this romantic, 90-seat restaurant with hardwood floors, soft lighting, smooth-plastered walls, and beam ceilings that create a slightly less formal feel than other big-ticket dining rooms in town. A plate of plump sea scallops with celery-root puree, corn-chorizo succotash, and 12-hour-cooked pork belly is available as a starter or main dish; other worthy entrées include roasted free-range local lamb with smoked eggplant and jalapeño croquettes, and chile-almond-crusted salmon with a blood orange butter sauce. A fun lighter menu (cheese plates, buffalo burger sliders, ahi tacos) is available on the

inviting patio, a fun spot for street-side people-watching, and in the cozy, convivial bar. Sunday brunch is superb. *Average main: $32* *113 Washington Ave., The Plaza* *505/988–3030* *www.innoftheanasazi.com.*

★ Fodor's Choice ✕ **La Boca and Taberna.** *Spanish.* Already a beacon of superbly crafted, authentic yet creatively updated Spanish tapas, La Boca expanded into two distinct spaces in 2012. There's the intimate and quieter original storefront dining room that's better for a leisurely romantic repast, and in back, spilling out into a cloistered courtyard, there's Taberna, a bustling tavern with live music, ample seating indoors and out, and late hours. Both spaces feature the delectable small-plates cooking of celebrated chef James Cambpell Caruso, and a full meal in either spot is similarly priced though just a tad pricier in the main restaurant, where the food also tends more toward contemporary: *bocadillos* (sandwiches) of pan-seared ahi or braised-beef tongue with green mustard, braised pork ribs with quince-clove glaze, grilled artichokes with Spanish goat cheese and mint. In both sections, there's a long list of fine Spanish wines and sherries, and great deals during the daily afternoon and (in Taberna) late-night happy hours. *Average main: $20* *72 W. Marcy St., The Plaza* *505/982–3433* *www.labocasf.com.*
$$

$$$ ✕ **La Casa Sena.** *American.* The Southwestern-accented and Continental fare served at La Casa Sena is beautifully presented and generally quite delicious. Weather permitting, get a table on the patio surrounded by hollyhocks, flowering shrubs, and centuries-old adobe walls. A favorite entrée is the braised Colorado lamb shank with chipotle-*huitlacoche* demi-glace, roasted purple- and Yukon-gold potatoes, braised *cipollini* onions, and orange *gremolata.* There's a knockout lemon crème brûlée as well as a tantalizingly sweet-and-tart sour cream–blueberry sundae with blue-corn crumble on the dessert menu. For a musical meal (evenings only), sit in the restaurant's adjacent, less-pricey Cantina ($$), where the talented and perky staff belt out Broadway show tunes. An on-site wine shop sells many of the estimable vintages offered on the restaurant's wine list. *Average main: $24* *Sena Plaza, 125 E. Palace Ave., The Plaza* *505/988–9232* *www.lacasasena.com.*

$$$ ✕ **Luminaria.** *American.* The casually sophisticated restaurant at Santa Fe's Inn at Loretto is one of the most inviting dining spaces in town. Inside, there's a contemporary dining room with a kiva-style fireplace, white-washed pine floors and vibrant artwork. On warm days or evenings, take a

seat on the lushly landscaped patio. Breakfast and Sunday brunch are great times to dine here—the breakfast burritos are almost comically gigantic, and the orange-poppy waffles are topped with blueberry compote, whipped cream, and maple syrup. But dinners are the main event. You might start with grilled achiote-marinated shrimp with pumpkin mole, or the exceptional tortilla soup, before moving on to blackened salmon *a la plancha* with scallion risotto and lemon beurre blanc, or lightly smoked duck breast with a cherry compote, ancho sauce, and marcona almonds. Take note of the impressive wine list. *Average main: $31 Inn at Loretto, 211 Old Santa Fe Trail, The Plaza 505/988–5531 www.innatloretto.com.*

$$ **Plaza Café.** *Eclectic.* Run with homespun care by the Razatos family since 1947, this café has been a fixture on the Plaza since 1918. The decor—red leather banquettes, black Formica tables, tile floors, a coffered tin ceiling, and a 1940s-style service counter—hasn't changed much in the past half century. The food runs the gamut, from cashew mole enchiladas to New Mexico meat loaf to chile-smothered burritos to a handful of Greek favorites, but the ingredients tend toward Southwestern. You'll be hard put to find a better tortilla soup. You can cool it off with an old-fashioned ice-cream treat from the soda fountain or a slice of one of the delicious, homemade pies. It's a good, tasty stop for breakfast, lunch, or dinner. The newer South Side branch (*3466 Zafarano Dr. 505/424–0755*) is close to Cerrillos Road hotels. *Average main: $16 54 Lincoln Ave., The Plaza 505/982–1664 www.thefamousplazacafe.com Reservations not accepted.*

$$ **Rooftop Pizzeria.** *Pizza.* For sophisticated pizza, head to this slick indoor-outdoor restaurant on the upper level of Santa Fe Arcade. The kitchen here scores high marks for its rich and imaginative pizza toppings: consider the one topped with lobster, shrimp, mushrooms, apple-smoked bacon, caramelized leeks, truffle oil, Alfredo sauce, and four cheeses on a blue-corn crust. Antipasti and salads are impressive, too, as there's a wonderful smoked-duck-confit-and-peppercorn spread, or the smoked-salmon Caesar salad. There's also an extensive wine and microbrew beer list. Although the Santa Fe Arcade's main entrance is on the Plaza, it's easier to access the restaurant from the arcade's Water Street entrance. *Average main: $14 60 E. San Francisco St., The Plaza 505/984–0008 www.rooftoppizzeria.com.*

$$$ ✕ **Santacafé.** *Southwestern.* Fans of this long-acclaimed member of Santa Fe's culinary vanguard most appreciate it as a destination for lunch or afternoon happy hour on the inviting shaded patio, which is one of the prettiest and quietest outdoor venues in Downtown Santa Fe. This minimalist, elegant restaurant two blocks north of the Plaza in the historic Padre Gallegos House focuses on seasonally driven, inventive cuisine, which might include grilled pomegranate-marinated Colorado lamb chops with roasted red potatoes and Swiss chard; or citrus-crusted pan-seared wild Alaskan halibut with Israeli couscous, baby bok choy, and orange-cilantro beurre blanc. Sunday brunch is also highly regarded. *Average main: $28 231 Washington Ave., The Plaza 505/984–1788 www.santacafe.com.*

★ Fodor's Choice ✕ **The Shed.** *Mexican.* The lines at lunch attest
$$ to the status of this Downtown New Mexican eatery. The rambling, low-doored, and atmospheric adobe dating from 1692 is decorated with folk art, and service is downright neighborly. Even if you're a devoted green-chile sauce fan, consider trying the locally grown red chile the place is famous for; it is rich and perfectly spicy. Specialties include red-chile enchiladas, green-chile stew with potatoes and pork, comforting posole, and their charbroiled Shedburgers. The mushroom bisque is a milder and delicious starter. Homemade desserts, like the mocha cake, are a yummy way to smooth out the spice. There's a full bar, too. *Average main: $16 113½ E. Palace Ave., The Plaza 505/982–9030 www.sfshed.com Closed Sun.*

$$$ ✕ **Shohko.** *Japanese.* Shohko and her family run this first-rate Japanese restaurant that's known for the freshest, best-prepared sushi and sashimi in town. On any given night there are two-dozen or more varieties of fresh fish available. The soft-shell crab tempura is feather-light, and the salad with crispy panko-crusted calamari is delicious. Sit at the sushi bar and watch the expert chefs, including Shohko, work their magic, or at one of the tables in this old adobe with whitewashed walls, dark-wood vigas, and Japanese decorative details. Table service is friendly, but can be slow. *Average main: $21 321 Johnson St., The Plaza 505/982–9708 www.shohkocafe.com Closed Sun. No lunch Sat.*

$$ ✕ **TerraCotta Wine Bistro.** *Wine Bar.* Locals familiar with the considerable culinary talents of Catherine O'Brien and Glenda Griswold, longtime owners of Peas 'n' Pod Catering, rejoiced when the duo opened this affordable, warmly decorated bistro and wine bar in summer 2013 inside a cozy late-19th-century Territorial-style house near the O'Keeffe

Museum. The menu favors snacking and sharing—salmon salad with pomegranate vinaigrette, bruschetta with Brie and fig-port jam, flatbread pizzas, panini, grilled flank steak. These are the perfect complements to a glass of rosé or Cotes du Rhone from the long, value-driven list of wines by the glass. There's a great Sunday brunch, too, best enjoyed in warm weather on the front porch when the fragrant flower garden is in bloom. *Average main: $18* *304 Johnson St., The Plaza* *505/989–1166* *www.terracottawinebistro.com.*

$ ✕ **Tia Sophia's.** *Southwestern.* This Downtown joint serves strictly New Mexican breakfasts and lunches (open until 2 pm most days and 1 on Sundays). You're as likely to be seated next to a family from a remote village in the mountains as you are to a legislator or lobbyist from the nearby state capitol. Tia's ("Auntie's") delicious burritos stuffed with homemade chorizo disappear fast on Saturdays; get there early. Order anything and expect a true taste of local tradition, including perfectly flaky, light sopaipillas. Mammoth chile-smothered breakfast burritos will hold you over for hours on the powdery ski slopes during winter. Be warned, though: the red and green chiles are spicy, and you're expected to understand this elemental fact of local cuisine. Alcohol is not served here. *Average main: $8* *210 W. San Francisco St., The Plaza* *505/983–9880* *No dinner.*

OLD SANTA FE TRAIL AND SOUTH CAPITOL

$$$ ✕ **315 Restaurant & Wine Bar.** *French.* As if it were on a thoroughfare in Paris rather than on Old Santa Fe Trail, 315 has a Continental, white-tablecloth sophistication, but the offbeat wall art and unfussy ambience gives it a light, fun feel. Chef-owner Louis Moskow uses traditional techniques to prepare contemporary French bistro fare using organic vegetables and locally raised meats. Daily specialties on the ever-evolving menu might include squash-blossom beignets with local goat cheese, basil-wrapped shrimp with apricot chutney and curry sauce, or grilled boneless lamb loin with crispy polenta, spring vegetables, and green peppercorn sauce. The garden patio opens onto the street scene. There's also a wine bar with an exceptional list of vintages and light snacks, like crispy monkfish "nuggets" and house-made tater tots with wasabi tobiko caviar and crème fraîche. *Average main: $24* *315 Old Santa Fe Trail, Old Santa Fe Trail and South Capitol* *505/986–9190* *www.315santafe.com* *No lunch.*

$$ × **Mariscos La Playa.** *Seafood.* Yes, even in landlocked Santa Fe it's possible to find incredibly fresh and well-prepared seafood served in big portions. This cheery, colorful Mexican restaurant surrounded by strip malls is just a short hop south of Downtown. Favorite dishes include the absolutely delicious shrimp wrapped in bacon with Mexican cheese and *caldo vuelve a la vida* ("come back to life"), a hearty soup of shrimp, octopus, scallops, clams, crab, and calamari. There are also ceviche tostadas, fresh oysters on the half shell, and *pescado a la plancha,* super-tender trout cooked with butter and paprika. The staff and service are delightful. *Average main: $14* *537 W. Cordova Rd., South Side* *505/982–2790.*

$$$ × **Restaurant Martin.** *American.* After cooking at some of the best restaurants in town (Geronimo, the Old House, Anasazi), acclaimed chef Martin Rios now flexes his culinary muscles in his own place, a simple, elegant restaurant with a gorgeous patio. Martin prepares progressive American cuisine, which is heavily influenced by his French culinary training. Lunch favorites include his superb Cobb salad, and a deftly prepared Atlantic salmon BLT sandwich. Dinner entrées include a delicious vegetarian tasting plate that might feature a butternut squash Napoleon, curried quinoa–French lentil salad, and garlic-spinach tempura Jasmine rice, and a grilled Kurobuta pork striploin with *guajillo* chile–and–plum glaze with sweet potato and crispy young vegetables. The Sunday brunch menu includes classic huevos rancheros prepared with typical Martin flair, and crispy Alaskan halibut Baja fish tacos. *Average main: $31* *526 Galisteo St., Old Santa Fe Trail and South Capitol* *505/820–0919* *www.restaurantmartinsantafe.com* *Closed Mon. No lunch Sat.*

$ × **Santa Fe Bite.** *Burger.* John and Bonnie Eckre, the former owners of the legendary Bobcat Bite burger joint have brought their juicy green-chile cheeseburgers and humongous 16-ounce "Big Bite" burgers to a much bigger audience. There's breakfast and weekend brunch, too—morning highlights include brioche French toast with strawberries and maple-caramel sauce, and traditional steak-and-eggs. The casually contemporary dining room is light and attractive, if lacking the funky vibe of Bobcat Bite, but you come here chiefly for the great food. *Average main: $10* *Garrett's Desert Inn, 311 Old Santa Fe Trail, Old Santa Fe Trail and South Capitol* *505/982–0544* *www.santafebite.com* *Closed Mon.*

FAMILY

3

EAST SIDE AND CANYON ROAD

★ $$$$ Fodor's Choice ✕ **The Compound.** *Eclectic.* Chef Mark Kiffin has transformed this gracious, folk-art-filled old restaurant into one of the state's culinary darlings. It's a fancy place, thanks to decor by famed designer Alexander Girard and a highly attentive staff, but it maintains an easygoing, distinctly Santa Fe feel. From chef Kiffin's oft-changing menu devoted to seasonal and local ingredients, consider a starter of ravioli filled with "forever-braised" short ribs and tossed in Parmesan cream with black truffles. Memorable entrées include Muscovy duck with steamed baby bok choy, wild mushrooms, and a rhubard-ginger compote, and Scottish salmon with crispy pancetta–fingerling potato salad and a Riesling-apple glaze. The extensive and carefully chosen wine list will please the most discerning oenophile. Lunch is as delightful as dinner, featuring one of the best burgers in town, especially if you dine amid the gardens on the patio. *Average main: $35 ✉ 653 Canyon Rd., East Side and Canyon Road ☎ 505/982–4353 ⊕ www.compound-restaurant.com ⊙ No lunch Sun.*

★ $$$$ Fodor's Choice ✕ **Geronimo.** *American.* At this bastion of high cuisine, the complex dishes range from New Mexico lamb chops with panfried red potato cakes, candied shallots, and hot mustard–chile-mint sauces to mesquite-grilled Maine lobster tails over angel hair pasta, served with a creamy garlic-chile sauce. Chef Eric DiStefano's peppery elk tenderloin with apple-smoked bacon remains a perennial favorite. Desserts are artful and rich—note the chocolate hazelnut cake with blood-orange sauce and caramel crème anglaise. Located in the Borrego House, a massive-walled adobe dating from 1756, the intimate, white dining rooms have beamed ceilings, wood floors, fireplaces, and cushioned *bancos* (banquettes). The restaurant is renowned for both its cuisine and its highly refined service. In summer you can dine under the front portal; in winter the bar with fireplace is inviting. For a less formal experience, dine in the dark, seductive bar—the cocktails are excellent. *Average main: $38 ✉ 724 Canyon Rd., East Side and Canyon Road ☎ 505/982–1500 ⊕ www.geronimorestaurant.com ⊙ No lunch.*

$$ ✕ **Teahouse.** *Café.* A delightful spot toward the end of gallery row at the intersection of Canyon Road and East Palace Avenue, the Teahouse has several bright dining rooms throughout the converted adobe home, and a tranquil outdoor seating area in a rock garden. In addition to

fine teas from all over the world, you can find extremely well-prepared breakfast and lunch fare, including baked polenta with poached eggs and romesco sauce, bagels and lox, and wild-mushroom panini. Light fare as well as wine and beer are served in the evenings. The service tends to be leisurely but friendly. *Average main: $14 821 Canyon Rd., East Side and Canyon Road 505/992–0972 www.teahousesantafe.com.*

RAILYARD DISTRICT

$$ **Andiamo.** *Italian.* A longtime locals' favorite, Andiamo scores high marks for its friendly staff, consistently good food, and comfortable dining room. Produce from the farmers' market down the street adds to the seasonal surprises of this intimate northern Italian restaurant set inside a sweet cottage in the Railyard District. Start with the addictively delectable crispy polenta with rosemary and Gorgonzola sauce; move on to the white pizza with roasted garlic, fontina, grilled radicchio, pancetta, and rosemary; and consider such hearty entrées as crispy duck legs with grilled polenta, roasted turnips, and sautéed spinach; or linguine with spicy grilled shrimp and olives in a white wine tomato cream sauce. There's a super wine list with varied prices. Save room for the chocolate *pot de crème. Average main: $17 322 Garfield St., Railyard District 505/995–9595 www.andiamoonline.com No lunch weekends.*

$ **Cowgirl BBQ.** *Southern.* A rollicking, popular bar and grill
FAMILY with several rooms overflowing with Old West memorabilia, Cowgirl has reasonably priced Southwestern, Tex-Mex, barbecue, and Southern fare. Highlights include barbecue, buffalo burgers, chiles rellenos, and salmon tacos with tomatillo salsa. If you catch one of the nightly music acts—usually rock or blues—you're likely to leave smiling. When the weather is good, grab a seat on the spacious patio out front, order a delicious margarita and some green-chile cheese fries, and settle in for great people-watching. The attached pool hall has a great jukebox to keep toes tapping. Alas, service can be spotty. *Average main: $12 319 S. Guadalupe St., Railyard District 505/982–2565 www.cowgirlsantafe.com.*

$ **El Tesoro.** *Latin American.* One of the Railyard District's better-kept secrets, this small café occupies a spot in the high-ceilinged center of the Sanbusco Center, steps from several chic boutiques. The tiny kitchen turns out a mix of Central American, New Mexican, and American dishes, all of them reliable. Grilled tuna tacos with *salsa fresca*, black beans, and rice; and Salvadorian chicken tamales wrapped in banana leaves are among the tastiest treats. El Tesoro also serves breakfast fare (including great French toast with strawberries), pastries, gelato, lemon bars, hot cocoa, and other snacks, making it a perfect break from shopping. *Average main: $9 Sanbusco Market Center, 500 Montezuma Ave., Railyard District 505/988–3886 www.eltesorocafe.com No dinner.*

$ FAMILY **Flying Star Cafe.** *Café.* The lone Santa Fe outpost of the popular Albuquerque minichain occupies a spacious, high-ceilinged modern building in the heart of the Railyard District. With comfy booths, ample access to outlets (for plugging in laptops or smartphones), and long hours (7 am until 9 or 10 pm daily), this lively spot serves many functions: office-away-from-home, bar (wine and beer only), coffeehouse, and full-service restaurant. You order at the counter, and service is quick and friendly. Check out the extensive list of blackboard specials, or go with a Flying Star classic, like the Southwest eggs Bennie (with turkey sausage and a cheesy-chile sauce), Chinese "crunch" salad with chicken or tofu, or grilled sirloin sandwich with Jack cheese, green chiles, and horseradish sauce. Breakfast is served all day, and there's also a huge selection of decadent cakes and cookies. *Average main: $11 500 Market St., Railyard District 505/216–3939 www.flyingstarcafe.com.*

★ $ FAMILY Fodor's Choice **La Choza.** *Mexican.* The off-the-beaten-path and less expensive sister to the Shed, La Choza (which means "the shed" in Spanish), serves supertasty, super-traditional New Mexican fare. It's hard to go wrong here: chicken or pork *carne adovada* (marinated in red chile and slow-cooked until tender) burritos, white clam chowder spiced with green chiles, and the classic huevos rancheros are exceptional. The dining rooms are dark and cozy, with vigas across the ceiling and local art on the walls. The staff is friendly and competent, and the margaritas are potent and flavorful. *Average main: $12 905 Alarid St., Railyard District 505/982–0909 www.lachozasf.com Closed Sun.*

$$ **Raaga.** *Indian.* In a town with some surprisingly good Indian restaurants, this intimate spot in a cozy Railyard District bungalow earns kudos for the modern interpretations of talented chef Paddy Rawal, who frequently uses New Mexican ingredients in his delicious creations. Among the starters, don't miss the *lasooni gobhi* (cauliflower florets sautéed in garlic sauce) and chicken-mint

salad with mango and mint chutny and pico de gallo. Notable main dishes include mahimahi marinated in yogurt, lime leaf, green chile, and saffron, and *paneer mutter* (garden peas and farmers cheese in a mild cashew sauce). The honey-soaked "milk puffs" make a nice ending to a hearty meal. *Average main: $15 ✉ 544 Agua Fria St., Railyard District ☎ 505/820–6440 ⊕ www.raagacuisine.com ⊙ Closed Sun.*

$$ ✕ **Vinaigrette.** *American.* A novel and noble alternative to the many Santa Fe restaurants that favor filling (and often fattening) fare, Vinaigrette is all about the greens, which are sourced organically, with the majority of produce raised on owner Erin Wade's 10-acre farm in nearby Nambé. This isn't mere rabbit food, however; the hearty salads make a satisfying meal, especially when you add toppings like grilled flank steak, hibiscus-cured duck confit, or seared sea scallops. The apple-cheddar chop and classic French frissée salads are among the highlights. For a casual space with sometimes uneven service (especially during the busy lunch rush), Vinaigrette is a bit spendy—but you're paying those few extra dollars for high-quality, local ingredients. There's a branch in Albuquerque's Old Town neighborhood, too. ■ TIP→ **While you're here, check out the new next-door burger joint Shake Foundation**, which as of this writing is set to open in early 2014, with renowned chef Brian Knox at the helm. *Average main: $16 ✉ 709 Don Cubero Alley, Railyard District ☎ 505/820–9205 ⊕ www.vinaigretteonline.com ⊙ Closed Sun.*

$ ✕ **Zia Diner.** *American.* In a renovated coal warehouse from the 1880s, this quirky diner with a low-key, art-deco-style interior serves comfort food with a twist (green-chile-piñon meat loaf, for example). Stop in for a full meal or just snack on their classic banana split with homemade hot fudge sauce. Zia's Cobb salad is one of the best in town, and the amazingly fluffy corn, green chile, and Asiago pie served with a mixed green salad is hard to match. There's a small patio and a friendly bar known for its tasty mixed drinks and personable bartenders. Breakfast here is great start to the day: try the smoked-salmon eggs Benedict. *Average main: $12 ✉ 326 S. Guadalupe St., Railyard District ☎ 505/988–7008 ⊕ www.ziadiner.com.*

WEST OF THE PLAZA

★ Fodor's Choice ✕ **Arroyo Vino.** *Wine Bar.* It's worth making
$$ the 15-minute trek out to Santa Fe's western mesa to dine at this outstanding bistro–cum–wine shop that's quickly developed a devout following among locals. At the store, stock up on often hard-to-find vintages from all over the world—for a $20 corkage fee, you can also enjoy your new Bordeaux or Albariño in the airy dining room, where tables are set around a central wine bar and the night's specials are handwritten on a chalkboard. The menu of deftly prepared contemporary American fare is in a small-plate format, with dishes like braised veal cheeks with polenta and tomato confit, and housemade pappardelle pasta with lamb ragu and feta running $10–$15, but you'll want to order two to four portions per person. *Average main: $16 ✉ 218 Camino la Tierra, off NM 599, 4 miles west of U.S. 285/84, West of the Plaza ☎ 505/983–2100 ⊕ www.arroyovino.com ⊗ Closed Sun.–Mon. No lunch.*

$ ✕ **Atrisco Café & Bar.** *Southwestern.* Run by the family behind Tia Sophia's and Tomasita's, this first-rate, affordable New Mexican restaurant is in a cheerfully decorated space inside the humdrum but conveniently located DeVargas shopping center (just five minutes north of the Plaza). At Atrisco, delightful, authentic classics are upgraded with local organic meats and high-quality produce—the sopaipilla stuffed with roasted leg of lamb and smothered in red chile is highly recommended, as is the meat loaf with jalapeño-mashed potatoes. Breakfast is available on weekends. *Average main: $11 ✉ DeVargas Center, 193 Paseo de Peralta, West of the Plaza ☎ 505/983–7401 ⊕ www.atriscocafe.com.*

$ ✕ **Bert's Burger Bowl.** *Burger.* This unassuming, old-fashioned
FAMILY burger stand has brought fans back year after year since 1954 with favorites like their flame-broiled green-chile cheeseburgers (veggie burgers are available, too), crispy onion rings, jalapeño cheese fries, and hand-mixed cherry-lime Cokes. More recently, they've added higher-end burger options like Kobe beef, organic local lamb, and bison (these all come with specific toppings). Tacos, breakfast sandwiches, and breakfast burritos are also served. *Average main: $7 ✉ 235 N. Guadalupe St., West of the Plaza ☎ 505/982–0215 ⊕ www.bertsburgerbowl.com.*

★ Fodor's Choice ✕ **Bouche.** *French.* Talented chef-owner Charles
$$$ Dale (who previously cooked at Rancho Encantado's Terra, Daniel Boulud's Le Cirque, and at his own James Beard–lauded Renaissance restaurant in Aspen) opened this lively,

modern take on a traditional French neighborhood bistro in 2013. Choose a cozy table by the fireplace and try the consistently stellar renditions of calf's liver Dijonnaise, tenderloin steak tartare with a fresh farm egg, sautéed sweetbreads, and truffle frites—prices are more than fair compared with similarly upscale eateries around town. On warm days, take a seat on the quieter ramada-covered patio, where it feels like dining at a chic friend's house. *Average main: $24* *451 W. Alameda St., West of the Plaza* *505/982–6297* *www.bouchebistro.com* *Closed Sun.–Mon. No lunch.*

$ × **Bumble Bee's Baja Grill.** *Southwestern.* A bright, vibrantly
FAMILY colored restaurant with closely spaced tables, piñatas, and ceiling fans wafting overhead, Bumble Bee's (the nickname of the ebullient owner, Bob) delights locals with its super-fresh Cal Mex–style food. If you like fish tacos, the mahimahi ones with creamy, nondairy slaw are outstanding; try them with a side of salad instead of beans and rice. Mammoth burritos with a wide range of fillings (including asparagus—yum!), roasted chicken with cilantro-lime rice, char-grilled trout platters, and plenty of vegetarian options keep folks pouring through the doors. You order at the counter, grab some chips and a variety of freshly made salsas from the bar, and wait for your number to come up. Beer, wine, and Mexican soft drinks are served. Try a homemade Mexican chocolate brownie for dessert. There's another location on Cerrillos Road. *Average main: $10* *301 Jefferson St., West of the Plaza* *505/820–2862* *www.bumblebeesbajagrill.com.*

★ Fodor's Choice × **Clafoutis.** *Café.* Undeniably French, this bus-
$ tling café serves authentic, delicious food. Walk through the door of this bright, open space and you'll almost certainly be greeted with a cheery *"bonjour"* from Anne-Laure, who owns it with her husband, Philippe. Start your day with a crepe, one of the fluffy omelets, or *les gauffres* (large house waffles). Lunch offers quiches with perfectly flaky crusts, an enticing selection of large salads (the *salade de la maison* has pears, pine nuts, blue cheese, Spanish chorizo, tomatoes, and cucumbers atop mixed greens), and savory sandwiches, like the classic *croque madame* (grilled ham, egg, and cheese) on homemade bread. The classic onion soup is comforting on a cold day. The café's namesake dessert, clafoutis, is worth saving room for. The baguettes and pastries are perfectly prepared—no small feat at this elevation. *Average main: $10* *402 N. Guadalupe St., West of the Plaza* *505/988–1809* *Reservations not accepted* *Closed Sun. No dinner.*

3

$$ ✕ **Los Mayas.** *Latin American.* Owners Fernando Antillas and Reyes Solano brought the spirit of Latin America with them when they opened this restaurant. The cozy, tile-floored space has a shady patio—albeit with less-than-ambient plastic patio chairs. The menu mixes New Mexican, Latin American, and South American recipes. The guacamole made table-side is a sure bet, as is the *chile en nogada,* a stuffed pepper in a smooth, rich, and slightly sweet walnut sauce. Entrées, such as the charbroiled skirt steak and cheese rellenos with rice and black beans, or shrimp sautéed with butter and garlic, are equally reliable. There's guitar music every night, including flamenco on Saturday. Downsides are the busloads of tourists sometimes deposited here for prearranged meals and a building in need of some upgrades. *Average main: $10 ✉ 409 W. Water St., Santa Fe ☎ 505/986–9930 ⊕ www.losmayas.com ⊙ No lunch.*

$$$ ✕ **Vanessie.** *Steakhouse.* This classy, lodgelike space with high ceilings and a tremendously popular piano cabaret serves hefty portions of well-prepared chops and seafood to a well-heeled, older clientele. New Zealand rack of lamb, tenderloin of elk, and dry-aged steaks are among the specialties. Burgers, onion loaf, and salads are served in the piano bar, where noted musicians Doug Montgomery and Charles Tichenor perform classical and Broadway favorites well into the evening (no cover). *Average main: $10 ✉ 434 W. San Francisco St., Santa Fe ☎ 505/982–9966 ⊕ www.vanessiesantafe.com ⊙ No lunch.*

NORTH SIDE

$ ✕ **Gabriel's.** *Southwestern.* This rambling and often very busy restaurant has a great location (convenient for pre-opera and post-high-road tours), a gorgeous setting (the Spanish Colonial style art, the building, the flower-filled courtyard, and those mountain views!), and the outstanding made-to-order guacamole going for it. The margaritas aren't too shabby either. The overall food quality can be a little uneven, but given the reasonable prices, friendly service, and sunset views, it's a great all-around option, especially if you're staying on this side of town. *Average main: $13 ✉ 4 Banana La., off U.S. 285/84, Exit 176, just south of Buffalo Thunder Resort, 5 miles north of Santa Fe Opera, North Side ☎ 505/455–7000 ⊕ www.restauranteur.com/gabriels.*

★ Fodor's Choice ✕ **Terra.** *American.* Among the many reasons
$$$$ guests of the Four Seasons Rancho Encantado often find it difficult to ever leave the gloriously situated property is

this handsome yet down-to-earth restaurant that serves tantalizingly delicious and creative contemporary American and Southwestern cuisine. Young and charismatic chef Andrew Cooper cooked previously at Hawaii's Four Seasons Hualalai, which perhaps accounts for his knack for exquisitely plated seafood, from tuna tartare with avocado purée and crispy purple potato to pan-seared sea scallops with foie gras, caramelized pears, frisée, and a blood-orange reduction. Other dishes reflect a more Southwestern approach, including green chile–braised short ribs with smoked pumpkin, wilted chard, and a coffee glaze. The high-ceilinged dining room is lined with tall windows overlooking the mountains, and a side bar with a patio and fire pit is a fun hangout for cocktails and lighter bar nibbles. There's also a decadent Sunday brunch. *Average main: $34 Four Seasons Rancho Encantado, 198 State Road 592, North Side 505/946–5700 www.fourseasons.com/santafe/dining/restaurants/terra.*

3

$$ ✕ **Tesuque Village Market.** *Eclectic.* Nestled in the heart of the artsy, country-chic village of Tesuque (just a 10-minute drive from the Plaza and a couple of miles from the opera house), this laid-back café and impressively stocked neighborhood grocery store has long been famous for its eclectic crowd and charming patio dining area (the inside room can feel a little cramped). Breakfast, especially on weekends, draws sizable crowds—try the Big Ass Breakfast Sandwich, stuffed with eggs, bacon, lettuce, tomato, and cheddar. Later in the day, favorites include a justly famous tortilla soup, a housemade black-bean burger, and green-chile and pork tamales. A bakery doles out tempting sweets, and the corkage fee for wine purchased in the adjacent market is just $10. *Average main: $16 138 Tesuque Village Rd., North Side 505/988–8848 www.tesuquevillagemarket.com.*

SOUTH SIDE

$$ ✕ **Chocolate Maven.** *Café.* Although the name of this cheery bakery suggests sweets, and it does sweets especially well, Chocolate Maven produces impressive savory breakfast and lunch fare. Dinner is "farmers' market–inspired" and features seasonal dishes. Favorite treats include wild-mushroom-and-goat-cheese focaccia sandwiches, eggs ménage à trois (one each of eggs Benedict, Florentine, and Madison—the latter consisting of smoked salmon and poached egg), and Caprese salad of fresh mozzarella, basil, and tomatoes. Pizzas are thin-crusted and delicate. Some of the top desserts include

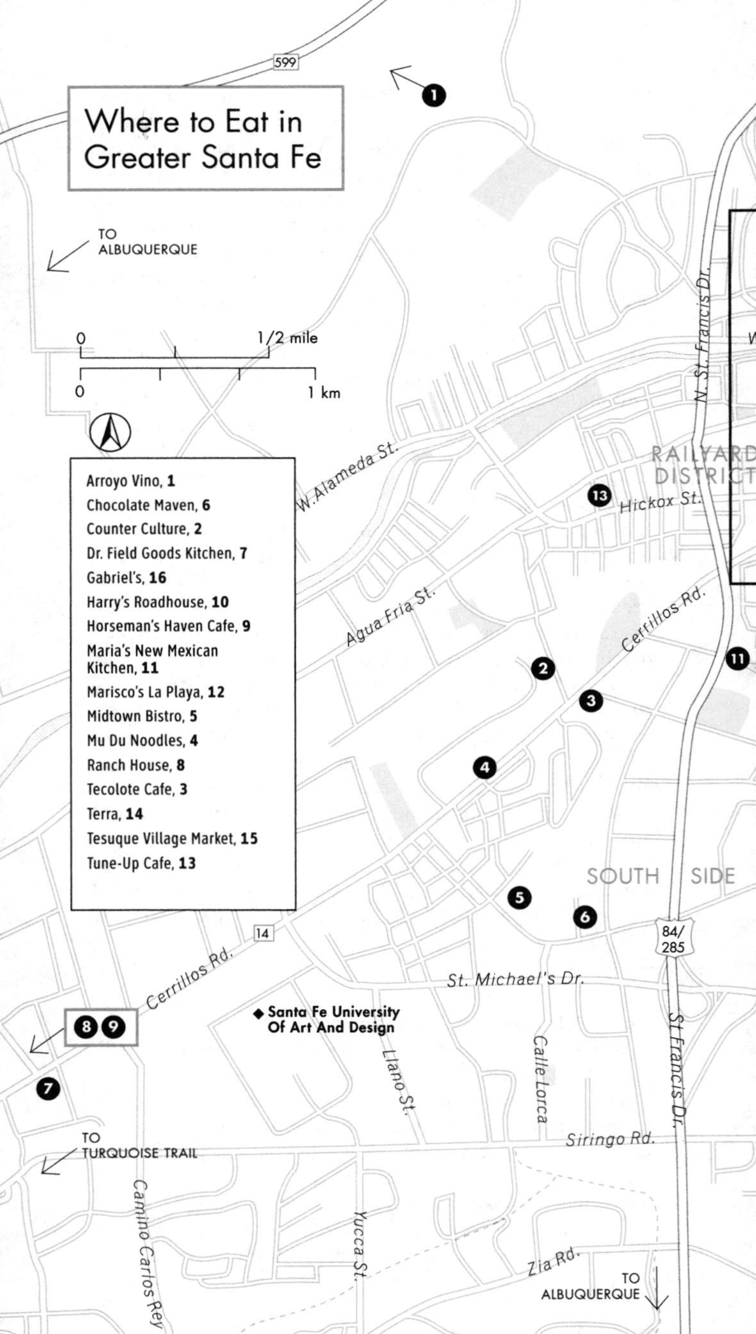

Where to Eat in Greater Santa Fe
Arroyo Vino, 1
Chocolate Maven, 6
Counter Culture, 2
Dr. Field Goods Kitchen, 7
Gabriel's, 16
Harry's Roadhouse, 10
Horseman's Haven Cafe, 9
Maria's New Mexican Kitchen, 11
Marisco's La Playa, 12
Midtown Bistro, 5
Mu Du Noodles, 4
Ranch House, 8
Tecolote Cafe, 3
Terra, 14
Tesuque Village Market, 15
Tune-Up Cafe, 13
599
TO ALBUQUERQUE
0
1/2 mile
0
1 km
W. Alameda St.
Agua Fria St.
N. St. Francis Dr.
RAILYARD DISTRICT
Hickox St.
Cerrillos Rd.
SOUTH SIDE
84/285
14
Cerrillos Rd.
St. Michael's Dr.
Santa Fe University Of Art And Design
Llano St.
Calle Lorca
St Francis Dr.
TO TURQUOISE TRAIL
Siringo Rd.
Camino Carlos Rey
Yucca St.
Zia Rd.
TO ALBUQUERQUE

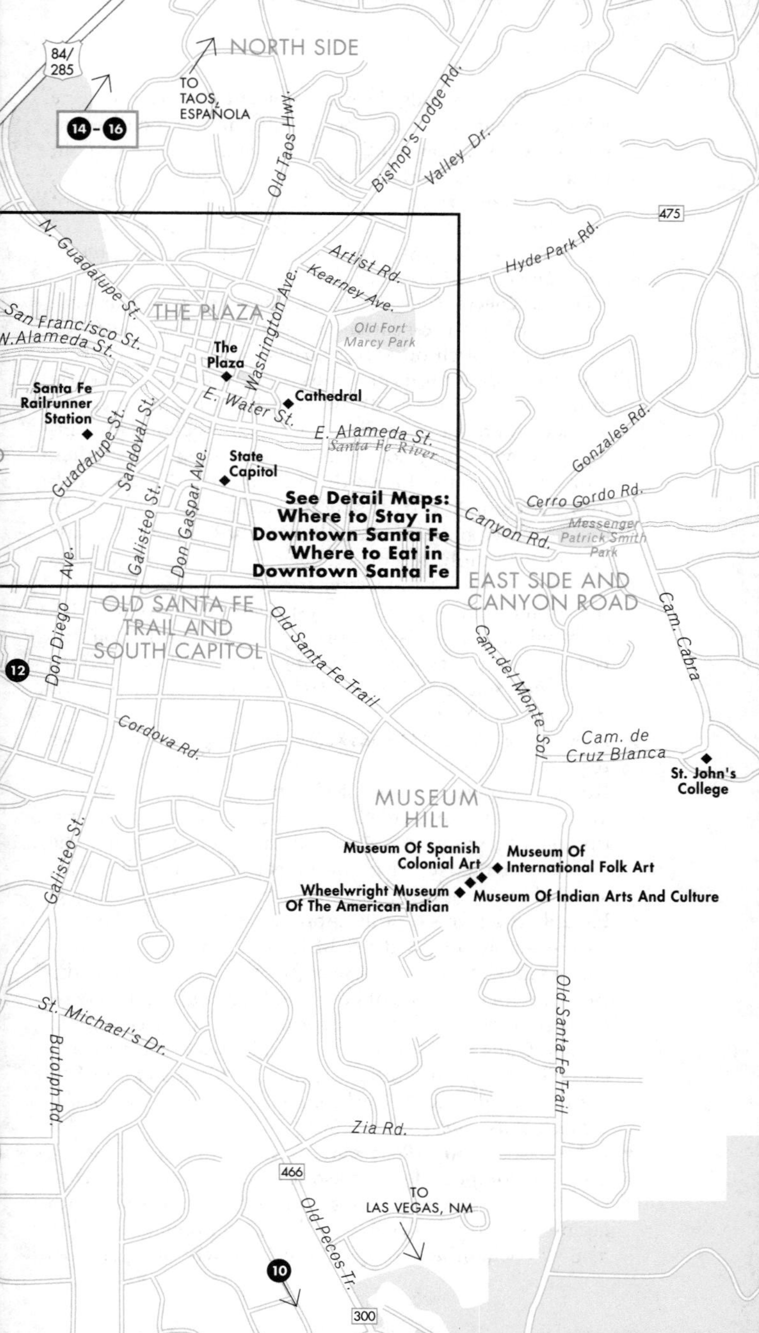

84/
285
14-16
TO
TAOS,
ESPAÑOLA
NORTH SIDE
Old Taos Hwy.
Bishop's Lodge Rd.
Valley Dr.
475
Hyde Park Rd.
N. Guadalupe St.
Artist Rd.
Kearney Ave.
Washington Ave.
THE PLAZA
San Francisco St.
N.Alameda St.
Old Fort
Marcy Park
The
Plaza
Santa Fe
Railrunner
Station
Cathedral
E. Water St.
E. Alameda St.
Santa Fe River
Guadalupe St.
Sandoval St.
State
Capitol
Gonzales Rd.
Cerro Gordo Rd.
See Detail Maps:
Where to Stay in
Downtown Santa Fe
Where to Eat in
Downtown Santa Fe
Canyon Rd.
Messenger
Patrick Smith
Park
Galisteo St.
Don Gaspar Ave.
Don Diego
Ave.
EAST SIDE AND
CANYON ROAD
OLD SANTA FE
TRAIL AND
SOUTH CAPITOL
Old Santa Fe Trail
Cam. del Monte Sol
Cam. Cabra
12
Cordova Rd.
Cam. de
Cruz Blanca
St. John's
College
MUSEUM
HILL
Museum Of Spanish
Colonial Art
Museum Of
International Folk Art
Wheelwright Museum
Of The American Indian
Museum Of Indian Arts And Culture
Galisteo St.
Old Santa Fe Trail
St. Michael's Dr.
Butolph Rd.
Zia Rd.
466
TO
LAS VEGAS, NM
Old Pecos Tr.
10
300

Belgian chocolate fudge brownies, mocha-buttercream torte with chocolate-covered strawberries, and French lemon-raspberry cake. Don't let the industrial building put you off; the interior is light, bright, and cozy. Try the Mayan Mocha, espresso mixed with steamed milk and a delicious combo of chocolate, cinnamon, and red chiles. *Average main: $14* *821 W. San Mateo St., South Side* *505/984–1980* *www.chocolatemaven.com* *No dinner.*

$ **Counter Culture.** *Café.* It's taken a few years for this low-key, slightly off-the-beaten-path café that's well-regarded by locals to catch on with tourists, but Counter Culture is worth finding for its delicious breakfasts, lunches, early dinners (they close at 8), or even just afternoon coffee breaks—there's a spacious covered patio beyond the dining room with long communal tables and a few smaller, more private ones. Inside this hip industrial space, tuck into plates of huevos rancheros and other eggy fare in the morning, and grilled rainbow trout with sautéed kale and saffron aioli, or curried veggies with lentils, mango chutney, and mint raita later in the day. There's a good selection of baked goods and espresso drinks as well. It's cash-only and casual—you order your food at the counter. But prices are very low. *Average main: $11* *930 Baca St., South Side* *505/995–1105* *No credit cards* *No dinner Mon.–Sun.*

★ $ Fodor's Choice **Dr. Field Goods Kitchen.** *Eclectic.* Ardent foodies regularly trek 4 miles south along traffic-choked Cerrillos Road to experience one of the more memorable dining adventures in Santa Fe. Chef Josh Gerwin ran this operation out of a wildly popular food truck before opening the airy and attractive brick-and-mortar restaurant in 2013, situated in a nondescript shopping center beside Jackalope. He utilizes a farm-to-table approach in his boldly flavored cuisine—note the "Bad Ass BLT," piled high with ground bacon sculpted into a massive patty. Start with the queso dip (served with two types of housemade salsa), which may be the best in town, before considering the wood-fired buffalo burger, Cuban sandwich, or the addictive carne adovada egg roll with peanut dipping sauce. *Average main: $12* *2860 Cerrillos Rd., South Side* *505/471–0043* *www.drfieldgoods.com* *Closed Sun.*

★ $ FAMILY Fodor's Choice **Harry's Roadhouse.** *Eclectic.* This busy, friendly, art-filled compound 6 miles southeast of Downtown consists of several inviting rooms, from a diner-style space with counter seating to a cozier nook with a fireplace—there's also an enchanting courtyard out back with juniper trees and flower gardens. The varied menu of contemporary diner favorites, pizzas, New Mexican fare, and bountiful salads is supplemented by a long list of daily specials—which often include delicious ethnic dishes. Favorites include smoked-chicken quesadillas and grilled-salmon tacos with tomatillo salsa and black beans. Breakfast is fantastic. On weekends, if you're there early, you might just get a chance at one of co-owner–pastry chef Peyton Young's phenomenal cinnamon rolls. Desserts here are homey favorites, from the chocolate pudding to the blueberry cobbler. Many gluten-free and veggie options are available, and Harry's is also known for stellar margaritas. The owners are committed to recycling and sustainable business practices. *Average main: $11 ✉ 96-B Old Las Vegas Hwy., 1 mile east of Old Pecos Trail exit off I–25, South Side ☎ 505/989–4629 ⊕ www.harrysroadhousesantafe.com.*

★ Fodor'sChoice ✕ **Horseman's Haven Cafe.** *Southwestern.* Tucked
$ behind the Giant gas station, this no-frills diner-style restaurant close to the many chain hotels along lower Cerrillos Road has long been a standout for some of the spiciest and tastiest Northern New Mexican fare in town, including superb green chile–bacon-cheeseburgers, blue-corn tacos packed with beef or chicken, huevos rancheros, and the hearty *plato sabroso* (a 12-ounce rib steak with rolled enchilada, beans, posole, rice, and hot sopaipillas with honey). Grab one of the comfy red-leatherette corner booths or a stool at the counter, and enjoy the people-watching. *Average main: $10 ✉ 4354 Cerrillos Rd., South Side ☎ 505/471–5420 ⊗ No dinner Sun.*

$ ✕ **Maria's New Mexican Kitchen.** *Mexican.* Creaky wood floors and dark-wood vigas set the scene for reliable, if predictable, traditional New Mexican cuisine. This rustic restaurant's real claim to fame is its selection of more than 100 types of margaritas. The house version is one of the best in town (and you may have surmised that we take our margaritas seriously here). Get the SilverCoin if you want to go top-shelf and leave the rest of the super tequilas to sip on without intrusion of other flavors. The place holds its own as a reliable, supertasty source of authentic New Mexican fare, including chiles rellenos, blue-corn enchiladas, and green-chile tamales. The Galisteo chicken, parboiled and covered in red chiles, is simple and satisfying. Don't be surprised to have to wait for a table—the line moves quickly. *Average main: $14 ✉ 555 W. Cordova Rd., South Side ☎ 505/983–7929 ⊕ www.marias-santafe.com.*

3

SANTA FE COOKING

Fodor's Choice ★ **Santa Fe School of Cooking.** If you'd like to bring the flavors of the Southwest to your own kitchen, consider taking one of the wildly popular and fun cooking classes at the Santa Fe School of Cooking, which moved into a much larger and more inviting building in 2012. Regular classes are taught during days and evenings, and more elaborate courses include the three-day Southwest Culinary Boot Camp, regional wine-tasting classes, and walking tours on which you visit several of Santa Fe's most notable restaurants. Reservations are advised. The school also operates an online market where you can purchase all sorts of New Mexico culinary goods and gifts. ✉ *125 N. Guadalupe St., West of the Plaza* ☎ *505/983–4511, 800/982–4688* 🌐 *www.santafeschoolofcooking.com.*

$$$ ✕ **Midtown Bistro.** *American.* A couple of miles south of downtown in a spacious adobe building with pitched ceilings and a charming patio, Midtown Bistro opened in 2012 with an aim to present creative, artfully prepared modern American cuisine at prices a couple of notches below what the upscale heavy hitters near the Plaza and Canyon Road charge. In every sense, chef Angel Estrada and his smiling staff have succeeded. Dishes like grilled French-cut pork chop with sweet potato purée, bok choy, and habanero-pineapple syrup, and filet mignon with roasted poblano gratin, broccoli, and truffle-butter are at once boldly flavorful, accessible, and filling. Lunch is more casual, with an emphasis on salads and sandwiches. A short but smart wine list delivers bottles from all over the world. $ *Average main: $24* ✉ *901 W. San Mateo St., South Side* ☎ *505/820–3121* 🌐 *www.midtownbistrosf.com* ⊗ *No dinner Sun.*

$$ ✕ **Mu Du Noodles.** *Asian.* This warm and cozy eatery on a busy stretch of Cerrillos Road excels both in its friendly and helpful staff and its interesting pan-Asian fare. Dinner specials are always good, though if you're fond of spice be sure to ask for "hot" as their food tends to be mild. Sample the *martabak*, Indonesian dumplings filled with minced lamb, scallions, garlic, and spices and served with a mint-cilantro dipping sauce; fragrant lemongrass soup with house-made fish balls, shrimp, and fried shallots; and Singapore-style rice vermicelli noodles with barbecue pork or tofu and a mild yellow curry. Mu, the proprietor, is a strong advocate of cooking with local, organic ingredients. Average main: $18 1494 Cerrillos Rd., South Side 505/988–1411 www.mudunoodles.com Closed Sun.–Mon. No lunch.

$ **The Pantry.** *American.* Since 1948, this beloved, family-owned greasy spoon with a familiar blue neon sign has been pleasing budget-minded locals and visitors with consistently tasty diner fare, including buckwheat pancakes, *huevos consuelo* (a corn tortilla topped with two eggs, a spicy chile sauce, and cheese, with the Pantry's famous home fries), green-chile stew, tortilla burgers, and chicken-fried steak. *Average main: $9 1820 Cerrillos Rd., South Side 505/986–0022 www.pantrysantafe.com.*

$$ **Ranch House.** *Barbecue.* Given New Mexico's deep ties to its easterly neighbor, the Lone Star State, it's hardly surprising that the region has some top-notch barbecue joints. This bright, spacious contemporary adobe building with two large patios may look a bit fancy for down-home, fall-off-the-bone barbecue brisket, baby-back ribs, pulled pork, and smoked half-chicken, but the cooks here know what they're doing. Fish tacos, steaks, and traditional New Mexican dishes round out the extensive menu. Don't mind the location near several car dealers just off Cerrillos Road (about a 15-minute drive from the Plaza)—the Ranch House is quite inviting inside. The afternoon happy hour is a sweet deal. *Average main: $16 2571 Cristo's Rd., South Side 505/424–8900 www.theranchhouse-santafe.com.*

$ **Tecolote Café.** *Southwestern.* The mantra here is "no toast," and you won't miss it. Since 1980, the bellies of locals and tourists alike have been satisfied with delicious breakfasts and lunches founded primarily on northern New Mexican cuisine. The simple rooms and comfortable seating allow you to focus on such dishes as the Sheepherder's Breakfast (red potatoes browned with jalapeños and topped with red and green chiles and two eggs), delicious carne adovada (lean pork slow-cooked in their homemade red chile), and a green-chile stew that locals swear by to cure colds. French toast is prepared with homemade breads. When the server asks if you'd like a tortilla or the bakery basket, go for the basket—it's full of warm, fresh muffins and biscuits that are out of this world. *Average main: $8 1203 Cerrillos Rd., South Side 505/988–1362 www.tecolotecafe.com Reservations not accepted No dinner.*

$ ✕ **Tune-Up Cafe.** *Southwestern.* This cozy locals' favorite has colorful walls and wood details, booths, a few tables, and a community table. The shaded patio out front is a great summertime spot to enjoy the toothsome Southwest-inspired cooking. Start the day with savory breakfast rellenos, fluffy buttermilk pancakes, or the *huevos salvadoreños* (eggs scrambled with scallions and tomatoes, served with refried beans, panfried bananas, and a tortilla). Lunch and dinner offerings include the superjuicy Dave Was Here burger served with crispy home-cut fries, a ginger-chicken sandwich on ciabatta bread, and Salvadoran treats called *pupusas,* which are most like griddled, flattened, soft tamales. Homemade baked goods include a variety of pies and cakes. The staff is friendly and efficient and the care taken by the owners, Chuy and Charlotte Rivera, is evident. *Average main: $8 ✉ 115 Hickox St., South Side ☎ 505/983–7060 🌐 tuneupsantafe.com ✍ Reservations not accepted.*

4

WHERE TO STAY

In Santa Fe you can ensconce yourself in quintessential Southwestern style or anonymous hotel-chain decor, depending on how much you want to spend—the city has costlier accommodations than anywhere in the Southwest. Cheaper options are available on Cerrillos (pronounced sir-*ee*-yos) Road, the rather unattractive business thoroughfare southwest of Downtown. Quality varies greatly on Cerrillos, but some of the best-managed, most attractive properties are (from most to least expensive) the DoubleTree, Hyatt Place, Courtyard Marriott, Hampton Inn, Comfort Suites, and the Econolodge. You generally pay more as you get closer to the Plaza, but for many visitors it's worth it to be within walking distance of many attractions. Some of the best deals are offered by bed-and-breakfasts—many of those near the Plaza offer much better values than the big, touristy hotels. Rates drop, often from 30% to 50%, from November to April (excluding Thanksgiving and Christmas).

Prices in the reviews are the lowest cost of a standard double room in high season. For expanded reviews, facilities, and current deals, visit Fodors.com.

WHERE TO STAY

RENTALS AND RENTAL AGENCIES

In addition to the usual array of inns and hotels here, Santa Fe has a wide range of long-and short-term vacation rentals. Rates generally range from $150 to $300 per night for double-occupancy units, with better values at some of the two- to four-bedroom properties. Many have fully stocked kitchens. Another route is to rent a furnished condo or casita at one of several compounds geared to travelers seeking longer stays. Here are some top vacation-rental options in town.

Kokopelli Properties. A large, well-established agency, Kokopelli represents more than 70 vacations rentals in town, including everything from cozy two-bedroom casitas that rent for as low as $150 per day to ultra-posh mountain compounds that will set you back $800 per day during the busy months. Many of these rentals have seven-day minimums in summer and early fall. ☎ *855/982–2823, 505/982–1013* 🌐 *www.santaferentals.com.*

★ Fodor'sChoice **Campanilla Compound.** *Rental.* A luxurious,
$$$ secluded, yet centrally located tract of about 15 spacious
FAMILY one-and-two-bedroom vacation rentals on a hill just north of Downtown. Kitchens are especially impressive in these units, which also have kiva-style fireplaces, patios with gas grills, washers and dryers, and plenty of off-street parking. Rates run from about $1,500 to $2,000 per week in summer (and about one-third less the rest of the year). **Pros:** perfect for extended stays; beautiful furnishings and high-end appliances; close to Plaza but still very private. **Cons:** the walk from Plaza is uphill; there's a two-night minimum stay. *Rooms from: $225 334 Otero St., North Side 505/988–7585, 800/828–9700 www.campanillacompound.com 15 homes No meals.*

$$ **Fort Marcy Suites.** *Rental.* On a bluff just a 10-minute
FAMILY walk northeast of the Plaza with great views, this large, older compound comprises individually furnished units that accommodate two to six guests and come with full kitchens, wood fireplaces, DVDs, and CD stereos. They're a good value for families and groups, and although these units aren't especially fancy, the management has been steadily upgrading decor and amenities in recent years. **Pros:** nice views of the Sangre de Cristo range; handy amenities for extended stays. **Cons:** some units are showing their age; the walk from the Plaza is uphill. *Rooms from: $189 321 Kearney Ave., North Side 888/570–2775 www.allseasonsresortlodging.com 100 units No meals.*

THE PLAZA

$$$ **Antigua Inn.** *B&B/Inn.* Tucked down a narrow, unpaved lane, this peaceful, upscale four-room inn feels private and secluded but is actually just steps from the lively shops and restaurants on nearby Marcy Street and just a 10-minute walk from the Plaza. **Pros:** central but quiet location; elegant decor; great for a few friends traveling together. **Cons:** pricier than many B&Bs in town. *Rooms from: $249 622 Castillo Pl., The Plaza 505/954–1231 www.antiguainn.com 4 rooms Breakfast.*

$$$ **Eldorado Hotel & Spa.** *Hotel.* Because it's the closest thing Santa Fe has to a convention hotel, the Eldorado sometimes gets a bad rap, but it's actually quite inviting, with individually decorated rooms and stunning mountain views. **Pros:** attractive accommodations three blocks from Plaza, fun bar with great late-night food menu; great view from rooftop pool (especially at sunset). **Cons:** staff's attention to service varies considerably; can be very expensive during

BEST BETS

Fodor's Choice ★
El Rey Inn, Four Seasons Resort Rancho Encantado, Hacienda Nicholas, Hotel Santa Fe, Inn of the Anasazi, Inn of the Five Graces, Inn of the Governors, Inn on the Alameda, La Fonda, Madeleine Inn, Silver Saddle Motel, Ten Thousand Waves

BEST HOTEL BAR
Four Seasons Resort Rancho Encantado, Hotel St. Francis, Inn of the Anasazi, Inn of the Governors, La Fonda

BEST FOR KIDS
Bishop's Lodge Resort and Spa, El Rey Inn, Inn and Spa at Loretto, La Posada de Santa Fe Resort and Spa, Lodge at Santa Fe

BEST LOCATION
Hotel St. Francis, Inn on the Alameda, Inn of the Anasazi, La Fonda

BEST FOR ROMANCE
Inn of the Five Graces, Inn and Spa at Loretto, Madeleine Inn, Ten Thousand Waves

BEST SERVICE
Four Seasons Resort Rancho Encantado, Inn of the Anasazi, Inn of the Governors, Inn of the Five Graces, Inn on the Alameda

BEST VIEWS
Four Seasons Resort Rancho Encantado, La Fonda

BEST-KEPT SECRET
Don Gaspar Inn, El Farolito, Hacienda Nicholas, Old Santa Fe Inn

busy periods. *Rooms from: $259* *309 W. San Francisco St., The Plaza* *505/988–4455, 800/955–4455* *www.eldoradohotel.com* *213 rooms* *No meals.*

$$ **Hotel Chimayó de Santa Fe.** *Hotel.* Among the handful of
FAMILY mid-price, full-service hotels within a couple of blocks of the Plaza, this attractive, Territorial-style adobe hotel with a mix of spacious standard rooms and even bigger suites is a terrific option, especially given the extensive amenities available in many units—wet bars, kitchenettes, spacious sitting areas. **Pros:** unbeatable location; spacious rooms and extensive in-room perks are nice for families or groups. **Cons:** in a crowded part of Downtown; no pool or gym. *Rooms from: $170* *125 Washington Ave., The Plaza* *505/988–4900, 855/752–9273* *www.hotelchimayo.com* *40 rooms, 16 suites* *No meals.*

$$ **Hotel St. Francis.** *Hotel.* Just one block south of the Plaza, this stately three-story hotel retains a historic vibe but has been given a modern flair—with expansive stone floors, plaster walls, and spare furnishings lit by massive pillar

candles at night, the lobby feels a bit like a Tuscan monastery. **Pros:** highly distinct ambience; two blocks from the Plaza and near many shops. **Cons:** service can be spotty; some rooms (and especially bathrooms) are quite small. *Rooms from: $179 ✉ 210 Don Gaspar Ave., The Plaza ☎ 505/983–5700, 800/529–5700 ⊕ www.hotelstfrancis.com ⇨ 79 rooms, 2 suites No meals.*

$$$ FAMILY **Inn and Spa at Loretto.** *Hotel.* This plush, oft-photographed, pueblo-inspired property attracts a loyal clientele, many of whom swear by the friendly staff and high decorating standards. **Pros:** ideal location; gorgeous grounds; distinctive architecture. **Cons:** expensive parking and resort fees; some rooms can be dark. *Rooms from: $249 ✉ 211 Old Santa Fe Trail, The Plaza ☎ 505/988–5531, 800/727–5531 ⊕ www.innatloretto.com ⇨ 129 rooms, 5 suites No meals.*

★ $$$$ Fodor's Choice **Inn of the Anasazi.** *Hotel.* Unassuming from the outside, this first-rate boutique hotel steps from the Plaza is one of Santa Fe's finest, with superb architectural detail. **Pros:** staff is thorough, gracious, and highly professional; superb restaurant and charming bar. **Cons:** standard rooms are a bit small for the price; few rooms have balconies; no hot tub or pool. *Rooms from: $385 ✉ 113 Washington Ave., The Plaza ☎ 505/988–3030, 888/688–8100 ⊕ www.innoftheanasazi.com ⇨ 58 rooms No meals.*

★ $$ Fodor's Choice **Inn of the Governors.** *Hotel.* This rambling, reasonably priced hotel by the Santa Fe River is staffed by a polite, enthusiastic bunch. **Pros:** close to Plaza; year-round, heated pool; free parking (a rarity downtown). **Cons:** standard rooms are a bit small; some rooms view parking lot. *Rooms from: $179 ✉ 101 W. Alameda St., The Plaza ☎ 505/982–4333, 800/234–4534 ⊕ www.innofthegovernors.com ⇨ 100 rooms Breakfast.*

$$ **Inn on the Paseo.** *B&B/Inn.* This inn is on a busy road, but at least this stretch of Paseo de Peralta is just two lanes wide and is in a semiresidential neighborhood a short walk from the Plaza. **Pros:** just a few blocks from the Plaza. **Cons:** rooms facing the road receive some traffic noise. *Rooms from: $140 ✉ 630 Paseo de Peralta, The Plaza ☎ 505/984–8200, 855/457–9045 ⊕ www.innonthepaseo.com ⇨ 16 rooms, 2 suites Breakfast.*

★ $$$ Fodor's Choice **La Fonda.** *Hotel.* This venerable Downtown landmark underwent its biggest renovation in nearly a century in 2013, its rooms upgraded with more modern amenities and better climate controls, but with a warm, artful design—including whimsical painted headboards

4

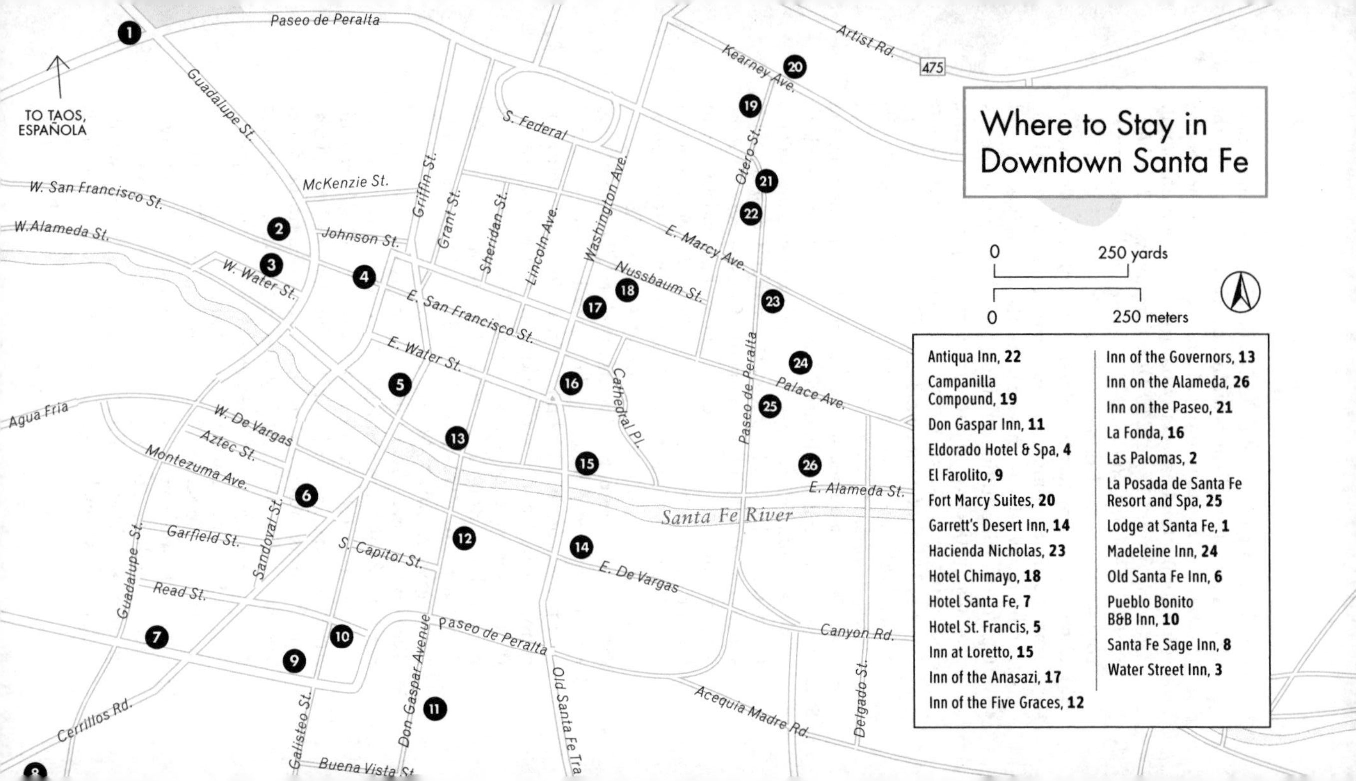
Where to Stay in Downtown Santa Fe
0 250 yards
0 250 meters
Antiqua Inn, 22
Campanilla Compound, 19
Don Gaspar Inn, 11
Eldorado Hotel & Spa, 4
El Farolito, 9
Fort Marcy Suites, 20
Garrett's Desert Inn, 14
Hacienda Nicholas, 23
Hotel Chimayo, 18
Hotel Santa Fe, 7
Hotel St. Francis, 5
Inn at Loretto, 15
Inn of the Anasazi, 17
Inn of the Five Graces, 12
Inn of the Governors, 13
Inn on the Alameda, 26
Inn on the Paseo, 21
La Fonda, 16
Las Palomas, 2
La Posada de Santa Fe Resort and Spa, 25
Lodge at Santa Fe, 1
Madeleine Inn, 24
Old Santa Fe Inn, 6
Pueblo Bonito B&B Inn, 10
Santa Fe Sage Inn, 8
Water Street Inn, 3
TO TAOS, ESPAÑOLA
Paseo de Peralta
Artist Rd.
475
Kearney Ave.
Guadalupe St.
S. Federal
Otero St.
W. San Francisco St.
McKenzie St.
Griffin St.
Grant St.
Sheridan St.
Lincoln Ave.
Washington Ave.
E. Marcy Ave.
W.Alameda St.
Johnson St.
W. Water St.
Nussbaum St.
E. San Francisco St.
E. Water St.
Cathedral Pl.
Palace Ave.
Agua Fria
W. De Vargas
Aztec St.
Montezuma Ave.
E. Alameda St.
Santa Fe River
Garfield St.
Sandoval St.
S. Capitol St.
E. De Vargas
Read St.
Canyon Rd.
Paseo de Peralta
Don Gaspar Avenue
Old Santa Fe Tra
Acequia Madre Rd.
Delgado St.
Cerrillos Rd.
Galisteo St.
Buena Vista St.

and handcrafted furniture—that's faithful to the vision of Mary Elizabeth Jane Colter, the vaunted architect responsible for the hotel's elegant Southwestern aesthetic. **Pros:** iconic building steeped in history; gracious service; Plaza is right outside the door. **Cons:** lobby often packed with tourists and nonguests; fitness facilities are modest for an upscale hotel. *Rooms from: $199 100 E. San Francisco St., The Plaza 505/982–5511, 800/523–5002 www.lafondasantafe.com 149 rooms, 14 suites No meals.*

OLD SANTA FE AND SOUTH CAPITOL

$$$ **Don Gaspar Inn.** *B&B/Inn.* One of the city's most charming little finds, this exquisitely landscaped and attractively decorated compound is on a pretty residential street a half-mile south of the Plaza. **Pros:** beautiful decor; delicious and generous breakfasts; lush gardens. **Cons:** occasional noise from nearby elementary school. *Rooms from: $189 623 Don Gaspar Ave., Old Santa Fe Trail and South Capitol 505/986–8664, 888/986–8664 www.dongaspar.com 4 rooms, 3 suites, 2 casitas, 1 house Breakfast.*

$$ **El Farolito.** *B&B/Inn.* All the beautiful Southwestern and Mexican furniture in this small, upscale compound is custom-made, and all the art and photography original. **Pros:** attentive service; special dietary requests accommodated; ample free off-street parking. **Cons:** no on-site pool or hot tub. *Rooms from: $195 514 Galisteo St., Old Santa Fe Trail and South Capitol 505/988–1631, 888/634–8782 www.farolito.com 7 rooms, 1 suite Breakfast.*

$ **Garrett's Desert Inn.** *Hotel.* This sprawling, U-shaped motel may surround a parking lot and offer relatively little in the way of ambience, but it's fairly well maintained and you'll be hard-pressed to find more affordable accommodations just a few blocks from the Plaza, smack in the middle of historic Barrio de Analco. **Pros:** super location; nice pool and patio; excellent restaurant. **Cons:** $8 per night parking fee; not much curb appeal. *Rooms from: $109 311 Old Santa Fe Trail, Old Santa Fe Trail and South Capitol 505/982–1851, 800/888–2145 www.garrettsdesertinn.com 83 rooms No meals.*

★ Fodor's Choice **Inn of the Five Graces.** *B&B/Inn.* There isn't

$$$$ another property in Santa Fe to compare to this sumptuous yet relaxed inn with an unmistakable East-meets-West feel. **Pros:** tucked into a quiet, ancient neighborhood; loads of cushy perks and in-room amenities; fantastic staff, attentive but not overbearing. **Cons:** very steep rates. *Rooms*

from: $500 ✉ *150 E. DeVargas St., Old Santa Fe Trail and South Capitol* ☎ *505/992–0957, 866/992–0957* 🌐 *www.fivegraces.com* ⇨ *22 suites, 1 house* 🍽 *Breakfast.*

$$ **Pueblo Bonito B&B Inn.** *B&B/Inn.* Rooms in this 1873 adobe compound have handmade and hand-painted furnishings, Navajo weavings, brick and hardwood floors, sand paintings and pottery, locally carved santos (Catholic saints), and Western art. **Pros:** intimate, cozy inn on peaceful grounds; hot tub. **Cons:** bathrooms tend to be small; breakfast is Continental. 💲 *Rooms from: $135* ✉ *138 W. Manhattan Ave., Old Santa Fe Trail and South Capitol* ☎ *505/984–8001, 800/461–4599* 🌐 *www.pueblobonitoinn.com* ⇨ *12 rooms, 6 suites* 🍽 *Breakfast.*

EAST SIDE AND CANYON ROAD

★ Fodor's Choice $$ **Hacienda Nicholas.** *B&B/Inn.* This classic Santa Fe hacienda is just blocks from the Plaza yet set in a quiet residential area and sheltered from outside noises by thick adobe walls. **Pros:** reasonable rates for such a lovely, upscale inn; the inn uses eco-friendly products and practices. **Cons:** no hot tub or pool, but guests have privileges at El Gancho Health Club (a 15-minute drive). 💲 *Rooms from: $150* ✉ *320 E. Marcy St., East Side and Canyon Road* ☎ *505/986–1431, 888/284–3170* 🌐 *www.haciendanicholas.com* ⇨ *4 rooms, 3 suites, 3 cottages* 🍽 *Breakfast.*

★ Fodor's Choice $$$ **Inn on the Alameda.** *Hotel.* Near the Plaza and Canyon Road is one of the Southwest's best small hotels. **Pros:** the solicitous staff is first-rate; excellent, expansive breakfast buffet with lots of extras. **Cons:** rooms closest to Alameda can be a bit noisy; no pool. 💲 *Rooms from: $221* ✉ *303 E. Alameda St., East Side and Canyon Road* ☎ *505/984–2121, 888/984–2121* 🌐 *www.innonthealameda.com* ⇨ *59 rooms, 10 suites* 🍽 *Breakfast.*

$$$$ FAMILY **La Posada de Santa Fe Resort and Spa.** *Resort.* Rooms on the beautiful, quiet grounds of this hotel vary, but extensive renovations have enhanced all rooms to a level of luxury befitting the somewhat steep rates. **Pros:** numerous amenities, including a top-notch spa and restaurant; two blocks from Plaza and similarly close to Canyon Road. **Cons:** resort can sometimes feel crowded; daily resort fee. 💲 *Rooms from: $289* ✉ *330 E. Palace Ave., East Side and Canyon Road* ☎ *505/986–0000, 866/331–7625* 🌐 *www.laposadadesantafe.com* ⇨ *118 rooms, 39 suites* 🍽 *No meals.*

★ Fodor's Choice $$ **Madeleine Inn.** *B&B/Inn.* Santa Fe hasn't always been a town of pseudopueblo buildings, and this lovely Queen Anne Victorian is a dramatic reminder of the city's more eclectic architectural heritage. **Pros:** excellent value; great service; eco-friendly. **Cons:** steep stairs; no elevators in this three-story Victorian. *Rooms from: $150 ✉ 106 Faithway St., East Side and Canyon Road ☎ 505/982–3465, 888/877–7622 ⊕ www.madeleineinn.com ⇨ 5 rooms, 2 suites 🍽 Breakfast.*

RAILYARD DISTRICT

★ Fodor'sChoice **Hotel Santa Fe.** *Hotel.* Picurís Pueblo has controlling interest in this handsome Pueblo-style three-story hotel on the Railyard District's edge and a 15-minute walk from the Plaza. **Pros:** professional, helpful staff; lots of amenities; easy access to Railyard District's trendy shopping and dining. **Cons:** standard rooms are fairly small; resort fee. *Rooms from: $205 ✉ 1501 Paseo de Peralta, Railyard District ☎ 505/982–1200, 800/825–9876 ⊕ www.hotelsantafe.com ⇨ 40 rooms, 91 suites 🍽 No meals.*
$$$

$$ **Old Santa Fe Inn.** *Hotel.* This contemporary motor-court-style inn looks like an attractive, if fairly ordinary, adobe motel, but it has stunning and spotless rooms with elegant Southwestern furnishings. **Pros:** rooms are more inviting than several more-expensive Downtown hotels; short walk to the Plaza; free parking. **Cons:** minimal, though friendly and professional, staffing; rooms set around parking lot. *Rooms from: $172 ✉ 320 Galisteo St., Railyard District ☎ 505/995–0800, 800/745–9910 ⊕ www.oldsantafeinn.com ⇨ 34 rooms, 9 suites 🍽 Breakfast.*

$ **Santa Fe Sage Inn.** *Hotel.* On the southern edge of the Railyard District, this smartly renovated motel offers affordable comfort and surprisingly attractive (given the low rates) Southwestern decor within walking distance of the Plaza (six blocks). **Pros:** comfortable and affordable; small but nice pool; close to Plaza and train station. **Cons:** rooms nearest the street can be noisy; $5 nightly parking charge. *Rooms from: $94 ✉ 725 Cerrillos Rd., Railyard District ☎ 505/982–5952, 866/433–0335 ⊕ www.santafesageinn.com ⇨ 156 rooms 🍽 Breakfast.*
FAMILY

WEST OF THE PLAZA

$$ **Las Palomas.** *B&B/Inn.* It's a pleasant 10-minute walk west of the Plaza to reach this group of properties consisting of a few historic, luxurious compounds, one of them Spanish Pueblo–style adobe, another done in the Territorial style, and others ranging from rooms in renovated Victorian houses to contemporary condos with up to three bedrooms. **Pros:** kid-friendly, with swings and a play yard; on-site fit-

4

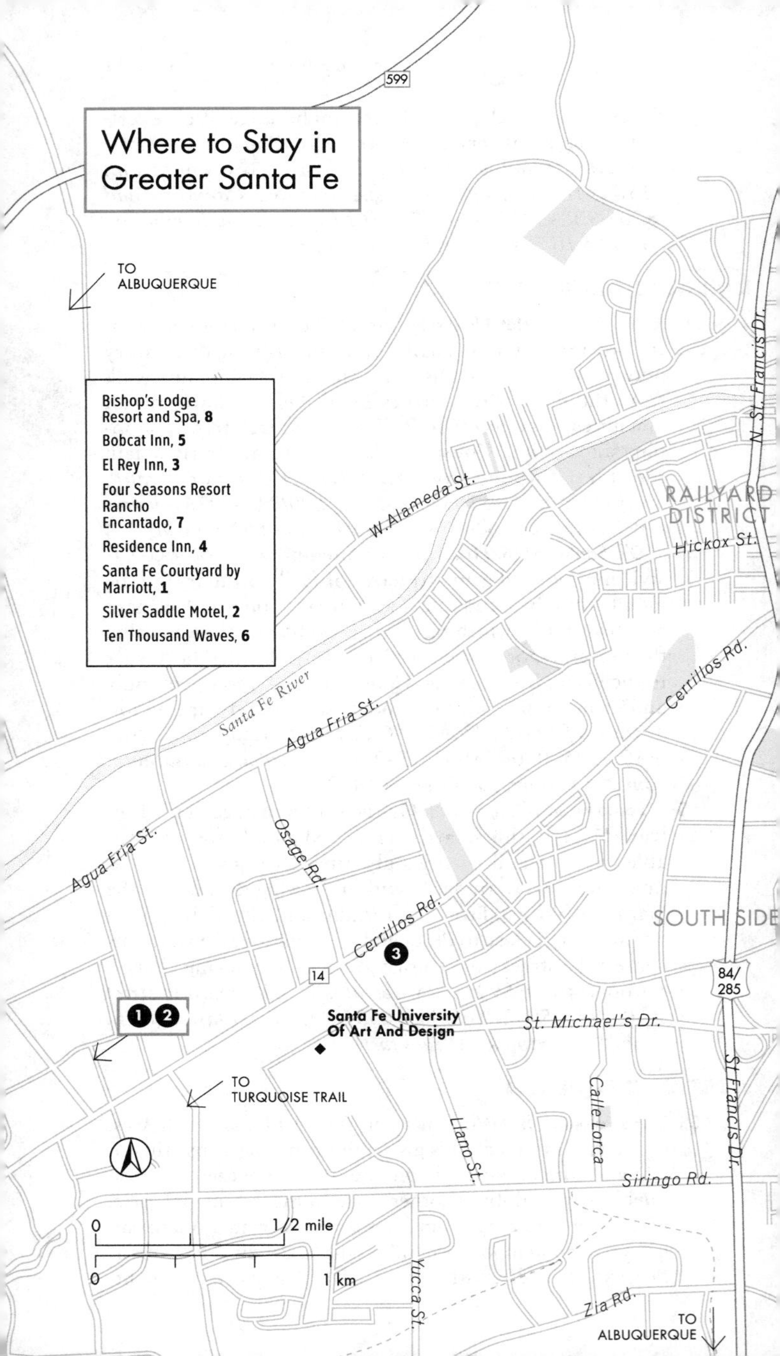
Where to Stay in Greater Santa Fe
Bishop's Lodge Resort and Spa, 8
Bobcat Inn, 5
El Rey Inn, 3
Four Seasons Resort Rancho Encantado, 7
Residence Inn, 4
Santa Fe Courtyard by Marriott, 1
Silver Saddle Motel, 2
Ten Thousand Waves, 6
TO ALBUQUERQUE
599
W. Alameda St.
RAILYARD DISTRICT
Hickox St.
N. St. Francis Dr.
Cerrillos Rd.
Santa Fe River
Agua Fria St.
Osage Rd.
SOUTH SIDE
Cerrillos Rd.
14
84/285
Santa Fe University Of Art And Design
St. Michael's Dr.
TO TURQUOISE TRAIL
Calle Lorca
Llano St.
St Francis Dr.
Siringo Rd.
0
1/2 mile
1 km
Yucca St.
Zia Rd.
TO ALBUQUERQUE

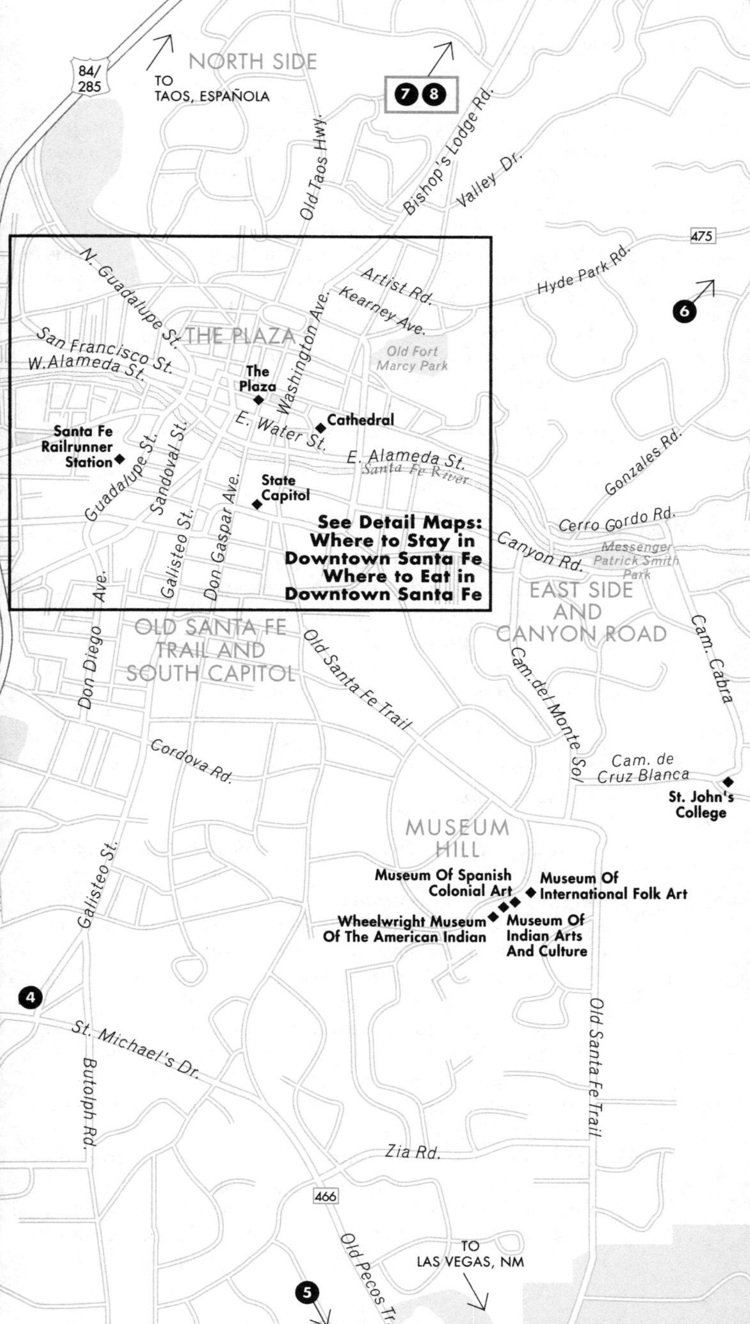

84/
285
TO
TAOS, ESPAÑOLA
NORTH SIDE
7 8
Old Taos Hwy.
Bishop's Lodge Rd.
Valley Dr.
475
Hyde Park Rd.
6
Artist Rd.
Kearney Ave.
N. Guadalupe St.
THE PLAZA
Washington Ave.
San Francisco St.
W.Alameda St.
Old Fort
Marcy Park
The
Plaza
Cathedral
E. Water St.
Santa Fe
Railrunner
Station
Guadalupe St.
Sandoval St.
E. Alameda St.
Santa Fe River
Gonzales Rd.
State
Capitol
Don Gaspar Ave.
Galisteo St.
See Detail Maps:
Where to Stay in
Downtown Santa Fe
Where to Eat in
Downtown Santa Fe
Cerro Gordo Rd.
Canyon Rd.
Messenger
Patrick Smith
Park
EAST SIDE
AND
CANYON ROAD
Ave.
Don Diego
OLD SANTA FE
TRAIL AND
SOUTH CAPITOL
Old Santa Fe Trail
Cam.del Monte Sol
Cam. Cabra
Cordova Rd.
Cam. de
Cruz Blanca
St. John's
College
MUSEUM
HILL
Museum Of Spanish
Colonial Art
Museum Of
International Folk Art
Wheelwright Museum
Of The American Indian
Museum Of
Indian Arts
And Culture
Galisteo St.
4
St. Michael's Dr.
Old Santa Fe Trail
Butolph Rd.
Zia Rd.
466
Old Pecos Tr.
TO
LAS VEGAS, NM
5

ness center; most units feel very private and self-contained. **Cons:** big variations among the accommodations; no hot tub or pool on-site (guests may use pool at the Hotel Santa Fe). *Rooms from: $152* *460 W. San Francisco St., West of the Plaza* *505/982–5560, 877/982–5560* *www.laspalomas.com* *63 units* *Breakfast.*

$$ **Water Street Inn.** *B&B/Inn.* The large rooms in this restored adobe 2½ blocks from the Plaza are decorated with reed shutters, antique pine beds, viga-beam ceilings, hand-stenciled artwork, and a blend of cowboy, Hispanic, and Native American art and artifacts. **Pros:** elegant decor; gracious, noteworthy staff. **Cons:** grounds are restricted—the inn overlooks a parking lot. *Rooms from: $152* *427 W. Water St., Santa Fe* *505/984–1193, 800/646–6752* *www.waterstreetinn.com* *8 rooms, 4 suites* *Breakfast.*

NORTH SIDE

$$$ FAMILY **Bishop's Lodge Resort and Spa.** *Resort.* Although this historic resort and tranquil ShâNah Spa is just a 10-minute drive from the Plaza, its setting in a bucolic valley at the foot of the Sangre de Cristo Mountains makes it feel worlds apart. **Pros:** staff is friendly and well-trained; stunning bucolic setting. **Cons:** resort is spread out over 700 acres and some rooms seem rather far-flung; resort fee. *Rooms from: $210* *1297 Bishop's Lodge Rd., 2½ miles north of Downtown, North Side* *505/983–6377, 888/419–0492* *www.bishopslodge.com* *91 rooms, 12 suites 7 villas* *No meals.*

★ Fodor's Choice $$$$ **Four Seasons Resort Rancho Encantado Santa Fe.** *Resort.* Four Seasons assumed control of this stunning property on a dramatic, sunset-facing bluff in the Sangre de Cristo foothills in 2012, bringing the brand's famously flawless sense of gracious hospitality and efficiency to an already ultra-plush resort. **Pros:** freestanding couples spa suites; complimentary minibar (nonalcoholic beverages only); stunning rooms and views. **Cons:** several of the private terraces overlook parking lots; remote location. *Rooms from: $375* *198 NM 592, North Side* *505/946–5700, 866/954–4840* *www.fourseasons.com/santafe* *65 rooms* *No meals.*

$$ FAMILY **Lodge at Santa Fe.** *Hotel.* Rooms at this midprice property have pleasant Southwestern furnishings and earth-tone fabrics. **Pros:** away from the crowds and noise of the Plaza. **Cons:** service can be lackluster; not much within walking distance. *Rooms from: $159* *750 N. St. Francis*

Dr., North Side ☎ *505/992–5800, 888/563–4373* 🌐 *www.lodgeatsantafe.com* 🛏 *102 rooms, 25 suites* 🍴 *No meals.*

★ Fodor's Choice **Ten Thousand Waves.** *B&B/Inn.* Devotees appreciate the authentic *onsen* (Japanese-style baths) atmosphere of this 20-acre Japanese-inspired spa and boutique inn a few miles northeast of town. **Pros:** artful furnishings; peaceful setting; warm service. **Cons:** a bit remote. $ *Rooms from: $199* ✉ *3451 Hyde Park Rd., 4 miles northeast of the Plaza, East Side and Canyon Road* ☎ *505/982–9304* 🌐 *www.tenthousandwaves.com* 🛏 *13 cottages* 🍴 *Breakfast.*

$$$

SOUTH SIDE

4

$$ **Bobcat Inn.** *B&B/Inn.* A delightful, affordable, country hacienda that's a 15-minute drive southeast of the Plaza, this adobe bed-and-breakfast sits amid 10 secluded acres of piñon and ponderosa pine, with grand views of the Ortiz Mountains and the area's high-desert mesas. **Pros:** gracious, secluded inn; wonderful hosts. **Cons:** located well outside town; no pets; no children under age 6. $ *Rooms from: $120* ✉ *442 Old Las Vegas Hwy., South Side* ☎ *505/988–9239* 🌐 *www.nm-inn.com* 🛏 *5 rooms* 🍴 *Breakfast.*

★ Fodor's Choice **El Rey Inn.** *Hotel.* The kind of place where Lucy and Ricky might have stayed during one of their cross-country adventures, the El Rey was built in 1936 but has been brought gracefully into the 21st century, its rooms and bathrooms handsomely updated without losing any period charm. **Pros:** excellent price for a distinctive, charming property. **Cons:** rooms closest to Cerrillos can be noisy; some rooms are quite dark. $ *Rooms from: $105* ✉ *1862 Cerrillos Rd., South Side* ☎ *505/982–1931, 800/521–1349* 🌐 *www.elreyinnsantafe.com* 🛏 *86 rooms* 🍴 *Breakfast.*

$ FAMILY

$$ **Residence Inn.** *Hotel.* This compound consists of clusters of three-story adobe town houses with pitched roofs and tall chimneys. **Pros:** complimentary full breakfast; evening socials; grocery-shopping service. **Cons:** not within easy walking distance of many restaurants or attractions. $ *Rooms from: $149* ✉ *1698 Galisteo St., South Side* ☎ *505/988–7300, 800/331–3131* 🌐 *www.marriott.com/safnm* 🛏 *120 suites* 🍴 *Breakfast.*

$ **Santa Fe Courtyard by Marriott.** *Hotel.* Of the dozens of chain properties along prosaic Cerrillos Road, this one stands out for especially high standards of comfort and service, even though it looks like all the others: clad in faux adobe and surrounded by parking lots and strip malls. **Pros:** rooms have the usual chain doodads: mini-refrigerators, coffeemakers, and hair dryers. **Cons:** hotel lacks character; Cerrillos Road is unattractive; a 10-minute drive from Plaza. *Rooms from: $109 3347 Cerrillos Rd., South Side 505/473–2800, 800/777–3347 www.santafecourtyard.com 178 rooms, 31 suites No meals.*

★ Fodor's Choice **Silver Saddle Motel.** *Hotel.* This low-slung

$ adobe property significantly transcends the generally sketchy quality of the several other budget motels along Cerrillos Road, thanks to the tireless efforts of its owner. **Pros:** superaffordable; good-sized rooms, some with refrigerators; friendly, helpful staff. **Cons:** rooms toward the front get noise from Cerrillos Boulevard; basic; a 15-minute drive from the Plaza. *Rooms from: $62 2810 Cerrillos Rd., South Side 505/471–7663 www.santafesilversaddlemotel.com 27 rooms Breakfast.*

5

NIGHTLIFE AND THE ARTS

Few, if any, small cities in America can claim an arts scene as thriving as Santa Fe's—with opera, symphony, and theater in splendid abundance. The music acts here tend to be high-caliber, but rather sporadic. Nightlife, as in dance clubs, is considered fairly "bleak." When popular acts come to town the whole community shows up and dances like there's no tomorrow. A super, seven-week series of music on the Plaza bandstand runs through the summer with performances four nights a week. Gallery openings, poetry readings, plays, and dance concerts take place year-round, not to mention the famed opera and chamber-music festivals. Check the arts and entertainment listings in Santa Fe's daily newspaper, the *New Mexican* (⊕ *www.santafenewmexican.com*), particularly on Friday, when the arts and entertainment section, "Pasatiempo," is included, or check the weekly *Santa Fe Reporter* (⊕ *www.sfreporter.com*) for shows and events. As you probably suspect by now, activities peak in the summer.

NIGHTLIFE

Culturally endowed though it is, Santa Fe has a pretty mellow nightlife scene; its key strength is live music, which is presented at numerous bars, hotel lounges, and restaurants. Austin-based blues and country groups and other acts wander into town, and members of blockbuster bands have been known to perform unannounced at small clubs while vacationing in the area. But on most nights your best bet might be quiet cocktails beside the flickering embers of a piñon fire or under the stars out on the patio.

BARS AND LOUNGES

Agave Lounge. The side bar at the Hotel Eldorado is stylish and contemporary, making it just as much of a hit with locals and nonguests as with those staying on property. The well-made cocktails, natty decor, and stellar late-night bar-food menu (seared tuna with avocado, steak frites) are among Agave's key assets. ✉ *Eldorado Hotel, 309 W. San Francisco St., The Plaza* ☎ *505/995–4530* ⊕ *www.eldoradohotel.com/agave_lounge_bar*.

Cowgirl Santa Fe. This rollicking spot is one of the most popular places in town for live blues, country, rock, folk, and even comedy, on occasion. The bar is friendly and the cheap happy hour margaritas provide a lot of bang for the buck. The pool hall is fun and can get wild as the night gets late. ✉ *319 S. Guadalupe St., Railyard District* ☎ *505/982–2565* ⊕ *www.cowgirlsantafe.com*.

Del Charro. The laid-back saloon at the centrally located Inn of the Governors serves one of the better green-chile cheeseburgers in town, plus fine margaritas and the like. It's less fancy than some of the other hotel bars in town, with old-fashioned Western decor, dark-wood paneling (warmed by the glow of a wood-burning fireplace), and an airy patio. ✉ *Inn of the Governors, 101 W. Alameda St., The Plaza* ☎ *505/954–0320* 🌐 *www.delcharro.com.*

El Farol. With its long front portal and expansive back patio, this ancient adobe restaurant is a lovely spot to enjoy the afternoon and evenings of summer. The roomy, rustic lounge has a true Old West atmosphere—there's been a bar on the premises since 1835—and you can order some fine Spanish brandies and sherries in addition to cold beers, sangria, and margaritas, and the kitchen turns out authentic Spanish fare, from hearty paellas to lighter tapas. It's a great place to see a variety of music; the dance floor fills up with a friendly crowd. ✉ *808 Canyon Rd., East Side and Canyon Road* ☎ *505/983–9912* 🌐 *www.elfarolsf.com.*

5

Evangelo's. The quintessential old-school dive bar, this street-side spot a couple of blocks from the Plaza has pool tables downstairs, a good selection of imported and domestic beers, rock bands on many weekends, and a gruff but lovable staff. ✉ *200 W. San Francisco St.* ☎ *505/982–9014.*

Santa Fe Brewing Company. A little off the beaten path, about a 20-minute drive south of the Plaza right where the Turquoise Trail intersects with Interstate 25, this first-rate brewery—the state's oldest—hosts all sorts of music and serves fine ales as well as offering tours. Although food isn't served, visitors are encouraged to bring their own to enjoy while they knock back a couple of pints. There's sometimes live music on the weekends. ✉ *35 Fire Pl., off NM 14, South Side* ☎ *505/424–3333* 🌐 *www.santafebrewing.com.*

Second Street Brewery. This long-popular brewpub has two locations in town, the newest of which, at the Railyard, is especially spiffy and within easy walking distance of Downtown hotels. At both venues, there's great live music (usually rock or folk) or DJs most nights, large patios, and a rotating selection of terrific beers. Good burgers and pub favorites are served at outposts. ✉ *1607 Paseo de Peralta, in back of farmers' market building, Railyard District* ☎ *505/982–3030* 🌐 *www.secondstreetbrewery.com.*

★ Fodor'sChoice **Secreto Lounge.** This beautifully designed bar inside the dramatically renovated Hotel St. Francis makes the best and most interesting craft cocktails in town, including a classic Manhattan with clove tincture spritzed over the top, and a smoked-sage margarita. There's a nice selection of appetizers and light entrées, too, prepared by the kitchen at the hotel's Tabla de Los Santos restaurant. When the weather is good, try to get a seat on the loggia out front. ✉ *210 Don Gaspar Ave., The Plaza* ☎ *505/983–5700* 🌐 *www.hotelstfrancis.com.*

Tiny's. This retro-fabulous restaurant serving steaks and New Mexican fare is a legend in this town with politicos, reporters, and deal makers. The real draw is the kitsch-filled '50s cocktail lounge. ✉ *1015 Pen Rd., Cerrillos Rd. at St. Francis Dr., South Side* ☎ *505/983–9817* 🌐 *www.tinyssantafe.com.*

THE ARTS

The performing arts scene in Santa Fe blossoms in summer when the calendar is filled with classical or jazz concerts, Shakespeare on the grounds of St. John's campus, experimental theater at Santa Fe Stages, and nearly 100 free concerts on the Plaza. . . . "Too many choices!" is the biggest complaint. The rest of the year is a bit quieter, but several notable performing-arts groups are prolific from fall through spring, including Santa Fe Pro Musica, Santa Fe Concert Association, Santa Fe Symphony, Santa Fe Playhouse, and Theaterwork. The "Pasatiempo" section of the *Santa Fe New Mexican*'s Friday edition, which is also distributed as a free stand-alone in newspaper stands around town, or the *Santa Fe Reporter*, released on Wednesday, are great sources for current happenings.

ARTS CENTERS

Center for Contemporary Arts (CCA). The city's most interesting multiuse arts venue, the Center for Contemporary Arts (CCA) presents indie and foreign films, art exhibitions, provocative theater, and countless workshops and lectures. ✉ *1050 Old Pecos Trail, Old Santa Fe Trail and South Capitol* ☎ *505/982–1338* 🌐 *www.ccasantafe.org.*

SITE Santa Fe. The events at this nexus of international contemporary art include lectures, concerts, author readings, performance art, and gallery shows. The facility hosts a biennial exhibition every even-numbered year. Exhibitions are often provocative, and the immense, open space is ideal for taking in the many larger-than-life installations. ✉ *1606 Paseo de Peralta, Railyard District* ☎ *505/989–1199* 🌐 *www.sitesantafe.org* 🎫 *$10, free Fri., free Sat. 10–noon during Santa Fe Farmers' Market* ⏲ *Thurs. and Sat. 10–5, Fri. 10–7, Sun. noon–5 (also Wed. 10–5 in July and Aug.).*

CONCERT VENUES

Lensic Performing Arts Center. Santa Fe's vintage Downtown movie house has been fully restored and converted into the 850-seat Lensic Performing Arts Center. The grand 1931 building, with Moorish and Spanish Renaissance influences, hosts the Santa Fe Symphony, theater, classic films, lectures and readings, noted world, pop, and jazz musicians, and many other noteworthy events. ✉ *211 W. San Francisco St., The Plaza* ☎ *505/988–1234* 🌐 *www.lensic.com.*

St. Francis Auditorium. This historic space with colorful murals is inside the Museum of Fine Arts and is a top venue for many cultural events, such as theatrical productions and concerts. ✉ *107 W. Palace Ave., The Plaza* ☎ *505/476–5072* 🌐 *www.nmartmuseum.org.*

DANCE

Aspen Santa Fe Ballet. The esteemed company presents several ballet performances throughout the year at the Lensic Performing Arts Center. ☎ *505/983–5591* 🌐 *www.aspensantafeballet.com.*

FILM

Jean Cocteau Cinema. Author and longtime Santa Fe resident George R. R. Martin, of *Game of Thrones* fame, purchased this intimate, funky, and at the time defunct Railyard District art-movie house in summer 2013. This single-screen theater is a great place to catch first-run films, indie flicks, and cult classics, and "midnight movies" (really at 11 pm) are shown on weekends. ✉ *418 Montezuma Ave., Railyard District* ☎ *505/466–5528* 🌐 *www.jeancocteaucinema.com.*

Santa Fe Film Festival. With the film industry booming in New Mexico, this four-day event held in early December has become increasingly well-attended and independent films, workshops, and discussion panels take place at venues around the city. Film buffs should also mark their calendars for the Santa Fe Independent Film Festival (🌐 *www.santafeindependentfilmfestival.com*), which is unrelated to the December festival and takes place over four days in mid-October, with an emphasis, of course, on indie flicks. ☎ *505/988–7414* 🌐 *www.santafefilmfestival.com.*

The Screen. An intimate art-house theater on the campus of the Santa Fe University of Art and Design, The Screen presents a steady rotation of high-quality indie movies using state-of-the-art video and sound. ✉ *1600 St. Michael's Dr., South Side* ☎ *505/473–6494* 🌐 *www.thescreensf.com.*

MUSIC

New Mexico Jazz Festival. Begun in 2006 and rapidly growing in acclaim and popularity, this two-week festival presents numerous concerts in both Santa Fe and Albuquerque in mid-July. Recent performers have included Stanley Clarke, the Yellowjackets, Dianne Reeves, and Allen Toussaint. 🌐 *www.newmexicojazzfestival.org.*

Santa Fe Bandstand Concerts. Each night from mid-June through late August, the bandstand at Downtown's festive and historic Plaza is the site of a free concert. A number of nationally noteworthy artists have appeared for this event, where the music ranges from Spanish guitar to blues to rockabilly. ✉ *Old Santa Fe Trail and Palace Ave., The Plaza* ☎ *505/986–6054* 🌐 *www.santafebandstand.org.*

Santa Fe Chamber Music Festival. This outstanding festival runs mid-July through late August, with performances nearly every night at the art-filled St. Francis Auditorium, or, occasionally, the Lensic Performing Arts Center. There are also free youth-oriented concerts given on several summer mornings. ☎ *505/983–2075, 888/221–9836* 🌐 *www.sfcmf.org.*

Santa Fe Concert Association. From September through May, the venerable organization founded in 1937 presents symphony and solo classical concerts, lectures, dance recitals, opera, and family-minded shows at several venues around town, including the Lensic, the Cathedral, St. John's College, St. Francis Auditorium, and the Scottish Rite Temple. SFCA has brought a number of prestigious talents to Santa Fe in recent years, including Wynton Marsalis, Kronos Quartet, and the Academy of St. Martin in the Fields Chamber Ensemble. ☎ *505/984–8759* 🌐 *www.santafeconcerts.org.*

Santa Fe Desert Chorale. Performances take place throughout the summer at a variety of intriguing venues, from the Cathedral Basilica St. Francis to Loretto Chapel. This highly regarded singing group, which was started in 1982, also performs during the December holiday season. ☎ *505/988–2282, 800/244–4011* ⊕ *www.desertchorale.org.*

★ Fodor'sChoice **Santa Fe Opera.** To watch opera in this strikingly modern structure—a 2,126-seat, indoor-outdoor amphitheater with excellent acoustics and sight lines—is a memorable visual and auditory experience. Carved into the natural curves of a hillside 7 miles north of the Plaza, the opera overlooks mountains, mesas, and sky. Add some of the most acclaimed operatic talents from Europe and the United States, and you begin to understand the excitement that builds every June. This world-renowned company presents five works in repertory each summer—a blend of seasoned classics, neglected masterpieces, and world premieres. Many evenings sell out far in advance, but less expensive standing-room tickets are often available on the day of the performance. A favorite pre-opera pastime is tailgating in the parking lot before the evening performance—many guests set up elaborate picnics of their own, but you can also preorder picnic meals at the opera website or by calling 24 hours in advance. Or you can dine at the Preview Buffet, set up 2½ hours before each performance by the Guilds of the Santa Fe Opera. These meals include a large spread of very good food along with wine, held on the opera grounds. During dessert, a prominent local expert on opera gives a talk about the evening's performance. The Preview Buffet is by reservation only, and the cost is $55 per person. ✉ *301 Opera Dr., off U.S. 285/84, North Side* ☎ *505/986–5900, 800/280–4654* ⊕ *www.santafeopera.org.*

Santa Fe Pro Musica. First-rate orchestra and chamber concerts are given at St. Francis Auditorium and the Lensic Performing Arts Center by the Grammy-nominated Santa Fe Pro Musica from September through April. Baroque and other classical compositions are the normal fare; the annual Christmas performance, held at Loretto Chapel, is a highlight. ☎ *505/988–4640, 800/960–6680* ⊕ *www.santafepromusica.com.*

Santa Fe Symphony. This highly respected symphony performs about 10 concerts each season (September to May) in the Lensic Performing Arts Center. ☎ *505/983–1414, 800/480–1319* ⊕ *www.sf-symphony.org.*

5

THEATER

Santa Fe Playhouse. The oldest extant theater company west of the Mississippi, the Santa Fe Playhouse occupies a converted 19th-century adobe stable and has been presenting an adventurous mix of avant-garde pieces, classical drama, and musical comedy since 1922—the season runs August through July. The Fiesta Melodrama—a spoof of the Santa Fe scene—is presented late August to mid-September. ✉ *142 E. De Vargas St., Old Santa Fe Trail and South Capitol* ☎ *505/988–4262* 🌐 *www.santafeplayhouse.org.*

Theaterwork. This well-respected community theater group performs five plays each season, which runs from September through June. ✉ *James A. Little Theater at the New Mexico School for the Deaf, 1060 Cerrillos Rd.* ☎ *505/471–1799* 🌐 *www.twnm.org.*

6

SHOPS, GALLERIES, AND SPAS

Santa Fe has been a trading post for eons. Nearly a thousand years ago the great pueblos of the Chacoan civilizations were strategically located between the buffalo-hunting tribes of the Great Plains and the Indians of Mexico. Native Americans in New Mexico traded turquoise and other valuables with Indians from Mexico for metals, shells, parrots, and other exotic items. After the arrival of the Spanish and the West's subsequent development, Santa Fe became the place to exchange silver from Mexico and natural resources from New Mexico for manufactured goods, whiskey, and greenbacks from the United States. The construction of the railroad in 1880 brought Santa Fe access to all kinds of manufactured goods.

The trading legacy remains, but now Downtown Santa Fe caters increasingly to those looking for handcrafted furniture and crafts, and bespoke apparel and accessories. Sure, a few chains have moved in and a handful of fairly tatty souvenir shops still proliferate, but shopping in Santa Fe consists mostly of high-quality, one-of-a-kind independent stores. Canyon Road, packed with internationally acclaimed galleries, is the perfect place to browse for art and collectibles. The Downtown district around the Plaza has unusual gift and curio shops, as well as clothiers and shoe stores that range from theatrical to conventional. You'll find quite a few art galleries here, too. The hip, revitalized Railyard District (sometimes referred to as the Guadalupe District), less touristy than the Plaza, is on Downtown's southwest perimeter and includes an eclectic mix of trendy boutiques, gift shops, and avant-garde contemporary art galleries—it's the most cosmopolitan of Santa Fe's shopping areas.

ART GALLERIES

Over the past two decades, Santa Fe has outgrown its reputation as a provincial, albeit respected, market for traditional Southwest art. Galleries carrying works by both vintage and contemporary artists who specialize in Western landscapes and scenes still thrive, but Santa Fe now rivals cities many times its size when it comes to edgy, provocative, and often high-priced abstract and contemporary works in every imaginable media. The following are only a limited but notable sampling of the roughly 200 galleries in greater Santa Fe—with the best of representational, nonobjective, Native American, Latin American, cutting-edge, photographic, and soulful works that defy categorization. *The Collectors Guide to Santa Fe, Taos, and Albuquerque* is a good resource for learning about more galleries; you can pick up this free resource at hotels and shops around town, or browse listings online at *www.collectorsguide.com*. Check the "Pasatiempo" pullout in the *Santa Fe New Mexican* on Friday for a preview of weekly gallery openings.

★ Fodor'sChoice **Andrew Smith Gallery.** This highly esteemed photo gallery deals in works by Edward S. Curtis and other 19th-century chroniclers of the American West. Other major figures are Ansel Adams, Edward Weston, O. Winston Link, Henri Cartier-Bresson, Eliot Porter, Laura Gilpin, Dorothea Lange, Alfred Stieglitz, Annie Liebovitz, and regional artists like Barbara Van Cleve. ✉ *122 Grant Ave., The Plaza* ☎ *505/984–1234* *www.andrewsmithgallery.com.*

Art of Russia Gallery. The art communities of Santa Fe and Taos have a surprisingly strong connection with those of Russia, and this Canyon Road space carries a particularly strong collection of works by contemporary and historic Russian artists, including a number of Impressionist paintings. A highlight here is the selection of USSR Propaganda posters. ✉ *225 Canyon Rd., East Side and Canyon Road* ☎ *505/466–1718* *www.artofrussiagallery.com.*

Bellas Artes. A sophisticated gallery with a serene sculpture garden, Bellas Artes has a captivating collection of ceramics, paintings, photography, and sculptural work, and represents internationally renowned artists like Judy Pfaff, David Kimball Anderson, and Olga de Amaral. The vanguard modernist work of sculptor Ruth Duckworth is also well-represented. ✉ *653 Canyon Rd., East Side and Canyon Road* ☎ *505/983–2745* *www.bellasartes-gallery.com.*

Charlotte Jackson Fine Art. This Railyard District notable focuses primarily on monochromatic "radical" painting and sculpture and is set in a fantastic, open space in a renovated warehouse. Many of the pieces here are large scale, with "drama" the guiding force. Mala Breuer, Joe Barnes, William Metcalf, Constance DeJong, and Joseph Marioni are among the artists producing minimalist works dealing with light and space. ✉ *554 S. Guadalupe St., Railyard District* ☎ *505/989–8688* *www.charlottejackson.com.*

Eight Modern. In an unassuming building just off Canyon Road, this increasingly renowned gallery showcases modern and contemporary painting, photography, and sculpture by established artists from around the world. Eight Modern has staked a notable claim in Santa Fe's art world by bringing a number of internationally acclaimed artists here for the first time. ✉ *231 Delgado St., East Side and Canyon Road* ☎ *505/995–0231* 🌐 *www.eightmodern.net.*

★ Fodor's Choice **Gerald Peters Gallery.** Santa Fe's most impressive gallery of American and European art from the 19th century to the present. Contained are works by Max Weber, Albert Bierstadt, Frederic Remington, the Taos Society, the New Mexico modernists, and Georgia O'Keeffe, as well as contemporary artists. ✉ *1011 Paseo de Peralta, East Side and Canyon Road* ☎ *505/954–5700* 🌐 *www.gpgallery.com.*

Giacobbe-Fritz. Stop inside this late-1890s adobe building to admire a truly diverse collection of paintings, drawings, and sculpture, much of it with a regional and traditional approach, including impressionist New Mexico landscapes by Connie Dillman and whimsical bronze sculptures of burros, bats, and other animals by Copper Tritscheller. The owners also operate the excellent GF Contemporary, across the street, which focuses more on modern and abstract works. ✉ *702 Canyon Rd., East Side and Canyon Road* ☎ *505/986–1156* 🌐 *www.giacobbefritz.com.*

★ Fodor's Choice **James Kelly Contemporary.** Instrumental in transforming the Railyard District into Santa Fe's hub for contemporary art, James Kelly Contemporary mounts sophisticated, high-caliber shows by international and regional artists—such as Johnnie Winona Ross, Nic Nicosia, Peter Sarkisian, Tom Joyce, and Sherrie Levine—in a renovated warehouse directly across from SITE Santa Fe. ✉ *550 S. Guadalupe St., Railyard District* ☎ *505/989–1601* 🌐 *www.jameskelly.com.*

LewAllen Contemporary. This is a leading center for a variety of contemporary arts by both Southwestern and other acclaimed artists, among them Judy Chicago and Janet Fish; sculpture, photography, ceramics, basketry, and painting are all shown in this dynamic space near the Plaza. There's a second outpost in the Railyard District, near the farmers' market building. ✉ *129 W. Palace Ave., The Plaza* ☎ *505/988–8997* 🌐 *www.lewallencontemporary.com.*

★ Fodor's Choice **Manitou Galleries.** Known for presenting the much-celebrated two-day Auction in Santa Fe (🌐 *www.auctioninsantafe.com*) each year in mid-August, this respected gallery near the Plaza carries mostly contemporary representational paintings and sculptures by such world-class artists as Albert Dreher, Tong Luo, and Martha Pettigrew. Manitou has a second location, every bit as impressive, at 225 Canyon Road. ✉ *123 W. Palace Ave., The Plaza* ☎ *505/986–0440* 🌐 *www.manitougalleries.com.*

Meyer Gallery. One of the oldest and most prestigious galleries in the Southwest, Meyer is a good place to begin a stroll up Canyon Road—it's at the bottom of the hill, and the work shown in this expansive gallery gives a good sense of the traditional Santa Fe art scene. The owners also operate adjacent Meyer East Gallery, which contains another 6,000 square feet of exhibit space devoted somewhat more to modern and contemporary, though still primarily representational, artists. ✉ *225 Canyon Rd., East Side and Canyon Road* ☎ *505/983–1434* 🌐 *www.meyergalleries.com.*

Monroe Gallery. In this attractive storefront space a couple of blocks from the Plaza, you can admire works by the most celebrated black-and-white photographers of the 20th century, from Margaret Bourke-White to Alfred Eisenstaedt. The focus is on humanist and photojournalist style photography, and many iconic images are sold here. ✉ *112 Don Gaspar Ave., The Plaza* ☎ *505/992–0800* 🌐 *www.monroegallery.com.*

★ Fodor's Choice **Nedra Matteucci Galleries.** One of the Southwest's premier galleries, Matteucci Galleries exhibits works by California regionalists, members of the early Taos and Santa Fe schools, and masters of American impressionism and modernism. Spanish-colonial furniture, Indian antiquities, and a fantastic sculpture garden are other draws of this well-respected establishment. The old adobe building that the gallery is in is a beautifully preserved example of Santa Fe–style architecture. Matteucci also owns Morning Star Gallery around the corner on Canyon Road. ✉ *1075 Paseo de Peralta, East Side and Canyon Road* ☎ *505/982–4631* 🌐 *www.matteucci.com.*

Peyton Wright. Tucked inside the historic Spiegelberg house, this gallery represents some of the most talented emerging and established contemporary artists in the country; historic notables featured here include Dorothy Brett and Maurice Prendergast as well as antique and even ancient New Mexican, Russian, and Latin works. ✉ *237 E. Palace Ave., The Plaza* ☎ *505/989–9888* 🌐 *www.peytonwright.com.*

★ FAMILY Fodor's Choice **Shidoni Foundry and Galleries.** This picturesque compound is home to a foundry that casts work for established and up-and-coming artists from all over North America. On the grounds of an old chicken ranch, Shidoni has a rambling sculpture garden and a gallery. Self-guided foundry tours ($3) are permitted weekdays noon to 1, but the sculpture garden (free) is open daily during daylight hours; you can watch bronze pourings ($5) and take the foundry tour most Saturday afternoons. This is a dream of a place to expose your kids to large-scale art and enjoy a lovely and, in this area, rare expanse of green grass at the same time. ✉ *1508 Bishop's Lodge Rd., 5 miles north of Santa Fe, North Side, Tesuque* ☎ *505/988–8001* 🌐 *www.shidoni.com.*

Ventana Fine Art. Set in a dramatic and expansive Victorian redbrick schoolhouse on Canyon Road, Ventana has been at the forefront of Santa Fe's constantly shifting contemporary art scene since the mid-1980s. The gallery represents notable talents like Doug Dawson, John Axton, and John Nieto, and there's a lovely sculpture garden adjacent. ✉ *400 Canyon Rd., East Side and Canyon Road* ☎ *505/983–8815* 🌐 *www.ventanafineart.com.*

Verve Gallery of Photography. Opened in 2003 in an attractive Territorial-style house not far from the Plaza, Verve has become a leader in contemporary, often wonderfully innovative, fine art photography. It's worth contrasting the works here to those sold at some of the other photography galleries in town, where the focus is more on historic photojournalism. ✉ *219 E. Marcy St., The Plaza* ☎ *505/982–5009* 🌐 *www.vervegallery.com.*

★ Fodor's Choice **Waxlander Gallery.** Owned by Phyllis Kapp, who helped bring Canyon Road's art scene to world acclaim and is one of the most respected names of the Santa Fe creative community, this exceptional gallery showcases works that tend to share one consistent trait: magnificent, vibrant colors. Note the stunning landscape watercolors of Kapp herself, along with similarly dynamic works by Sharon Markwardt, Sangita Phadke, Michael Ethridge, and Bruce King. ✉ *622 Canyon Rd., East Side and Canyon Road* ☎ *505/984–2202* 🌐 *www.waxlander.com.*

Zane Bennett Contemporary Art. The sleek design of this airy, two-story gallery with a skylighted atrium is a fitting venue for the cutting-edge photography, paintings, sculptures, and mixed-media works within. Zane Bennett has carried works by icons (Helen Frankenthaler, Robert Motherwell) but also presents rotating shows focused on everything from up-and-coming Native artists to the grid-based paintings of French artist François Morellet. ✉ *435 S. Guadalupe St., Railyard District* ☎ *505/982–8111* 🌐 *www.zanebennettgallery.com.*

SHOPS

ANTIQUES AND HOME FURNISHINGS

Antique Warehouse. If staying in a Santa Fe B&B or historic inn has you now yearning for the heavy, ornately carved chests, doors, tables, and decorative items that give these places their rustic old-world character, spend some time in this 9,000-square-foot repository of vintage New Mexican and Mexican furnishings and collectibles. ✉ *530 S. Guadalupe St., Railyard District* ☎ *505/984–1159* 🌐 *www.antiquewarehouse-santafe.com.*

Arrediamo. One of the top spots in the Southwest for handmade Turkish, Persian, and Afghan rugs, Arrediamo also carries a fine selection of authentic Navajo rugs and textiles. ✉ *214 Galisteo St., The Plaza* ☎ *505/820–8337* 🌐 *www.arrediamo.com.*

6

Asian Adobe. Browse porcelain lamps, ornate antique baby hats and shoes, red-lacquer armoires, and similarly stunning Chinese and Southeast Asian artifacts and antiques. The jewelry selection often includes hard-to-find ethnic Chinese pieces as well as exceptional one-of-a-kind finds from the owner's travels. ✉ *310 Johnson St., The Plaza* ☎ *505/992–6846* 🌐 *www.asianadobe.com.*

Casa Nova. A spacious shop that sells functional and decorative art from around the world, Casa Nova deftly mixes colors, textures, and cultural icons—old and new—from stylish pewter tableware from South Africa to vintage hand-carved ex-votos (votive offerings) from Brazil. There is a major emphasis here on goods produced by artists and cooperatives focused on sustainable economic development. ✉ *530 S. Guadalupe St., Railyard District* ☎ *505/983–8558* 🌐 *www.casanovagallery.com.*

Design Warehouse. A welcome antidote to Santa Fe's preponderance of shops selling Native American and Spanish-colonial antiques that carries hip, contemporary furniture, kitchenware, home accessories, and other sleek knickknacks, such as those made by the Italian firm Alessi. Note the select collection of amusing books for kids and adults. ✉ *101 W. Marcy St., The Plaza* ☎ *505/988–1555* 🌐 *www.designwarehousesantafe.com.*

Doodlet's. Check out the whimsical collection of stuff: pop-up books, silly postcards, tin art, hooked rugs, and stringed lights. Wonderment is in every display case, drawing the eye to the unusual. There's something for just about everyone at this delightfully quirky shop, and often it's affordable. ✉ *120 Don Gaspar Ave., The Plaza* ☎ *505/983–3771.*

★ Fodor's Choice **Jackalope.** You could easily spend a couple of hours wandering through this legendary indoor-outdoor bazaar, which sprawls over 7 acres, incorporating several pottery barns, a furniture store, endless aisles of knickknacks from Latin America and Asia, a huge greenhouse, and a prairie dog run (a fun diversion if you have kids along). There's also an area where craftspeople, artisans, and others sell their wares—sort of a mini flea market. ✉ *2820 Cerrillos Rd., South Side* ☎ *505/471–8539* 🌐 *www.jackalope.com.*

La Mesa. La Mesa has become well-known for showcasing contemporary handcrafted, mostly functional, works by more than two dozen, mostly local, artists including Kathy O'Neill, Gregory Lomayesva, and Nancy Udell. Collections include dinnerware, glassware, pottery, lighting, fine art, and accessories. ✉ *225 Canyon Rd., East Side and Canyon Road* ☎ *505/984–1688* 🌐 *www.lamesaofsantafe.com.*

Pachamama. Located on Canyon Road, Pachamama carries a diverse and captivating collection of Latin American folk art, including small tin or silver *milagros,* the stamped metal images used as votive offerings, and gorgeous jewelry. The shop also carries weavings, Spanish-colonial antiques, and other delightful trinkets. ✉ *223 Canyon Rd., East Side and Canyon Road* ☎ *505/983–4020* 🌐 *pachamamasantafe.com.*

Pandora's. Beautiful, carefully curated items for the home—some produced regionally and others from Peru, Uzbekistan, the Congo, and other far-flung lands—are the specialty of this colorful boutique in the Sanbusco Market Center. Keep an eye out for quilts made by a weaving co-op in Vietnam and brightly colored Missoni bath linens. ✉ *500 Montezuma Ave., Railyard District* ☎ *505/982–3298* 🌐 *www.pandorasantafe.com.*

BOOKS

Several shops in Santa Fe sell used books, and a handful of high-quality shops carry the latest releases from mainstream and small presses.

★ Fodor'sChoice **Collected Works Book Store.** You'll find a great selection of art and travel books here, including a generous selection of titles on Southwestern art, architecture, and general history, as well as the latest in contemporary literature. In a large, inviting space close to the Plaza, you can enjoy organic coffees, snacks, and sandwiches in the café, which also presents readings and music. The patio invites long, leisurely reads. The proprietress, Dorothy Massey, and her staff are well loved for their knowledge and helpfulness. ✉ *202 Galisteo St., The Plaza* ☎ *505/988–4226* 🌐 *www.collectedworksbookstore.com.*

Garcia Street Books. This outstanding independent shop is strong on art, architecture, cookbooks, literature, and regional Southwestern works—it's a block from the Canyon Road galleries and hosts frequent talks by authors under its portal during the summer. ✉ *376 Garcia St., East Side and Canyon Road* ☎ *505/986–0151* 🌐 *www.garciastreetbooks.com.*

6

Nicholas Potter. The specialty here is used, rare, and out-of-print books, along with an extensive collection of Southwest art and artifacts. Modern first editions and photography are other areas of focus. The quixotic shop also stocks used jazz and classical CDs. Potter is an amazing resource for those looking for a specific book or subject and his knowledge is encyclopedic. ✉ *211 E. Palace Ave., The Plaza* ☎ *505/983–5434* 🌐 *www.nicholaspotterbooks.com.*

★ Fodor'sChoice **Photo-eye Bookstore and Gallery.** This is your source of an almost unbelievable collection of new, rare, and out-of-print photography books; the staff is made up of photographers who are excellent sources of information and advice on great spots to shoot in and around Santa Fe. The adjacent gallery presents fine photography. ✉ *370 Garcia St., East Side and Canyon Road* ☎ *505/988–5152* 🌐 *www.photoeye.com.*

Travel Bug. Here you'll find a huge array of guides and books about travel, and USGS and other maps. You'll also find all sorts of gadgets for hikers and backpackers. There's also a cozy coffeehouse (excellent java) with Wi-Fi. ✉ *839 Paseo de Peralta, The Plaza* ☎ *505/992–0418* 🌐 *www.mapsofnewmexico.com.*

CLOTHING AND ACCESSORIES

Many tourists arrive in clothing from mainstream department stores and leave bedecked in Western garb. Although it's not difficult to find getups Annie Oakley herself might have envied, you'll see that at most boutiques in town Western gear is mixed with pieces from all over the globe to create a more eclectic and cosmopolitan Santa Fe style. There are few towns where you'll find more distinctive, sometimes downright eccentric, expressions of personal style on every age and every shape. It is worth asking specifically to see the work of locals during your wanderings. There are artists of every bent in this town and the surrounding areas, not only putting paint to canvas, but creating jewelry, clothing, hats, shoes, and other accessories. Informed by cultural traditions but as cutting-edge and innovative as anything you'll find in New York or San Francisco, the contemporary jewelry coming from Native American artists like Cody Sanderson and Pat Pruitt is incredible. The shops Downtown at the Museum of Contemporary Native Arts and up on Museum Hill at both the Museum of Indian Arts and Culture and the Wheelwright Museum (home of the Case Trading Post Museum Store) are great places to shop for works by Native artists.

★ Fodor'sChoice **Back at the Ranch.** This cozy space in an old, creaky-floored adobe is stocked with perhaps the finest handmade cowboy boots you will ever see—in every color, style, and embellishment imaginable. Other finds, like funky ranch-style furniture, 1950s blanket coats, jewelry, and belt buckles are also sold. The staff is top-notch and the boots are breathtaking. ⊠ *209 E. Marcy St., The Plaza* ☎ *505/989–8110* 🌐 *www.backattheranch.com.*

Cicada Collection. Modern European women's apparel in timeless styles and muted colors are the hallmark of this intimate boutique that provides a refreshing contrast to the sometimes florid and funky threads that dominate Santa Fe's fashion landscape. ⊠ *221 Galisteo St., The Plaza* ☎ *505/982–6260* 🌐 *www.cicadacollection.com.*

Cupcake Clothing. This hip store is just off Guadalupe Street in the busy Railyard District. Inside you'll find all sorts of stylish clothing, shoes, and accessories for women and a very friendly staff to boot. The clientele is pretty evenly split between tourists and locals. ⊠ *328 Montezuma Ave., Railyard District* ☎ *505/988–4744* 🌐 *www.cupcakeclothing.com.*

★ Fodor'sChoice **Double Take at the Ranch.** This rambling shop ranks among the best consignment stores in the West, carrying elaborately embroidered vintage cowboy shirts, hundreds of pairs of boots, funky old prints, and amazing vintage Indian pawn and Mexican jewelry. The store adjoins its sister consignment store, also called Double Take, which stocks a wide range of contemporary clothing and accessories for men and women; and Santa Fe Pottery, which shows the works of local artists. ✉ *321 S. Guadalupe St., Railyard District* ☎ *505/820–7775* 🌐 *www.santafedoubletake.com.*

Mirá. The women's clothing here is edgy and eclectic, combining the adventurous spirit of New Mexico with global contemporary fashion. The shop has jewelry, accessories, and collectibles from Latin America, the Flax line of natural-fiber clothing, and knockout dresses and separates not sold anywhere else in town. ✉ *101 W. Marcy St., The Plaza* ☎ *505/988–3585* 🌐 *www.mirastore.com.*

★ Fodor'sChoice **Nathalie.** There are many fans of Parisian-born owner Nathalie Kent's distinctive style and carefully curated collection of vintage and new pieces. Though Kent's passion clearly leans toward traditional Western wear, from cowboy boots to velvet skirts to exquisite Old Pawn jewelry, you'll also find gorgeous pieces from all over the globe—antique Moroccan treasures line up next to 100-year-old Navajo bracelets like long lost pals. Her home furnishings are stupendous, too. ✉ *503 Canyon Rd., East Side and Canyon Road* ☎ *505/982–1021* 🌐 *www.nathaliesantafe.com.*

★ Fodor'sChoice **O'Farrell Hats.** Scott O'Farrell (son of the shop's late founder, Kevin) and his highly trained staff carry on the tradition of producing carefully designed and constructed classic Western hats. The one-of-a-kind beaver-felt cowboy hats make the ultimate Santa Fe keepsake. This level of quality comes at a cost, but devoted customers—who have included everyone from cattle ranchers to U.S. presidents—swear by O'Farrell's artful creations. ✉ *111 E. San Francisco St., The Plaza* ☎ *505/989–9666* 🌐 *www.ofarrellhatco.com.*

Origins. Borrowing from many cultures, Origins carries pricey women's wear like antique kimonos and custom-dyed silk jackets, with the overall look of artsy elegance. One-of-a-kind accessories complete the spectacular look that Santa Fe inspires. ✉ *135 W. San Francisco St., The Plaza* ☎ *505/988–2323* 🌐 *www.originssantafe.com.*

★ Fodor'sChoice **Sangre de Cristo Mountain Works.** For gear related to just about any outdoor activity you can think of, check out this well-stocked shop that both sells and rents hiking, climbing, camping, trekking, snowshoeing, and skiing equipment. There's a great selection of clothing and shoes for men and women. The superactive, knowledgeable staff here can also advise you on the best venues for local recreation. ✉ *328 S. Guadalupe St. (front door is on Montezuma Ave.), Railyard District* ☎ *505/984–8221* 🌐 *www.sdcmountainworks.com.*

★ Fodor'sChoice **Santa Fe Dry Goods.** This spacious, venerable shop in a vintage storefront on the Plaza carries a who's who of haute, international designer brands for women, including Holly Masterson, Avant Toi, Issey Miyake, Greig Porter, and Casmari—contemporary Asian and European styles are especially well-represented, and there's a stellar selection of scarves, handbags, and jewelry, too. ✉ *53 Old Santa Fe Trail, The Plaza* ☎ *505/983–8142* 🌐 *www.santafedrygoods.com.*

FOOD, DRINK, AND COOKWARE

In addition to traditional gift shops selling gourmet goodies and candies, you'll find an increasing number of shops in Santa Fe specializing in high-quality edibles and craft beverages (wine, beer, liquor, coffee). *See the Side Trips from Santa Fe chapter, for information on the top wineries in the region, most of which are north of Santa Fe, en route to Taos, and see the Santa Fe Nightlife and the Arts chapter for listings of brewpubs that not only serve fine local beers on premises but also sell them to go.*

★ Fodor'sChoice **Kakawa.** Proprietor Mark Sciscenti is a self-described chocolate historian and chocolate alchemist, and you're unlikely to ever have tasted anything like the divine, agave-sweetened, artisanal creations that emerge from his kitchen. Historically accurate chocolate drinks, like the Aztec Warrior Chocolate Elixir, divine caramels, and agave-sweetened, gluten-free chocolate baked goods are served in this cozy, welcoming shop that's as much an educational experience as a chance to indulge in exceptional sweets. ✉ *1050 Paseo de Peralta* ☎ *505/982–0388* 🌐 *www.kakawachocolates.com.*

FAMILY

Kaune's Neighborhood Market. Although Santa Fe has no shortage of gourmet chain groceries, this cozy market near the Capitol building has been stocking its shelves with fine foods since 1896. Following a complete and much-needed overhaul in spring 2013, Kaune's is looking quite spiffy now, with its wide aisles and expanded selection of specialty and organic goods (many of them local), fine wines, artisan cheeses, chocolates, and so on. ✉ *511 Old Santa Fe Trail, Old Santa Fe Trail and South Capitol* ☎ *505/982–2629* 🌐 *www.kaunes.com.*

Las Cosas Kitchen Shoppe. In the DeVargas shopping center, Las Cosas Kitchen Shoppe stocks a fantastic selection of cookery, tableware, and kitchen gadgetry and gifts. The shop is also renowned for its cooking classes, which touch on everything from high-altitude baking to Asian-style grilling. ✉ *De Vargas Mall, N. Guadalupe St. at Paseo de Peralta, West of the Plaza* ☎ *505/988–3394, 877/229–7184* 🌐 *www.lascosascooking.com.*

★ Fodor'sChoice **Santa Fe Spirits.** Since its 2010 opening, this artisan distillery has been earning admiration for superb Silver Coyote Pure Malt Whiskey, Expedition Vodka, Santa Fe Spirits Apple Brandy (made in the dry style of French calvados), and Wheeler's Gin—an aged, mesquite-smoked, single-malt whiskey is planned soon. For the full experience, including a tour of the facility, stop by the main distillery, which is out near the airport off the NM 599 Relief Route; tours and tastings are given Wednesday–Saturday 3–5, and an on-site bar serves cocktails using Santa Fe Spirits on those same days from 5 until 9 pm. If you can't make it out that way, drop by the downtown tasting room at 308 Read Street, in the Railyard District, which is open Monday–Saturday 1:30–8:30. ✉ *7505 Mallard Way, Unit 1, South Side* ☎ *505/467–8892* 🌐 *www.santafespirits.com.*

The Spanish Table. Here you can satisfy all your Spanish culinary needs, and then some, including Spanish meats and cheeses, cookware and beautiful Majolica pottery, books, dry goods, and a wonderful world-music selection. The staff is always ready to help advise on a recipe or gift idea and will ship your purchases anywhere you like. ✉ *109 N. Guadalupe St., West of the Plaza* ☎ *505/986–0243* 🌐 *www.spanishtable.com.*

★ Fodor'sChoice **Todos Santos.** This tiny candy shop in the 18th-century courtyard of Sena Plaza sells must-be-seen-to-be-believed works of edible art, including chocolate milagros and altar pieces gilded with 23-karat gold or silver leaf. Truffles come in exotic flavors, like tangerine chile, rose caramel, and lemon verbena. The buttery, spicy, handmade

6

chipotle caramels melt in your mouth. Amidst the taste sensations and quirky folk art are amazing and delightful customized Pez dispensers from Albuquerque folk artist Steve White and astonishing, intricate recycled paper creations from local phenom Rick Phelps. ✉ *125 E. Palace Ave., The Plaza* ☎ *505/982–3855.*

JEWELRY

Eidos. Check out "concept-led" minimalist contemporary jewelry from European designers and Deborah Alexander and Gordon Lawrie, who own the store. It's a lovely, contemporary space with a fascinating array of materials, good range of prices, and helpful staff. ✉ *500 Montezuma Ave., inside Sanbusco Center, Railyard District* ☎ *505/992–0020* 🌐 *www.eidosjewelry.com.*

Golden Eye. In this pint-size shop (even by Santa Fe standards) you'll find gorgeous handcrafted jewelry in high-karat gold, often paired with gemstones. The experienced, helpful staff of artisans can help you pick out something beautiful and unusual. ✉ *115 Don Gaspar St., The Plaza* ☎ *505/984–0040* 🌐 *www.goldeneyesantafe.com.*

LewAllen & LewAllen Jewelry. Father-and-daughter silversmiths Ross and Laura LewAllen run this impressive shop. Handmade jewelry ranges from whimsical to mystical inside their tiny shop just off the Plaza. There's something for absolutely everyone in here, including delightful charms for your pet's collar. ✉ *105 E. Palace Ave., The Plaza* ☎ *800/988–5112, 505/983–2657* 🌐 *www.lewallen-jewelry.com.*

★ Fodor's Choice **Patina.** In this airy, museum-like space, you'll find outstanding contemporary jewelry, textiles, and sculptural objects of metal, clay, and wood. With a staff whose courtesy is matched by knowledge of the genre, artists-owners Ivan and Allison Barnett have used their fresh curatorial aesthetic to create a showplace for more than 110 American and European artists they represent—many of whom are in permanent collections of museums such as MoMA. ✉ *131 W. Palace Ave., The Plaza* ☎ *505/986–3432* 🌐 *www.patina-gallery.com.*

Rippel & Company. Proprieter and talented silversmith John Rippel fell in love with Santa Fe during a road trip in the late '60s. Inspired by the landscape and architecture, he's earned a devoted followed for his distinctive sterling-silver belt buckles, and gorgeous bracelets and necklaces set with turquoise and coral. His shop near the Plaza also carries jewelry, leather bags, and gifts designed by other noted local artisans. ✉ *111 Old Santa Fe Trail, The Plaza* ☎ *505/986–9115* 🌐 *www.johnrippel.com.*

MARKETS

★ Fodor's Choice **Santa Fe Farmers' Market.** Browse through the vast selection of local produce, meat, flowers, honey, wine, jams, and cheese—much of it organic—at the thriving Santa Fe Farmers' Market. Dozens of stalls are arranged inside a snazzy, modern building in the Railyard and adjacent to it; it's open year-round on Saturday mornings and additionally, in summer, on Tuesday mornings. The lively space also hosts an artisan market on Sundays from 10 to 4. It's a great people-watching venue, with entertainment for kids as well as food vendors selling terrific breakfast burritos, green-chile bread, Taos Cow ice cream, and other goodies. ✉ *1607 Paseo de Peralta, Railyard District* ☎ *505/983–4098* 🌐 *www.santafefarmersmarket.com.*

6

NATIVE AMERICAN ARTS AND CRAFTS

Andrea Fisher Fine Pottery. You can browse some of the nation's finest examples of both historic and contemporary Native pottery at this gallery a couple of blocks east of the Plaza and especially renowned for its collection of pieces from San Ildefonso Pueblo legend Maria Martinez and her illustrious family. ✉ *100 W. San Francisco St., The Plaza* ☎ *505/986–1234* 🌐 *www.andreafisherpottery.com.*

Morning Star Gallery. Owned by the prestigious Nedra Matteucci Galleries, this is a veritable museum of Native American art and artifacts. An adobe shaded by a huge cottonwood tree houses antique basketry, pre-1940 Navajo silver jewelry, Northwest Coast Native American carvings, Navajo weavings, and art of the Plains Indians. Prices and quality prohibit casual purchases, but the collection is magnificent. ✉ *513 Canyon Rd., East Side and Canyon Road* ☎ *505/982–8187* 🌐 *www.morningstargallery.com.*

Niman Fine Arts. This intimate space focuses on the prolific work of contemporary Hopi artists Arlo, Dan, and Michael Namingha. Arlo is a sculptor working in bronze, wood, and stone; Dan paints and sculpts; and Michael works with digital imagery. ✉ *125 Lincoln Ave., The Plaza* ☎ *505/988–5091* 🌐 *www.namingha.com.*

Rainbow Man. Established in 1945, this colorful, if a bit touristy, shop does business in an old, rambling adobe complex, part of which dates from before the 1680 Pueblo Revolt. The shop carries early Navajo, Mexican, and Chimayó textiles, along with photographs by Edward S. Curtis, a breathtaking collection of vintage pawn and Mexican jewelry, Day of the Dead figures, Oaxacan folk animals, New Mexican folk art, kachinas, and contemporary jewelry from local artists. The friendly staff possesses an encyclopedic knowledge of the art here. ✉ *107 E. Palace Ave., The Plaza* ☎ *505/982–8706* 🌐 *www.therainbowman.com.*

★ Fodor'sChoice **Robert Nichols Gallery.** This long-running establishment on Canyon Road represents a remarkable group of Native American ceramics artists doing primarily nontraditional work. Diverse artists such as Glen Nipshank, whose organic, sensuous shapes would be right at home in MoMA, and Diego Romero, whose Cochiti-style vessels are detailed with graphic-novel-style characters and sharp social commentary, are right at home here. It is a treat to see cutting-edge work that is clearly informed by indigenous traditions. ✉ *419 Canyon Rd., East Side and Canyon Road* ☎ *505/982–2145* 🌐 *www.robertnicholsgallery.com.*

★ Fodor'sChoice **Shiprock Santa Fe.** "Eclectic Modern Vintage" is Shiprock Santa Fe's tagline, and it accurately sums up their incredible collection of pottery, textiles, painting, furniture, and sculpture. The gallery is notable for its dedication to showcasing exquisite vintage pieces alongside vanguard contemporary works. ✉ *53 Old Santa Fe Trail, The Plaza* ☎ *505/982–8478* 🌐 *www.shiprocksantafe.com.*

SPAS

Santa Fe has established itself as a major spa destination. From intimate boutique spas to gleaming resort sanctuaries where you can spend days ensconced in beautiful surroundings with endless treatment options, there is a spa and a specialty for everyone in this town. Several of the larger, upscale hotels have spas, the best of which are included here.

Absolute Nirvana. This intimate spa set amid the gracious gardens beside the late-Victorian Madeleine Inn lives up to its name with its lush, peaceful Indonesian-inspired setting and sumptuous treatments, some of which—like the pumpkin-infused massage, exfoliation, and mask offered in the fall—are change seasonally. Master-level massage therapists use all-organic, delectable food-grade ingredients. Among year-round treatments, the Indo-Asian hot-stone massage and Chocolate Decadence facial are highly popular. Most treatments finish with homemade snacks, and a variety of add-ons are available, including 30-minute foot massages and leisurely rose-petal baths in a massive stone tub. Cozy, low-keyed, and eco-friendly (it's certified by the nonprofit Green Spa Network), Absolute Nirvana has more limited facilities than some of Santa Fe's major resort facilities, but that's a big part of its charm—the price is right, too. It's $105 for a 60-minute massage and $325–$375 for a half-day spa package. ✉ *Madeleine Inn, 106 Faithway St., East Side and Canyon Road* ☎ *505/983–7942* 🌐 *www.absolutenirvana.com.*

Body. This day spa just south of the Guadalupe District is known for having one of the most popular vegetarian restaurants in town (the specialty is raw, organic fare), plus a great little boutique and comprehensive child-care services. Other big strengths of Body are the dance classes and yoga school, with an extensive slate of classes like body sculpting, personal training, and Pilates. The spa here offers the full range of treatments that you'll find at the bigger resort properties, but at lower prices than at most. The staff is friendly and the space unpretentious. Consider body wraps, facials, and Thai, Swedish, and Japanese massages in addition to Rolfing, Reiki, and prenatal massage. Also popular are the lemon-verbena body glow, and custom facials using top lines of holistic products. It's $80 for a 60-minute massage; the gym has cardiovascular machines, free weights, and weight-training equipment. ✉ *333 Cordova Rd., South Side* ☎ *505/986–0362* 🌐 *www.bodyofsantafe.com.*

★ Fodor'sChoice **La Posada de Santa Fe Spa.** The first-rate, 4,500-square-foot spa at this historic Downtown resort emphasizes regional ingredients in its extensive offerings of treatments and services, including a signature Spirit of Santa Fe body rub that uses ground blue corn as a skin exfoliant, and a body wrap using chocolate and red chiles from nearby Chimayó. The 25-minute Collagen Quench is a great way to combat the effects on the skin of New Mexico's sunny, high-desert climate. Hair and nail services are also available, and there's an expansive fitness center (24-hour access for hotel guests) with Cybex equipment and personal-training as well as private yoga sessions offered. After working out, or being worked on, go for a swim in the heated outdoor pool, or just soak up the Sangre de Cristo views on the rooftop terrace. There's also a poolside patio grill serving light fare. It's $179 for an 80-minute massage. ✉ *330 E. Palace Ave., East Side and Canyon Road* ☎ *505/986–0000* 🌐 *www.laposadadesantafe.com.*

ShaNah Spa & Wellness Center. Possibly the best thing about staying at Bishop's Lodge Resort, apart from the magical setting, is blissing out at ShaNah Spa, a tranquil sanctuary set in the Sangre de Cristo foothills, north of Downtown. The amenities here are extensive, including six indoor and two garden-side outdoor treatment rooms, an outdoor pool for watsu massage, a Native American meditation and massage tepee, and a nicely outfitted gym. Using such top-of-the-line products as Kerstin Florian and Eminence Organic Skin Care, aestheticians perform a wide range of skin-nourishing services, including caviar facials, wild plum–and–parsley eye treatments, and clay body wraps. Both traditional and Ayurvedic massages are offered, along with hair, nail, and waxing in the salon. $130 for a 50-minute massage. There is also a gym with cardiovascular machines, free weights, and weight-training equipment. Classes and programs include cycling, guided hikes, meditation, nature walks, personal training, and yoga. ✉ *1297 Bishop's Lodge Rd., 2½ miles north of Downtown, North Side* ☎ *505/412–4067* 🌐 *www.bishopslodge.com/shanah-spa.*

★ Fodor's Choice **Spa at Four Seasons Rancho Encantado.** Set on a hilltop with spectacular mountain views, this intimate oasis has 15 treatment rooms, some of the best-trained body workers and estheticians in the Southwest, and a full complement of salon services. You'll pay more at the Four Seasons Spa than at most other properties in town (it's $150 for a 50-minute massage), but there's a reason both hotel guests and locals rave about their experiences here. Specialties include Ayurvedic rituals and traditional Eastern massages, like shiatsu and Thai massage, and the Blue Corn and Honey Renewal body wrap. Several treatments are themed for Santa Fe's famous summer festivals, from a body rub with ingredients inspired by the Santa Fe Wine & Chile Fiesta to an "Old Man Gloom" Zozobra Facial. Do stick around and enjoy time in the impressive fitness center or relaxing by the pool (closed winter). Many guests combine their spa day with lunch or dinner on the peaceful patio of the resort's outstanding restaurant, Terra. The resort's Adventure Center also offers all sorts of excursions designed to get your blood flowing, from mountain-biking to hiking at nearby waterfalls. ✉ *198 NM 592, North Side* ☎ *505/946–5700* 🌐 *www.fourseasons.com/santafe/spa.*

Spa at Loretto. Dark, polished wood surfaces, amber lighting, and candelit Kiva-style fireplaces infuse Inn at Loretto's intimate spa with a relaxed, understated elegance—especially during Santa Fe's cool winter months, this is a particularly cozy, inviting space for a massage, and the central location near the Plaza makes it a convenient choice for guests of the many nearby hotels. The old-world decor of the five treatment suites (plus a couples suite), some with Vichy showers and antique claw-foot soaking tubs, are especially nice for enjoying one of the spa's half-day packages, including a deluxe 365-minute session that includes sage-scented bath, hot-stone massage, facial, milk-and-honey wrap, manicure and pedicure, and chakra balancing. These services can be booked individually, along with a high-altitude massage geared specifically to Santa Fe's 7,000-foot elevation, and the bracing Café Olé Indonesian coffee scrub. An 80-minute massage is $175, and half-day packages are $229–$695. The gym includes cardiovascular machines, free weights, and weight-training equipment. Yoga classes are offered as well. One drawback: common areas are very limited, as there are no steam rooms, saunas, or hot tubs. ✉ *211 Old Santa Fe Trail, The Plaza* ☎ *505/984–7997* 🌐 *www.innatloretto.com.*

★ Fodor'sChoice **Ten Thousand Waves.** This renowned Japanese-style spa with outstanding facilities and treatments is just 10 minutes north of Santa Fe toward the ski basin, nestled peacefully among the piñon trees on a sheltered hillside. Primarily a day spa—the private and communal hot tubs, especially nice in the evening under a starry sky, are a popular option—Ten Thousand Waves also has 13 sleek and inviting overnight casitas and a lovely new *izayaka*-style restaurant, which opened in fall 2013. The treatment rooms and spa facilities here are simple yet elegant, with a zenlike vibe—perfect for relaxing while undergoing a four-hands massage, a salt-glow body exfoliation, or the Japanese organic facial, which includes a thorough neck and shoulder massage. If you've been skiing or hiking in the mountains up the road, stopping here on the way home is a great way to heal sore muscle. It's $109 for a 50-minute massage and $230–$480 for half-day packages. Nature walks are also offered. ✉ *3451 Hyde Park Rd., East Side and Canyon Road* ☎ *505/992–5025* 🌐 *www.tenthousandwaves.com.*

Wo' P'in Spa at Buffalo Thunder Resort. At 16,000 square feet, the expansive Wo' P'in Spa at this Hilton-managed Pojoaque Tribe–owned gaming resort just north of Santa Fe is one of the largest in the state. With its huge outdoor pool and Roman baths–inspired indoor pool, swanky salon, and extensive manicure and pedicure options, Wo' P'in is more a place for pampering—in the style of a Vegas resort—than meditative serenity or spiritual enrichment. The spa can tailor any massage or treatment with a number of add-ons, ranging from reflexology sessions to deep-foot massage to sugar-scrub exfoliations. Recommended treatments include the sage-and-stone facial, and the Dead Sea cocoon wrap, which uses mud, almond oil, and local honey. This is one of the few spas in the region with Vichy shower treatments, but these are sometimes suspended when water restrictions are in effect (which is often in Santa Fe). It's $170 for an 80-minute massage, and $380 for a four-hour package. ✉ *30 Buffalo Thunder Trail, off U.S. 285/84, Exit 177, North Side* ☎ *505/819–2140* 🌐 *www.buffalothunderresort.com.*

7

SPORTS AND THE OUTDOORS

When it comes to outdoor adventure, Santa Fe is a four-season destination. Low humidity and, thanks to the high elevation, cool temperatures—even in summer, for the most part—make north-central New Mexico a mecca for hiking, biking, wildlife viewing, rafting, and golfing from late spring through autumn. During the winter months, snow sports dominate in the mountains above the city, and at renowned ski areas like Taos and Angel Fire, which are both within day-tripping distance (although better suited to overnight excursions).

The Santa Fe National Forest is right in the city's backyard and includes the Dome Wilderness (more than 5,000 acres in the volcanically formed Jémez Mountains) and the Pecos Wilderness (about 225,000 acres of high mountains, forests, and meadows at the southern end of the Rocky Mountains chain). The 12,500-foot Sangre de Cristo Mountains (the name translates as "Blood of Christ," for the red glow they radiate at sunset) fringe the city's east side. To the south and west, sweeping high desert is punctuated by several less formidable mountain ranges. From the Plaza in the center of the city, you're within a 10-minute drive from truly rugged and breathtakingly beautiful wilderness.

New Mexico Public Lands Information Center. For a one-stop shop for information about recreation on public lands, which include national and state parks, contact the New Mexico Public Lands Information Center. It has maps, reference materials, licenses, permits, and myriad online resources—just about everything you need to plan an outdoor adventure in Santa Fe and the surrounding region. ⊠ *301 Dinosaur Trail, South Side* ☎ *505/954–2002, 877/276–9404* 🌐 *www.publiclands.org*.

Santa Fe National Forest Office. For information on general conditions in the forest, including advisories about areas closed because of forest fires (unfortunately, these are a fairly regular occurrence each summer), call or visit the helpful website of the Santa Fe National Forest Office. ⊠ *11 Forest La., South Side* ☎ *505/438–5300* 🌐 *www.fs.fed.us/r3/sfe*.

BICYCLING

You can pick up a map of bike trips—among them a 38-mile round-trip ride from Downtown Santa Fe to Ski Santa Fe at the end of NM 475—from the New Mexico Public Lands Information Center, *or at the bike shops listed below.* One excellent place to mountain bike is the Dale Ball Trail Network, which you can access from several points on the east side of town.

★ Fodor'sChoice **Mellow Velo.** This friendly bike shop near the Plaza offers group tours, privately guided rides, bicycle rentals ($20 per day for basic cruises to $60 for top-of-the-line mountain and road bikes), and repairs. The helpful staff at this well-stocked shop offers a great way to spend a day—or seven! ✉ *132 E. Marcy St., The Plaza* ☎ *505/995–8356* 🌐 *www.mellowvelo.com.*

New Mexico Bike N' Sport. Here at this large shop by Trader Joe's you can rent or buy bikes of all kinds and shop the great selection of clothing and gear. ✉ *524C W. Cordova Rd., South Side* ☎ *505/820–0809* 🌐 *www.nmbikensport.com.*

Santa Fe Mountain Sports. Here's another good source for bike rentals. ✉ *1221 Flagman Way, Suite B1, South Side* ☎ *505/988–3337* 🌐 *www.santafemountainsports.com.*

7

BIRD-WATCHING

★ Fodor'sChoice **Randall Davey Audubon Center.** At the end of FAMILY Upper Canyon Road, at the mouth of the canyon as it wends into the foothills, the 135-acre Randall Davey Audubon Center harbors diverse birds (nearly 200 species have been indentified) and other wildlife. Guided nature walks are given many weekends; there are also two major hiking trails that you can tackle on your own. The home and studio of Randall Davey, a prolific early Santa Fe artist, can be toured on Friday afternoons. There's also a nature bookstore. ✉ *1800 Upper Canyon Rd., East Side and Canyon Road* ☎ *505/983–4609* 🌐 *nm.audubon.org* 🎫 *Center $2, house tour $5* ⏲ *Mon.–Sat. 8–4; grounds daily dawn–dusk; house tours Fri. at 2.*

WingsWest Birding Tours. For a knowledgeable insider's perspective, take a tour with WingsWest Birding Tours. Gregarious and knowledgeable guide Bill West leads regular early morning or sunset tours throughout spring and summer in Santa Fe and elsewhere in New Mexico, including Santa Fe Ski Basin, Cochiti Lake, the Espanola Valley, the

Sandia Mountains, Rowe Mesa and Pecos Monastery, Elk Mountain, and several other spots known for bird-watching. West also leads popular tours in Mexico and Ecuador. ☎ *800/583–6928* ⊕ *www.wingswestnm.com.*

FISHING

There's excellent fishing spring through fall in the Rio Grande and the mountain streams that feed into it, as well as a short drive away along the Pecos River.

High Desert Angler. This is a superb fly-fishing outfitter and guide service, your one-stop shop for equipment rental, fly-fishing tackle, licenses, and advice. ✉ *460 Cerrillos Rd., Railyard District* ☎ *505/988–7688, 888/988–7688* ⊕ *www.highdesertangler.com.*

GOLF

Marty Sanchez Links de Santa Fe. This outstanding, reasonably priced municipal facility has a beautifully groomed 18-hole layout and a shorter 9-hole executive course. These sweeping courses meander over high prairie west of Santa Fe and afford fine mountain views. ✉ *205 Caja del Rio Rd., off NM 599, about 10 miles west of Plaza, South Side* ☎ *505/955–4400* ⊕ *www.linksdesantafe.com* *18 holes. 6,095 yds. Par 72. Greens fee: $27. 9 holes. 1,615 yrds. Par 28. Greens fee: $14.* ☞ *Facilities: driving range, putting green, golf carts, pull carts, rental clubs, pro shop, golf lessons, restaurant, bar.*

HIKING

Hiking around Santa Fe can take you into high-altitude alpine country or into lunaresque high desert as you head south and west to lower elevations. For winter hiking, the gentler climates to the south are less likely to be snow packed, while the alpine areas will likely require snowshoes or cross-country skis. In summer, wildflowers bloom in the high country, and the temperature is generally at least 10 degrees cooler than in town. The mountain trails accessible at the base of the Ski Santa Fe area and at nearby Hyde Memorial State Park (near the end of NM 475) stay cool on even the hottest summer days. Weather can change with one gust of wind, so be prepared with extra clothing, rain gear, food, and lots of water. Keep in mind that the sun at 10,000 feet is very powerful, even with a hat and sunscreen.

⇨ *See the Day Trips from Santa Fe chapter, for additional hiking areas near the city.*

For information about specific hiking areas, contact the New Mexico Public Lands Information Center. Any of the outdoor gear stores in town can also help with guides and recommendations.

★ Fodor's Choice **Aspen Vista.** Especially in autumn, when golden aspens shimmer on the mountainside, this trail up near Santa Fe's ski area makes for a lovely hike. Take Hyde Park Road 13 miles to the well-signed Aspen Vista Picnic Site, where there's ample parking. After walking a few miles through thick aspen groves you come to panoramic views of Santa Fe. The path, which is well marked and gradually inclines toward Tesuque Peak, becomes steeper with elevation—also note that snow has been reported on the upper portions of the trail as late as July. In winter, after heavy snows, the trail is great for intermediate-advanced cross-country skiing. The full hike to the peak makes for a long, rigorous day—it's 12 miles round-trip and sees an elevation gain of 2,000 feet, but it's just 3½ miles to the spectacular overlook, and this section is less steep than later spans of the trail. Note that the Aspen Vista Picnic Site is also the trailhead for the Alamo Vista Trail, which leads to the summit of the ski area. ✉ *Hyde Park Road (NM 475), 2 miles before ski area, East Side and Canyon Road.*

FAMILY

★ Fodor's Choice **Atalaya Trail.** Spurring off the Dale Ball trail system, the steep but rewarding (and dog-friendly) Atalaya Trail runs from the visitor parking lot of St. John's College, up a winding, ponderosa pine–studded trail to the peak of Mt. Atalaya, which affords incredible 270-degree views of Santa Fe. The nearly 6-mile round-trip hike climbs nearly 2,000 feet (to an elevation of 9,121 feet), so pace yourself. The good news: the return to the parking area is nearly all downhill. ✉ *1160 Camino de Cruz Blanca, East Side and Canyon Road.*

Dale Ball Foothills Trail Network. A favorite spot for a ramble, with a vast network of trails, is the Dale Ball Foothills Trail Network, a network of some 22 miles of paths that winds and wends up through the foothills east of town and can be accessed at a few points, including Hyde Park Road (en route to the ski valley) and the upper end of Canyon Road, at Cerro Gordo. There are trail maps and signs at these points, and the trails are very well marked. ✉ *East Side and Canyon Road* 🌐 *sfct.org/dale-ball-trails.*

Sierra Club. The Rio Grande chapter of the Sierra Club organizes group hikes of all levels of difficulty throughout the Santa Fe region and elsewhere in the state along the Rio Grande valley; a schedule and description of upcoming hikes is posted on the website. *nmsierraclub.org*.

HORSEBACK RIDING

New Mexico's rugged countryside has been the setting for many Hollywood Westerns. Whether you want to ride the range that Gregory Peck and Kevin Costner tamed or just head out feeling tall in the saddle, you can do so year-round.

Bishop's Lodge. Both hotel guests and others can book trail rides at this historic resort on Santa Fe's northside, in the Sangre de Cristo foothills. *1297 Bishop's Lodge Rd., North Side* *505/983–6377* *www.bishopslodge.com/horseback-riding*.

MULTIPURPOSE SPORTS CENTER

FAMILY **Genoveva Chavez Community Center.** The huge, well-maintained community recreation center on the south side of town is a reasonably priced (adults $6 per day) facility with a regulation-size ice rink (you can rent ice skates for the whole family), an enormous gymnasium, indoor running track, 50-meter pool, leisure pool with waterslide and play structures, aerobics center, fitness center (with classes), two racquetball courts, and a child-care center. *3221 Rodeo Rd., South Side* *505/955–4001* *www.chavezcenter.com*.

RIVER RAFTING

If you want to watch birds and wildlife along the banks, try the laid-back floats along the Rio Chama or the Rio Grande's White Rock Canyon. The season is generally between April and September. More rugged white-water rafting adventures take place from spring through early summer, farther north along the Rio Grande. Most outfitters have overnight package plans, and all offer half- and full-day trips. Be prepared to get wet, and wear secure water shoes.

Bureau of Land Management (BLM), Taos Resource Area Office. For a list of outfitters who guide trips on the Rio Grande and the Rio Chama, contact the Bureau of Land Management (BLM), Taos Resource Area Office, or stop by the Rio Grande Gorge Visitor Center along NM 68 (on the "Low Road" to Taos), 16 miles south of Taos in the small village of Pilar, which is where many rafting trips on the Rio

Grande begin. The visitor center is also an official part of the newly established, 243,000-acre Rio Grande del Norte National Monument, created in 2013 and administered by the BLM. ✉ *226 Cruz Alta Rd., Taos* ☎ *505/758–8851* 🌐 *www.nm.blm.gov.*

Kokopelli Rafting Adventures. This outfitter offers half-day and multiday river trips down the Rio Grande and Rio Chama. ✉ *551 W. Cordova Rd., #540, South Side* ☎ *505/983–3734, 800/879–9035* 🌐 *www.kokopelliraft.com.*

New Wave Rafting. Look to this company for full-day, half-day, and overnight river trips on the Rio Chama and Rio Grande, as well as fly-fishing trips, from its riverside location in Embudo, 45 miles north of Santa Fe, on the Low Road to Taos. ✉ *NM 68, mile marker 21, Embudo* ☎ *800/984–1444* 🌐 *www.newwaverafting.com.*

Santa Fe Rafting Company and Outfitters. This well-known tour company leads day trips down the Rio Grande and the Chama River and customizes rafting tours. Tell them what you want—they'll figure out a way to do it. ✉ *1000 Cerrillos Rd., South Side* ☎ *505/988–4914, 888/988–4914* 🌐 *www.santaferafting.com.*

7

SKIING

You may want to rent skis or snowboards in town the afternoon before the day you hit the slopes so you don't waste any time waiting during the morning rush.

Alpine Sports. This centrally located shop rents downhill and cross-country skis and snowboards. ✉ *121 Sandoval St., The Plaza* ☎ *505/983–5155* 🌐 *www.alpinesports-santafe.com.*

Cottam's Ski Rentals. Stop by this long-established outfitter on your way up to the ski valley; they rent all manner of winter gear, including skis, snowboards, sleds, and snowshoes. ✉ *740 Hyde Park Rd., 8 miles northeast of Downtown, toward Ski Santa Fe, at Hyde Memorial State Park, East Side and Canyon Road* ☎ *505/982–0495, 800/322–8267* 🌐 *www.cottamsskishops.com.*

Santa Fe Mountain Sports. This family-owned specialty mountain shop rents boots, skis, and snowboards for the whole family in the winter, as well as bicycles in the summertime. The super-helpful staff is great to work with. ✉ *1221 Flagman Way, Suite B1, South Side* ☎ *505/988–3337* 🌐 *www.santafemountainsports.com.*

Ski Santa Fe. Open roughly from late November through early April, this is a fine, somewhat underrated, midsize operation that receives an average of 225 inches of snow a year and plenty of sunshine. It's one of America's highest ski areas—the 12,000-foot summit has a variety of terrain and seems bigger than its 1,725 feet of vertical rise and 660 acres. There are some great powder stashes, tough bump runs, and many wide, gentle cruising runs. The 77 trails are ranked 20% beginner, 40% intermediate, and 40% advanced; there are seven lifts. Snowboarders are welcome, and there's the Norquist Trail for cross-country skiers. Chipmunk Corner provides day care and supervised kids' skiing. The ski school is excellent. Rentals, a ski shop, a good base-camp restaurant, and Totemoff Bar and Grill (located mid-mountain) round out the amenities. The area is fun for hiking during the summer months, and the Super Chief Quad Chairs operates from late August through mid-October, catering to hikers and shutterbugs eager to view the high-mountain fall foliage, including acres of shimmering golden aspens. ✉ *End of NM 475, 18 miles northeast of Downtown, East Side and Canyon Road* ☎ *505/982–4429 general info, 505/983–9155 snow report* 🌐 *www.skisantafe.com*.

8

DAY TRIPS FROM SANTA FE

Santa Fe makes a great base for exploring the entire North-central Rio Grande Valley, a region rich in Spanish Colonial and Native American heritage and abounding with scenic drives, dazzling geographical formations, colorful villages, and important historic sites. Every community and attraction covered in this chapter could be visited as a day trip, but consider planning overnight excursions, too—you'll find a handful of wonderfully distinctive accommodations in these smaller villages. *(Visit Fodors.com for additional points of interest, as well as recommended hotels and restaurants.)*

It's also practical to embark on some of these trips en route to Albuquerque or Taos. For example, you could drive the Turquoise Trail or visit Tent Rock National Monument on the way to Albuquerque. The side trips to points north—such as the High Road, Bandelier and Los Alamos, and Abiquiú and Georgia O'Keeffe Country—are worth investigating on your way to Taos.

THE TURQUOISE TRAIL

★ Fodor'sChoice The most prominent side trip south of the city is along the fabled Turquoise Trail, an excellent—and leisurely—alternative route from Santa Fe to Albuquerque that's far more interesting than Interstate 25. Etched out in the early 1970s, the scenic Turquoise Trail (or more prosaically, NM 14) is a National Scenic Byway that's dotted with ghost towns now popular with writers, artists, and other urban refugees. This 70 miles of piñon-studded mountain back road along the eastern flank of the sacred Sandia Mountains is a gentle roller coaster that also affords panoramic views of the Ortiz, Jémez, and Sangre de Cristo mountains. It's believed that 2,000 years ago Native Americans mined turquoise in these hills. The Spanish took up turquoise mining in the 16th century, and the practice continued into the early 20th century, with Tiffany & Co. removing a fair share of the semiprecious stone. In addition, gold, silver, tin, lead, and coal have been mined here. There's plenty of opportunity for picture taking and picnicking along the way. You can drive this loop in three hours with minimal stops, or make a full day of it, if you stop to explore the main attractions along the way and make the side excursion up to Sandia Crest, which overlooks Albuquerque. You'll find plenty of great information online at ⊕ *www.turquoisetrail.org*.

EL RANCHO DE LAS GOLONDRINAS

The "Williamsburg of the Southwest," El Rancho de las Golondrinas ("Ranch of the Swallows") is a reconstruction of a small agricultural village with buildings from the 17th to 19th century. Travelers on El Camino Real would stop at the ranch before making the final leg of the journey north, a half-day ride from Santa Fe in horse-and-wagon time. By car, the ranch is only a 25-minute drive from the Plaza, and it's a 10-minute drive from where the Turquoise Trail (NM 14) intersects with Interstate 25, making it a fun stop—especially for kids—en route. Self-guided tours survey Spanish colonial lifestyles in New Mexico from 1660 to 1890. Farm animals roam through the barnyards on the 200-acre complex. During the spring and harvest festivals, on the first weekends of June and October, respectively, the village comes alive with Spanish-American folk music, dancing, and food and crafts demonstrations. The ranch hosts several other festivals throughout the year. ✉ *334 Los Pinos Rd., South Side* ☎ *505/471–2261* 🌐 *www.golondrinas.org* 🎟 *$6* ⏲ *June–Sept., Wed.–Sun. 10–4; Apr.–May and Oct., by appointment.*

MADRID

28 miles southwest of Santa Fe and 4 miles southwest of Cerrillos on NM 14.

Totally abandoned when its coal mine closed in the 1950s, Madrid (locals put the emphasis on the first syllable: *mah*-drid) has gradually been rebuilt and is now—to the dismay of some longtime locals—actually a bit trendy. The entire town was offered for sale for $250,000 back in the '50s, but there were no takers. Finally, in the early 1970s, a few artists fleeing big cities settled in and began restoration. Weathered houses and old company stores have been repaired and turned into boutiques and galleries, some of them selling high-quality furniture, paintings, and crafts. Big events here include Old Timers Days on July 4th weekend, the Madrid and Cerrillos Studio Tour in early October, and the Christmas open house, held weekends in December, when galleries and studios are open and the famous Madrid Christmas lights twinkle brightly.

As you continue south down NM 14 from Madrid, after about 11 miles you pass through the sleepy village of **Golden,** the site of the first gold rush (in 1825) west of the Mississippi. It has a rock shop and a mercantile store.

The rustic adobe church and graveyard are popular with photographers.

SANDIA PARK

24 miles southwest of Madrid and 22 miles northeast of Albuquerque on NM 14.

The southern stretch of the Turquoise Trail, as you continue from Golden and begin encountering upscale housing developments around Paa-Ko Ridge Golf Club, is more densely populated than the northern section—it's almost a bit suburban in character, with the towns of Sandia Park (population 3,500) and Cedar Crest (population 1,200), considered part of metro Albuquerque, growing fast. The Turquoise Trail meanders along the eastern flanks of the Sandia Mountains before intersecting with Interstate 40, which leads east for the final 10 miles into Albuquerque proper.

EXPLORING

★ FAMILY Fodor's Choice **Tinkertown Museum.** It may take months for this odyssey of a place to completely sink in: quirky and utterly fascinating, Tinkertown Museum contains a world of miniature carved-wood characters. The museum's late founder, Ross Ward, spent more than 40 years carving and collecting the hundreds of figures that populate this cheerfully bizarre museum, including an animated miniature Western village, a Boot Hill cemetery, and a 1940s circus exhibit. Ragtime piano music, a 40-foot sailboat, and a life-size general store are other highlights. The walls surrounding this 22-room museum have been fashioned out of more than 50,000 glass bottles pressed into cement. This homage to folk art, found art, and eccentric kitsch tends to strike a chord with people of all ages. As you might expect, the gift shop offers plenty of fun oddities. ✉ *121 Sandia Crest Rd. (NM 536), Sandia Park, New Mexico, USA* ✣ *Take Cedar Crest Exit 175 north off I–40 east and follow signs on NM 14 to Sandia Crest turnoff* ☎ *505/281–5233* 🌐 *www.tinkertown.com* 🎟 *$3.50* ⏲ *Apr.–Oct., daily 9–6.*

KASHA-KATUWE TENT ROCKS NATIONAL MONUMENT

46 miles west of Santa Fe.

This is a terrific hiking getaway that can be accessed from Interstate 25 on the drive between Albuquerque and Santa Fe. If you have time for just one hike, this is a great choice.

EXPLORING

★ Fodor's Choice **Kasha-Katuwe Tent Rocks National Monument.** The sandstone rock formations here look like stacked tents in a stark, water- and wind-eroded box canyon. Tent Rocks offers excellent hiking year-round, although it can get hot in summer, when you should bring extra water. The drive to this magical landscape is equally awesome, as the road heads west toward Cochiti Dam and through the cottonwood groves around the pueblo. It's a good hike for kids. The round-trip hiking distance is only 2 miles, about 1½ leisurely hours, but it's the kind of place where you'll want to hang out for a while. Take a camera, but leave your pets at home—no dogs are allowed. There are no facilities here, just a small parking area with a posted trail map and a self-pay admission box; you can get gas and pick up picnic supplies and bottled water at Cochiti Lake Convenience Store. ✉ *1405 Cochiti Hwy., BIA 92, off NM 22 (follow signs), Cochiti Lake* ⊕ *Take I–25 south to Cochiti Exit 264; follow NM 16 for 8 miles, turning right onto NM 22; continue approximately 3½ miles farther past Cochiti Pueblo entrance; turn right onto BIA 92, which after 2 miles becomes Forest Service Rd. 266, a rough road of jarring, washboard gravel that leads 5 miles to well-marked parking area* ☎ *505/761–8700* 🌐 *www.nm.blm.gov* 🎫 *$5 per vehicle* ⏲ *Apr.–Oct., daily 7–7; Nov.–Mar., daily 8–5 (gates shut an hour before closing).*

FAMILY

8

THE SANTA FE TRAIL

In the mid-19th century, this vast tract of grasslands and prairies, along with the eastern foothills of the Sangre de Cristo range, became the gateway to New Mexico for American settlers headed here from the Midwest. Towns along the Santa Fe Trail's modern offspring, I–25—notably Las Vegas but also Raton up near the Colorado border—remain popular stops for road-tripping fans of Old West history.

PECOS NATIONAL HISTORIC SITE

30 miles southeast of Santa Fe via Interstate 25 and NM 63.

Pecos was the last major encampment that travelers on the Santa Fe Trail reached before Santa Fe. Today the little village is mostly a starting point for exploring the Pecos National Historic Park.

EXPLORING

Pecos National Historic Park. The centerpiece of this national park is the ruins of Pecos, once a major pueblo village with more than 1,100 rooms. Twenty-five hundred people are thought to have lived in this structure, as high as five stories in places. Pecos, in a fertile valley between the Great Plains and the Rio Grande Valley, was a trading center centuries before the Spanish conquistadors visited in about 1540. The Spanish later returned to build two missions. The pueblo was abandoned in 1838, and its 17 surviving occupants moved to the Jémez Pueblo. Anglo travelers on the Santa Fe Trail observed the mission ruins with a great sense of fascination. You can view the mission ruins and the excavated pueblo on a ¼-mile self-guided tour in about two hours. ✉ *NM 63, off I–25 at Exit 307, Pecos* ☎ *505/757–7241* 🌐 *www.nps.gov/peco* 🎟 *$3* ⏲ *Late May–early Sept., daily 8–5; early Sept.–late May, daily 8–4:30.*

LAS VEGAS

67 miles northeast of Santa Fe and 42 miles northeast Pecos National Historic Site via I–25.

The antithesis of the Nevada city that shares its name, Las Vegas, elevation 6,470 feet, is a town of about 15,000 that time appears to have passed by. For decades, Las Vegas was actually two towns divided by Rio Gallinas: West Las Vegas, the Hispanic community anchored by the Spanish-style plaza, and East Las Vegas, where German Jews and Midwesterners had established themselves around a proper town square. Once an oasis for stagecoach passengers en route to Santa Fe, it became—for a brief period after the railroad arrived in the late 19th century—New Mexico's major center of commerce, and its largest town, where more than a million dollars in goods and services were traded annually.

The seat of San Miguel County, Las Vegas lies where the Sangre de Cristo Mountains meet the high plains of New Mexico, and its name, meaning "the meadows," reflects

Day Trips from Santa Fe
Chama
Los Ojos
Brazos
Tierra Amarilla
CARSON NATIONAL FOREST
Questa
San Cristobal
Arroyo Hondo
El Vado
Cebolla
Canjilon
Vallecitos
Rio Chama
Rio Grande
Taos
La Madera
El Rito
Rancho de Taos
Ghost Ranch
Ojo Caliente
Pilar
Dixon
Peñasco
Abiquiú
Velarde
Medanales
Chamisal
Alcade
Truchas
SANTA FE NATIONAL FOREST
Española
Chimayó
Cordova
Santa Clara Pueblo
Santa Cruz
San Ildefonso Pueblo
Nambé Pueblo
Valles Caldera National Preserve
Los Alamos
Pojoaque Pueblo
Baldy Peak
Jémez Springs
Bandelier National Monument
Hyde Memorial State Park
Kasha-Katuwe Tent Rocks National Monument
Santa Fe Ski Area
Tesuque
Cañon
El Rancho de las Golondrinas
Santa Fe
Pecos National Historic Park
Jémez Pueblo
La Cienaga
Turquoise Trail
an Isidro
Glorieta
Pecos
Rowe
Lamy
Cerrillos
Galisteo
Fort Union National Historic Site
Madrid
Las Vegas
Turquoise Trail
0
20 miles
Sandia Park
Golden
0
40 km
17
64/84
64
519
522
111
554
285
84
518
126
4
84/285
475
599
14
25
285
41

its scenic setting. A few funky bric-a-brac shops and genial cafés line the Old Town Plaza and the main drag, Bridge Street. More than 900 structures here are listed on the National Register of Historic Places, and the town has nine historic districts, many with homes and commercial buildings of ornate Italianate design. Strolling around this very walkable town gives a sense of the area's rough-and-tumble history—Butch Cassidy is rumored to have tended bar here, and miscreants with names like Dirty-Face Mike, Rattlesnake Sam, and Web-Fingered Billy once roamed the streets. You may also recognize some of the streets and facades from films; Las Vegas is where scenes from *Wyatt Earp, No Country for Old Men,* and *All the Pretty Horses* were shot and where Tom Mix shot his vintage Westerns.

EXPLORING

Las Vegas Chamber of Commerce Visitors Center. To gain an appreciation of the town's architecture, follow the walking tours described in free brochures available at the Las Vegas Chamber of Commerce Visitors Center. Best bets include Stone Architecture of Las Vegas; the Carnegie Park Historic District, with the Carnegie Library; and the Business District of Douglas–6th Street and Railroad Avenue. The latter includes the Mission Revival La Casteneda, a former hotel from the famed Harvey House railroad chain, with a well-preserved grand lobby and dining room. ✉ *1224 Railroad Ave., Las Vegas* ☎ *505/425–8631* 🌐 *www.lasvegasnewmexico.com.*

FORT UNION NATIONAL HISTORIC SITE

30 miles north of Las Vegas via Interstate 25 and NM 161.

The ruins of New Mexico's largest American frontier–era fort sit on an empty windswept plain. It still echoes with the isolation surely felt by the soldiers stationed here between 1851 and 1890, when the fort was established to protect travelers and settlers along the Santa Fe Trail. It eventually became a military supply depot for the Southwest, but with the taming of the West it was abandoned.

EXPLORING

Fort Union Visitor Center. The Fort Union Visitor Center provides historical background about the fort and the Santa Fe Trail; guided tours are available when volunteers are on hand. ✉ *Off NM 161, exit 364 from I–25, Watrous* ☎ *505/425–8025* 🌐 *www.nps.gov/foun* 🎫 *$3 per vehicle* ⏲ *Late May–early Sept., daily 8–5; mid-Sept.–mid-May, daily 8–4.*

BANDELIER AND LOS ALAMOS

In the Jémez region, the 1,000-year-old ancestral Puebloan ruins at Bandelier National Monument present a vivid contrast to nearby Los Alamos National Laboratory, birthplace of the atomic bomb. The surrounding town of Los Alamos has two outstanding museums.

LOS ALAMOS

35 miles north of Santa Fe via U.S. 285/84 and NM 502 west.

Look at old books on New Mexico and you rarely find a mention of Los Alamos, now a busy town of 19,000 that has the highest per capita income in the state. Like so many other Southwestern communities, Los Alamos was created expressly as a company town; only here the workers weren't mining iron, manning freight trains, or hauling lumber—they were busy toiling at America's foremost nuclear research facility, Los Alamos National Laboratory (LANL). The facility still employs some 9,000 full-time workers, most living in town but many others in the Española Valley and even Santa Fe.

A few miles from ancient cave dwellings, scientists led by J. Robert Oppenheimer built Fat Man and Little Boy, the atom bombs that in August 1945 decimated Hiroshima and Nagasaki, respectively. LANL was created in 1943 under the auspices of the intensely covert Manhattan Project, whose express purpose it was to expedite an Allied victory during World War II. Indeed, Japan surrendered—but a full-blown Cold War between Russia and the United States ensued for another four and a half decades.

EXPLORING

FAMILY **Bradbury Science Museum.** Los Alamos National Laboratory's public showcase, the Bradbury provides a balanced and provocative examination of such topics as atomic weapons and nuclear power. You can experiment with lasers; witness research in solar, geothermal, fission, and fusion energy; learn about DNA fingerprinting; and view fascinating exhibits about World War II's Project Y (the Manhattan Project, whose participants developed the atomic bomb). ✉ *Los Alamos National Laboratory, 15th St. and Central Ave., Los Alamos* ☎ *505/667–4444* 🌐 *www.lanl.gov/museum* 🎟 *Free* ⏲ *Tues.–Sat. 10–5, Sun.–Mon. 1–5.*

Fuller Lodge Art Center. New Mexican architect John Gaw Meem designed Fuller Lodge, a short drive up Central Avenue from the Bradbury Science Museum. The massive log building was erected in 1928 as a dining and recreation hall for a small private boys' school. In 1942 the federal government purchased the school and made it the base of operations for the Manhattan Project. Part of the lodge contains an art center that shows the works of northern New Mexican artists; there's a gorgeous rose garden on the grounds. This is a bustling center with drop-in art classes, nine art shows per year, and an outstanding gallery gift shop featuring works by nearly 100 local artisans. ✉ *2132 Central Ave., Los Alamos* ☎ *505/662–9331* 🌐 *www.fullerlodgeartcenter.com* 🎫 *Free* 🕐 *Mon.–Sat. 10–4.*

BANDELIER NATIONAL MONUMENT

10 miles south of Los Alamos via NM 501 and NM 4, 44 miles northwest of Santa Fe via U.S. 285/84 and NM 502 to NM 4.

Seven centuries before the Declaration of Independence was signed, compact city-states existed in the Southwest. Remnants of one of the most impressive of them can be seen at Frijoles Canyon in Bandelier National Monument. At the canyon's base, near a gurgling stream, are the remains of cave dwellings, ancient ceremonial kivas, and other stone structures that stretch out for more than a mile beneath the sheer walls of the canyon's tree-fringed rim. For hundreds of years the ancestral Puebloan people, relatives of today's Rio Grande Pueblo Indians, thrived on wild game, corn, and beans. Suddenly, for reasons still undetermined, the settlements were abandoned.

EXPLORING

★ Fodor's Choice FAMILY **Bandelier National Monument.** Wander through the site on a paved, self-guided trail. Steep wooden ladders and narrow doorways lead you to the cave dwellings and cell-like rooms. There is one kiva in the cliff wall that is large, and tall enough to stand in. Bandelier National Monument, named after author and ethnologist Adolph Bandelier (his novel *The Delight Makers* is set in Frijoles Canyon), contains 33,000 acres of backcountry wilderness, waterfalls, and wildlife. Some 70 miles of trails traverse the park. A small museum in the visitor center focuses on the area's prehistoric and contemporary Native American cultures, with displays of artifacts from 1200 to modern times.

Note that from late May to late October, visitors arriving by car between 9 am and 3 pm must park at the White Rock Visitor Center 10 miles east on NM 4 and take a free shuttle bus into the park. ✉ *15 Entrance Rd., off NM 4, Los Alamos* ☎ *505/672–0343* 🌐 *www.nps.gov/band* 🎫 *$12 per vehicle, good for 7 days* ⏲ *Park grounds: daily sunrise–sunset. Visitor Center: Late May–late Oct., daily 8:30–4:30; Nov.–mid-May, daily 9–4:30.*

White Rock Visitor Center. Opened in 2012 by the Los Alamos Meeting & Visitor Bureau, this sleek, eco-friendly building is a one-stop for finding out about the many things to see and do in the area, from Bandelier and Los Alamos to the Jémez Mountain Trail National Scenic Byway, the hiking at nearby White Rock Overlook, and Valles Caldera National Preserve. You can also catch free shuttle buses into Bandelier (in fact, you can only visit the park in this way from late May to late October, 9–3) and downtown Los Alamos. The region's nicest chain hotel, the Hampton Inn & Suites Los Alamos, is next door. The bureau operates a second visitor center in Los Alamos at 109 Central Park Square. ✉ *115 NM 4, White Rock* ☎ *505/672–3183, 800/444–0707* 🌐 *www.visit.losalamos.com* ⏲ *Mid-Mar.–Oct., Daily 9–4; Nov.–early Mar., daily 10–2.*

VALLES CALDERA NATIONAL PRESERVE

8

20 miles northwest of Bandelier National Monument on NM 4.

A high-forest drive brings you to the awe-inspiring Valles Grande, which at 14 miles in diameter is one of the world's largest calderas and which became Valles (*vah*-yes) Caldera National Preserve in 2000.

EXPLORING

★ Fodor's Choice **Valles Caldera National Preserve.** The caldera resulted from the eruption and collapse of a 14,000-foot peak over 1 million years ago; the flow out the bottom created the Pajarito Plateau and the ash from the eruption spread as far east as Kansas. You can't imagine the volcanic crater's immensity until you spot what look like specks of dust on the lush meadow floor and realize they're elk. The Valles Caldera Trust manages this 89,000-acre multiuse preserve with the aim to "protect and preserve the scientific, scenic, geologic, watershed, fish, wildlife, historic, cultural, and recreational values of the Preserve, and to provide for multiple use and sustained yield of renewable resources within the Preserve."

The preserve is open to visitors for hiking, cross-country skiing, horseback riding, horse-drawn carriage rides, van wildlife photography tours, mountain-bike tours, bird-watching, fly-fishing, and may other outdoorsy endeavors. Some of the activities require reservations and a fee, although there are four free, relatively short hikes, two of them signposted from the parking area along NM 4, and two others near the information center by the check-in station. About 20 miles southwest of the preserve entrance, the Valles Caldera Visitor Center at 18161 NM 4 is another good place to learn about park activities. ✉ *NM 4, Mile Marker 39.2, 10 miles west of junction with NM 501, Jémez Springs* ☎ *505/661–3333, 866/382–5537* 🌐 *www.vallescaldera.gov* ⏲ *Visitor Center: weekdays 8–5, Sat. 9–5.*

GEORGIA O'KEEFFE COUNTRY

It's a 20-minute drive north of Santa Fe to reach the Española Valley, where you head west to the striking mesas, cliffs, and valleys that so inspired the artist Georgia O'Keeffe—she lived in this area for the final 50 years of her life. Passing through the small, workaday city of Española, U.S. 84 continues to the sleepy village of Abiquiú and eventually up past Ghost Ranch, areas where O'Keeffe both lived and worked. One other notable community in this area is tiny Ojo Caliente, famous for its hot-springs spa retreat.

ABIQUIÚ

50 miles northwest of Santa Fe on U.S. 84.

This tiny, very traditional Hispanic village was originally home to freed *genizaros,* indigenous and mixed-blood slaves who served as house servants, shepherds, and other key roles in Spanish, Mexican, and American households well into the 1880s. Many descendants of original families still live in the area, although since the late 1980s Abiquiú and its surrounding countryside have become a nesting ground for those fleeing big-city life, among them actresses Marsha Mason and Shirley MacLaine. Abiquiú—along with parts of the nearby Española Valley—is also a hotbed of organic farming, with many of the operations here selling their goods at the Santa Fe Farmers' Market and to restaurants throughout the Rio Grande Valley. Newcomers or visitors may find themselves largely ignored by locals; it's best to observe one very important local custom: no photography is allowed in and around the village.

GHOST RANCH

15 miles north of Abiquiú on U.S. 84.

For art historians, the name Ghost Ranch brings to mind Georgia O'Keeffe, who lived on a small parcel of this 22,000-acre dude and cattle ranch. The ranch's owner in the 1930s—conservationist and publisher of *Nature Magazine,* Arthur Pack—first invited O'Keeffe here to visit in 1934; Pack soon sold the artist the 7-acre plot on which she lived summer through fall for most of the rest of her life. In 1955 Pack donated the rest of the ranch to the Presbyterian Church, which continues to use Pack's original structures and part of the land as a conference center, but Ghost Ranch is also open to visitors for tours, hikes, workshops, and all sort of other cool activities.

If you have the time, consider continuing north another 30 miles along gorgeous U.S. 84 to the tiny weaving village of Los Ojos and 12 more miles to Chama, a forested town near the Colorado border that's famous as the terminus of the scenic Cumbres & Toltec Railroad. From Los Ojos, in summer (this route is closed from fall through spring because of snow) you can cut across to Taos (80 miles away) via U.S. 64, crossing one of the prettiest mountain passes in the state.

LOS OJOS

Los Ojos, midway between Tierra Amarilla and Chama, could well serve as a model for rural economic development worldwide. The little town has experienced an economic revival of sorts by returning to its ancient roots—the raising of Churro sheep (the original breed brought over by the Spanish, prized for its wool) and weaving. Ganados del Valle, the community-based, nonprofit economic development corporation headquartered here, has created jobs and increased prosperity by returning to the old ways, with improved marketing. You can also find a smattering of artists' studios, most of them in rustic buildings with corrugated metal roofs.

THE HIGH ROAD TO TAOS

★ Fodor's Choice The main route to Taos (NM 68, the so-called "Low Road") is a great, actually quite dramatic, drive if you've got limited time, but by far the most spectacular way is via what's known as the High Road. Towering peaks, lush hillsides, orchards, and meadows surround tiny, ancient Hispanic villages that are as picturesque as they are historically fascinating. The well-signed High Road follows U.S. 285/84 north to NM 503 (a right turn just past Pojoaque toward Nambé), to County Road 98 (a left toward Chimayó), to NM 76 northeast to NM 75 east, to NM 518 north. The drive takes you through the badlands of stark, weathered rock—where numerous Westerns have been filmed—quickly into rolling foothills, lush canyons, and finally into pine forests. Although most of these insular, traditional Hispanic communities offer little in the way of shopping and dining, the region has become a haven for artists.

Depending on when you make this drive, you're in for some of the state's most radiant scenery. In mid-April the orchards are in blossom; summer turns the valleys into lush green oases; and in fall the smell of piñon adds to the sensual overload of golden leaves and red-chile ristras hanging from the houses. In winter the fields are covered with quilts of snow, and the lines of homes, fences, and trees stand out like bold pen-and-ink drawings against the sky. But the roads can be icy and treacherous—if in doubt, stick with the Low Road to Taos. ■ TIP→ **If you decide to take the High Road just one way between Santa Fe and Taos, you might want to save it for the return journey—the scenery is even more stunning when traveling north to south.**

POJOAQUE AND NAMBÉ PUEBLOS

17 miles north of Santa Fe on U.S. 285/84.

EXPLORING

★ Fodor's Choice **Estrella del Norte Vineyard.** Surrounded by vineyards, gardens, and towering shade trees, the gracious tasting room just a 20-minute drive north of Santa Fe carries the house label's own well-balanced wines, focused on French and Italian—Cabernet Franc, Viogner, Nebbiolo, Barbera. You can also sample wines from a few other winemakers in the area, Santa Fe Vineyards, Black Mesa Winery, and Labajada Wines. When the weather's nice, enjoy your tasting on the landscaped patio. In the same vicinity, you might also check out Don Quixote Distillery & Winery (⊕ *www.dqdistillery.com*), which has one tasting room just off U.S. 285/84, across from Cities of Gold Casino, and another on NM 4 en route to Bandelier National Monument. ✉ *106 N. Shining Sun, North Side* ☎ *505/455–2826* ⊕ *www.estrelladelnortevineyard.com* ⊙ *Mon.–Sat. 10–6, Sun. noon–6.*

WHERE TO STAY

$$ **Buffalo Thunder Resort & Casino.** *Resort.* Managed by Hilton, this expansive, upscale gaming and golfing getaway is the closest full-service resort to Downtown Santa Fe—it's 15 miles north of the Plaza, just off a busy freeway but with spectacular views of the mountains and Rio Grande Valley. **Pros:** surprisingly affordable given the snazzy rooms and amenities; convenient to opera and Low and High roads to Taos; panoramic mountain and mesa views. **Cons:** just off of a busy highway; lobby is noisy and crowded with gamers on many evenings; a 15-minute drive from the Plaza. $ *Rooms from: $149* ✉ *30 Buffalo Thunder Trail, off U.S. 285/84, Exit 177, North Side* ☎ *505/455–5555, 877/455–7775* ⊕ *www.buffalothunderresort.com* *290 rooms, 85 suites* *No meals.*

CHIMAYÓ

28 miles north of Santa Fe and 12 miles northeast of Nambé/Pojoaque on NM 76.

From U.S. 285/84 north of Pojoaque, scenic NM 503 winds past horse paddocks and orchards in the narrow Nambé Valley, then ascends into the red-sandstone canyons with a view of Truchas Peaks to the northeast before dropping into the bucolic village of Chimayó. Nestled into hillsides where gnarled piñons seem to grow from bare bedrock, Chimayó is famed for its weaving, its red chiles, and its two chapels, particularly El Santuario de Chimayó.

8

EXPLORING

★ Fodor's Choice **El Santuario de Chimayó.** This small, frontier, adobe church has a fantastically carved and painted reredos (altar screen) and is built on the site where, believers say, a mysterious light came from the ground on Good Friday in 1810 and where a large wooden crucifix was found beneath the earth. The chapel sits above a sacred *pozito* (a small hole), the dirt from which is believed to have miraculous healing properties. Dozens of abandoned crutches and braces placed in the anteroom—along with many notes, letters, and photos—testify to this. The Santuario draws a steady stream of worshippers year-round—Chimayó is considered the Lourdes of the Southwest. During Holy Week as many as 50,000 pilgrims come here. The shrine is a National Historic Landmark. It's surrounded by small adobe shops selling every kind of religious curio imaginable and some very fine traditional Hispanic work from local artists. ✉ *15 Santuario Dr. (CR 94A), signed lane off CR 98, Chimayó* ☎ *505/351–4889* 🌐 *www.holychimayo.us* 🎫 *Free* ⏲ *May–Sept., daily 9–6; Oct.–Apr., daily 9–5.*

CORDOVA

5 miles east of Chimayó via NM 76.

You'll have to turn south off NM 76 to get down into the narrow, steep valley that this lovely village sits it in, but you'll be happy you did. A picturesque mountain village with a small central plaza, a school, a post office, and a church, Cordova is the center of the centuries-old regional wood-carving industry. The town supports more than 30 full-time and part-time carvers. Many of them are descendants of José Dolores López, who in the 1920s created the village's signature unpainted "Cordova style" of carving. Most of the *santeros* (makers of religious images) have signs outside their homes indicating that santos are for sale. Many pieces are fairly expensive, a reflection of the hard work and fine craftsmanship involved—ranging from several hundred dollars for small ones to several thousand for larger figures—but there are also affordable and delightful small carvings of animals and birds.

TRUCHAS

4 miles northeast of Cordova via NM 76.

Truchas (Spanish for "trout") is where Robert Redford shot the movie *The Milagro Beanfield War* (based on the novel written by Taos author John Nichols). This pastoral village is perched dramatically on the rim of a deep canyon beneath the towering Truchas Peaks, mountains high enough to be almost perpetually capped with snow. The tallest of the Truchas Peaks is 13,102 feet, the second-highest point in New Mexico. Truchas has been gaining appeal with artsy, independent-minded transplants from Santa Fe and Taos, who have come for the cheaper real estate and the breathtaking setting. There are several excellent galleries in town.

Continue 7 miles north on NM 76, toward Peñasco, and you come to the marvelous San José de Gracia Church in the village of Trampas. It dates from circa 1760.

PEÑASCO

15 miles north of Truchas and 25 miles southeast of Taos on NM 76.

Although still a modest-size community, Peñasco is one of the "larger" villages along the High Road and a good bet if you need to fill your tank with gas or pick up a snack at a convenience store.

DIXON

13 miles west of Peñasco, 47 miles north of Santa Fe, and 25 miles south of Taos on NM 75.

The small village of Dixon and its surrounding country lanes are home to a surprising number of artists as well as a few surprisingly good wineries that are helping put the northern Rio Grande Valley on the map among oenophiles. Artistic sensitivity, as well as generations of dedicated farmers, account for the community's well-tended fields, pretty gardens, and fruit trees—a source of produce for restaurants and farmers' markets such as the one in Santa Fe. It's simple to find your way around; there's only one main road.

If you're driving the High Road, Dixon is a slight detour from Peñasco. You can either return the way you come and continue from Peñasco over the mountains into Taos, or from Dixon you can pick up NM 68, the Low Road, and continue north to Taos through the scenic Rio Grande Gorge.

EXPLORING

La Chiripada Winery. Nestled under mature shade trees down a dirt lane in Dixon's quaint village center, this producer of first-rate wines is the oldest vintner in the northern part of the state. La Chiripada's Viogner, Reserve Riesling, and Dolcetto have all earned considerable acclaim. There's also a nicely crafted New Mexico Port as well as Vino de Oro, an aged Muscato, both of them great paired with dessert. The winery also has a tasting room in Taos at 103 Bent Street. ✉ *NM 75, 3 miles east of NM 68, Dixon* ☎ *505/579–4437* 🌐 *www.lachiripada.com* ⏲ *Mon.–Sat. 10–6, Sun. noon–6.*

8

★ Fodor'sChoice **Vivac Winery.** "Vivac" means "high-altitude refuge," and that's a pretty fitting name for this hip winery located right at the turnoff on NM 68 (the Low Road) to NM 75 (which leads to the High Road). Owned and run by young brothers Jesse and Chris Padberg (and their wives Michele and Liliana), the vineyards and charming tasting room, with an adjacent patio, are set deep in the Rio Grande gorge surrounded by sheer cliffs. It's a dramatic setting for sampling these elegant, generally dry wines, which feature a mix of grapes, including Italian Dolcetto, Spanish Tempranillo, French Cabernet Sauvignon, and German off-dry Riesling. The Tasting Room also sells artisan (and local) Ek.chuah Chocolates, house-made cheeses, and jewelry; there's a second tasting room at the farmers' market building in Santa Fe (open when the market is going on). ✉ *2075 NM 68, Dixon* ☎ *505/579–4441* 🌐 *www.vivacwinery.com* ⏲ *Mon.–Sat. 10–6, Sun. 11–6.*

ALBUQUERQUE

9

Updated by Lynne Arany

In spite of its urban sprawl, Albuquerque merits a second look, and perhaps a stay of more than a day or two before you journey on to Santa Fe or Taos. Perfectly set as the gateway to other New Mexico wonders like Acoma Pueblo and Chaco Canyon, Albuquerque's own rich history and dramatic terrain—desert volcanoes, the meandering Rio Grande, and a striking confluence of mountain ranges—have long captured the imagination of folks en route from here to there.

Native American populations have left centuries-old traces throughout the verdant Rio Grande Valley, and Albuquerque is no exception. Their trade routes are what drew the Spanish here; the little farming settlement was proclaimed "Alburquerque," after the Viceroy of New Spain—the 10th Duke of Alburquerque—in 1706. By the time Anglo traders arrived in the 1800s, that first "r" had been dropped, but that early settlement, now known as Old Town, was still the heart of town. In the 1880s though, with the railroad in place, the center of town moved east to meet it, in modern-day Downtown. Remnants of all linger today—and may readily be seen by a casual stroller in spectacular outdoor spaces, and in the many museums that explore these elements, present and past. Other snatches of history have contributed to Albuquerque's development: the Manhattan Project, the birth of desktop computers, and the earliest days of film (one of Edison's first silent films was shot at nearby Isleta Pueblo).

Albuquerque embraces its multicultural population and a wholeheartedly commits to protecting its exquisite Bosque lands along the Rio Grande. A renowned network of bicycle and hiking trails has been developed throughout the city. Prestige microbreweries, a nationally noted Public Art program, world-class museum collections, and its role as a primary hub for the New Mexico Railrunner, which daily transfers commuters and visitors alike to Santa Fe along the scenic Rio Grande corridor, further set this city apart.

A bit of quiet attention reveals Albuquerque's subtle beauty—a flock of sandhill cranes overhead; a hot-air balloon, seemingly within reach; vintage Art Deco buildings and the neon motel signs in Nob Hill; Pueblo Revival details on the University of New Mexico campus; the fabulous facade of the KiMO theater; a sudden glimpse across the western desert to a 100-mile distant snow-capped Mt. Taylor; and the Sandia Mountains lit pink by the fading sun.

ORIENTATION AND PLANNING

GETTING ORIENTED

Albuquerque contains a compact and well-defined core comprising just a handful of neighborhoods—Downtown, Old Town, the University of New Mexico (UNM) district, and adjacent Nob Hill—that's encircled by a somewhat sprawling and less clearly defined region. Colorful Historic Route 66 (Central Avenue) unifies the older, central neighborhoods, cutting west to east through the center of the city. This route, where crossed by the 1880s-era rail tracks, determines the city's quadrants; the Sandia Mountains to the east and the Rio Grande to the west define the core. Visitors tend to spend most of their time in the Old Town to Nob Hill corridor, as it contains the majority of the city's notable dining, lodging, shopping, and sightseeing. The outlying neighborhoods are mostly residential and encompass the historic Rio Grande valley's Los Ranchos/North Valley and Barelas/South Valley sections, and the less-defined areas of the Northeast Heights, East Side, Airport, and West Side.

ALBUQUERQUE NEIGHBORHOODS

Old Town. This historic neighborhood contains the oldest buildings in the city. It's also home to numerous galleries, shops, and museums, plus a few hotels. It's just west of and adjacent to Downtown.

Downtown/EDo. A handful of mid-century and more modern office towers create the modest Downtown skyline. Bisected by Central Avenue, this relatively compact district has a limited—but choice—set of attractions. There are also a number of noteworthy hotels, restaurants, and shops. Downtown is within walking distance of Old Town, which lies just to the west.

Barelas/South Valley. Extending just south of Downtown and Old Town, historic Barelas is home to the acclaimed National Hispanic Cultural Center and is an otherwise mostly residential area. It gradually gives way to the rural South Valley.

UNM/Nob Hill. Off-campus life is focused directly to the south and east of the University of New Mexico, stretching along Central Avenue from University Boulevard east through the Nob Hill neighborhood. Budget eateries, specialty shops, and music and arts venues are tightly clus-

TOP REASONS TO GO

Drive up the Camino Real (North 4th Street) or south into Barelas where you'll glimpse vintage shops and taquerias with hand-painted signage in idiosyncratic script and blazing-hot colors. Be sure to pause for a bite at Barelas Coffee House or Garcia's Kitchen.

Visit the KiMo Theatre, in the center of Downtown right on old Route 66.

Walk or bike the Paseo del Bosque along the Rio Grande. The scenery along the 16-mile trail is a menagerie of cottonwoods, migrating birds, and the ever-present river rippling quietly at your side.

Explore the National Hispanic Cultural Center, a one-of-a-kind music and arts venue.

Witness the sunset over the volcanoes in the Western desert—a brilliant pink flood that creeps over the valley, making its way east to illuminate the Sandias before disappearing. It's even better in late August when the scent of roasting green chiles fills the air.

tered within the college-named streets just to the south of Central; things get more upscale as you head farther east.

Los Ranchos/North Valley. The North Valley (along with its sister South Valley) is the agrarian heart of Albuquerque. All along the Rio Grande Valley, where first Pueblo peoples, then generations of Hispanic and Anglo families have resided, you will experience the city's deepest sense of tradition.

Northeast Heights. This is quite a large neighborhood, taking in the area north of Interstate 40 and rising steadily east into the foothills of the Sandias, where there's great hiking and an incredible aerial tram to the top of the peak. You'll mostly find houses and shopping centers in this part of town, but it's worth the drive for the mountain close-up.

East Side. Ranging east of Nob Hill through a somewhat seedy stretch of old Route 66 and state fairgrounds neighborhoods, this area is notable as the gateway to the Sandia Mountain route to Santa Fe and home to the must-see National Museum of Nuclear Science & History.

Airport. The mesa-top neighborhood immediately southwest of the airport has a lot of hotels, but, aside from great views, has little else to see or do. It is, however, a short drive from Downtown, UNM, and Nob Hill.

West Side. Head west across the Rio Grande and discover near its far banks the fascinating sandhill crane flyway and nesting ground at the Open Space Visitor center and memorable Petroglyph National Monument. The rest is residential sprawl.

ALBUQUERQUE PLANNER

WHEN TO GO

Albuquerque is sunny and relatively pleasant year-round. Fall is by far the most popular time to visit. On just about any day in late-August through November, big balloons sail across the sharp blue sky and the scent of freshly roasting green chiles permeates the air. Balloon Fiesta brings enormous crowds for nearly two weeks in early October (book hotels at this time as far in advance as possible). But shortly after, the weather's still great and hotel prices plummet. Albuquerque's winter days (usually 10°F warmer than those in Santa Fe) are usually mild enough for hiking, biking, and golf, or simply strolling around Old Town or Nob Hill. The occasional frigid spike usually thaws by morning. Spring brings winds, though plenty of sunshine, too, and rates stay low until the summer crowds flock in. Hot but dry temps in mid-May through mid-July stay well below Phoenix-like extremes, but can soar into the high 90s. This is followed by roughly six to eight weeks of cooler temperatures, a bit more humidity, and the spectacular late-afternoon cloud formations that herald the brief "monsoon" season.

GETTING HERE AND AROUND

AIR TRAVEL

Albuquerque International Sunport (*ABQ*). The major gateway to New Mexico is Albuquerque International Sunport, a well-designed and attractive facility that's just 5 miles southeast of Downtown and just 3 miles south of UNM/Nob Hill. There's a free ABQ Ride bus shuttle service *(⇨ Bus Travel)* on weekdays from the airport to Downtown's Alvarado Transportation Center, where you can connect with Rail Runner service *(⇨ Train Travel)*. ☎ *505/244–7700* 🌐 *www.cabq.gov/airport*.

BUS TRAVEL

If you're only visiting for a couple of days and not planning to explore beyond Old Town, Downtown, and Nob Hill, the city's public bus system, ABQ Ride, is a practical if somewhat slow-going option. It's speedier, Rapid Ride, Red Line service plies the Central Avenue corridor and runs until about 9 pm Monday through Saturday and until 6 pm Sunday. The service is extended until about 1 am on Friday and Saturday nights June through September. Rapid Ride also has a Blue Line that runs from UNM to the West Side, and a Green Line that can get you from Downtown into the Northeast Heights. You can download trip-planning apps or obtain a customized trip plan at the city's public bus website, ABQ Ride.

The Alvarado Transportation Center Downtown is Rapid Ride's central hub and offers direct connections to the NM Rail Runner Express train service north to Santa Fe and to the South Valley suburbs. Buses accept bicycles at no additional charge, although space is limited. Service is free on the Downtown D-RIDE shuttle route (available only on weekdays), or if you are transferring (to any route) from the Rail Runner; otherwise, the fare is $1 (bills or coins, exact change only; 25¢ transfers may be requested on boarding). Bus stops are well marked. *See also Bus Travel in the Travel Smart chapter.*

Bus Contact **ABQ Ride** ☎ *505/243–7433* 🌐 *www.cabq.gov/transit.*

CAR TRAVEL

Although the city's public bus service, ABQ Ride, provides good coverage, a car is the easiest and most convenient way to get around. Albuquerque sprawls in all directions, but getting around town is not difficult. The main highways through the city, north–south Interstate 25 and east–west Interstate 40, converge just northeast of Downtown and generally offer the quickest access to outlying neighborhoods and the airport. Rush-hour jams are common in the mornings and late afternoons, but they're still far less severe than in most big U.S. cities. All the major car-rental agencies are represented at Albuquerque's Sunport airport.

Because it's a driving city, most businesses and hotels have free or inexpensive off-street parking, and it's easy to find metered street parking in many neighborhoods as well as affordable garages Downtown. Problems usually arise only when there's a major event in town, such as a concert near the University of New Mexico or a festival Downtown or in Old Town, when you may want to arrive on the early side to get a space.

ALBUQUERQUE IN A DAY

One of the best places to kick off the day is the Downtown branch of Flying Star restaurant, where you can enjoy breakfast in the heart of Downtown before checking out the handful of shops and galleries on Gold and Central avenues. From here, it's a short drive or 30-minute walk west along Central to reach Old Town, where you can explore the shops and museums of the neighborhood. Once in Old Town, check out the Albuquerque Museum of Art and History, and also try to make your way over to the Albuquerque BioPark, which contains the aquarium, zoo, and botanic park. For lunch, try the atmospheric Monica's El Portal near the Old Town center.

Later in the afternoon, drive or take the Red Line bus a couple of miles east along Central to reach the University of New Mexico's main campus and the nearby Nob Hill District. Start with a stroll around the UNM campus with its many historic adobe buildings; if you have time, pop inside either the Maxwell Museum of Anthropology or the UNM Art Museum. When you're finished here, walk east along Central into Nob Hill and check out the dozens of offbeat shops. If you plan to have dinner in Nob Hill, try Nob Hill Bar and Grill or El Patio. If you're still up for more, check out one of the neighborhood's lively lounges or head back Downtown for a bit of late-night barhopping.

TAXI TRAVEL

Taxis are metered in Albuquerque, and service is around-the-clock. Given the considerable distances around town, cabbing it can be expensive; figure about $9 from Downtown to Nob Hill, and about $20 from the airport to Downtown or EDo. There's also a $1 airport fee.

Taxi Contacts **Albuquerque Cab** ☎ *505/883–4888* ⊕ *www.albuquerquecab.com*. **Yellow Cab** ☎ *505/247–8888*.

TRAIN TRAVEL

The New Mexico Rail Runner Express, a commuter-train line, provides a picturesque, hassle-free way to make a day trip to Santa Fe. These sleek bi-level trains with large windows run south for about 35 miles to the suburb of Belén (stopping in Isleta Pueblo and Los Lunas), and north about 65 miles on a scenic run right into the historic heart of Santa Fe, with stops in Bernalillo, Kewa Pueblo, and a few other spots. Albuquerque stops are Downtown, at the

Alvarado Transportation Center (where ABQ Ride offers free bus service to the airport), and at the north end of town at Journal Center/Los Ranchos. On weekdays, the trains run about eight or nine times per day, from about 6 am until 9 pm. There are also about five trains on Saturdays and three usually run on Sundays. Fares are zone-based (one-way from $2 to $8), but day passes are just $1 more; all are discounted with an online purchase, and bicycles always ride free. Connections to local bus service are available at most stations. *For information on Amtrak service, see Train Travel in the Travel Smart chapter.*

Train Contact **New Mexico Rail Runner Express** ☎ *866/795–7245* 🌐 *www.nmrailrunner.com.*

VISITOR INFORMATION

The Albuquerque Convention and Visitors Bureau operates tourism information kiosks at the airport (on the baggage-claim level) and in Old Town on Plaza Don Luis, across from San Felipe de Neri church.

Albuquerque Convention and Visitors Bureau ☎ *505/842–9918, 800/284–2282* 🌐 *www.itsatrip.org.*

GUIDED TOURS

ABQ Trolley Co. These narrated rides on open-air trolleys go to unique areas—such as *Breaking Bad* shooting locations. Or take an 18-mile, 75-plus-minute overview of the city's top attractions and neighborhoods. Tours are offered April through October, Tuesday through Sunday. ☎ *505/240–8000* 🌐 *www.abqtrolley.com.*

Albuquerque Museum of Art and History. With paid museum admission, the Albuquerque Museum of Art and History leads free, hour-long historical walks through Old Town, beginning at 11 am Tuesday through Sunday, mid-March through mid-December. ☎ *505/243–7255* 🌐 *www.cabq.gov/museum.*

NM Jeep Tours. Backcountry and local-history expert Roch Hart, owner of NM Jeep Tours, offers Jeep tours and guided hikes that start from Albuquerque and go as far as time and permits allow. He can suggest an itinerary (ghost towns, rock formations, petroglyphs), or tailor one to your interests and time frame. ☎ *505/252–0112* 🌐 *nmjeeptours.com.*

Tours of Old Town. Tours of Old Town offers guided walking strolls around Old Town. The standard tour lasts about 75 minutes and is offered Friday through Wednesday, four times daily. Longer ghost-hunting and moonlight tours are also offered on occasion—check for times. ☎ *505/246–8687* 🌐 *www.toursofoldtown.com*.

PLANNING YOUR TIME

Although the city sprawls, it does contain a handful of neighborhoods well suited to exploring on foot. In both Downtown and Old Town, you'll find plenty of garages and parking lots, and good areas to get out of the car and explore on foot. The same is true of the adjoining Nob Hill and UNM neighborhoods. For a short visit to the city, you could focus your time on these two areas.

The rest of the city stretches pretty far. Allow an average of 20 minutes to get from one part of town to the other. A helpful strategy is to bunch together more outlying attractions that interest you, perhaps hitting Bosque Brewing Co. and the Balloon Museum the same day you go out to Petroglyph National Monument or ride the Sandia Peak Tram.

EXPLORING

Albuquerque's terrain is diverse. Along the river in the North and South valleys, the elevation hovers at about 4,800 feet. East of the river, the land rises gently to the foothills of the Sandia Mountains, which rise to over 6,000 feet; the 10,378-foot summit is a grand spot from which to view the city below. West of the Rio Grande, where Albuquerque is growing most aggressively, the terrain rises abruptly in a string of mesas topped by five volcanic cones. The changes in elevation from one part of the city to another result in corresponding changes in temperature, as much as 10°F at any time. It's not uncommon for snow or rain to fall on one part of town but for it to remain dry and sunny in another, and because temperatures can rise and fall considerably throughout the day and evening, it's a good idea to bring along a couple of layers when exploring large areas or for several hours.

OLD TOWN

Albuquerque's social and commercial anchor since the settlement was established in 1706. Old Town and the surrounding blocks contain the wealth of the city's top cultural attractions, including several excellent museums. The action extends from the historic Old Town Plaza for several blocks in all directions—most of the museums are

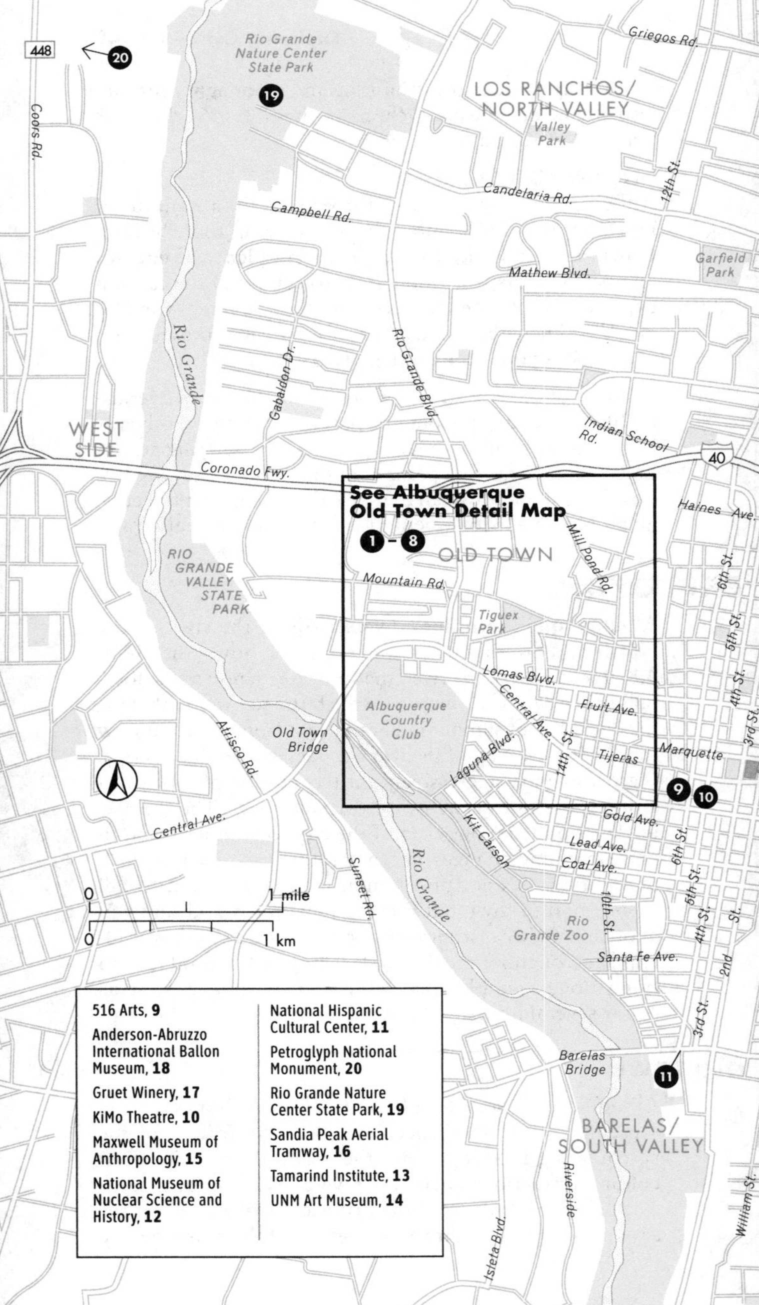

448
20
Rio Grande Nature Center State Park
19
Griegos Rd.
LOS RANCHOS/ NORTH VALLEY
Valley Park
Coors Rd.
12th St.
Candelaria Rd.
Campbell Rd.
Garfield Park
Mathew Blvd.
Rio Grande
Gabaldon Dr.
Rio Grande Blvd.
WEST SIDE
Indian School Rd.
40
Coronado Fwy.
See Albuquerque Old Town Detail Map
1 - 8
Haines Ave.
Mill Pond Rd.
OLD TOWN
RIO GRANDE VALLEY STATE PARK
Mountain Rd.
6th St.
Tiguex Park
5th St.
4th St.
Lomas Blvd.
Central Ave.
Fruit Ave.
3rd St.
Albuquerque Country Club
Atrisco Rd.
Old Town Bridge
Laguna Blvd.
14th St.
Tijeras
Marquette
9
10
Central Ave.
Kit Carson
Gold Ave.
Lead Ave.
Coal Ave.
6th St.
Sunset Rd.
Rio Grande
5th St.
0
1 mile
0
1 km
10th St.
Rio Grande Zoo
4th St.
2nd St.
Santa Fe Ave.
3rd St.
516 Arts, 9
Anderson-Abruzzo International Ballon Museum, 18
Gruet Winery, 17
KiMo Theatre, 10
Maxwell Museum of Anthropology, 15
National Museum of Nuclear Science and History, 12
National Hispanic Cultural Center, 11
Petroglyph National Monument, 20
Rio Grande Nature Center State Park, 19
Sandia Peak Aerial Tramway, 16
Tamarind Institute, 13
UNM Art Museum, 14
Barelas Bridge
11
BARELAS/ SOUTH VALLEY
Riverside
Isleta Blvd.
William St.

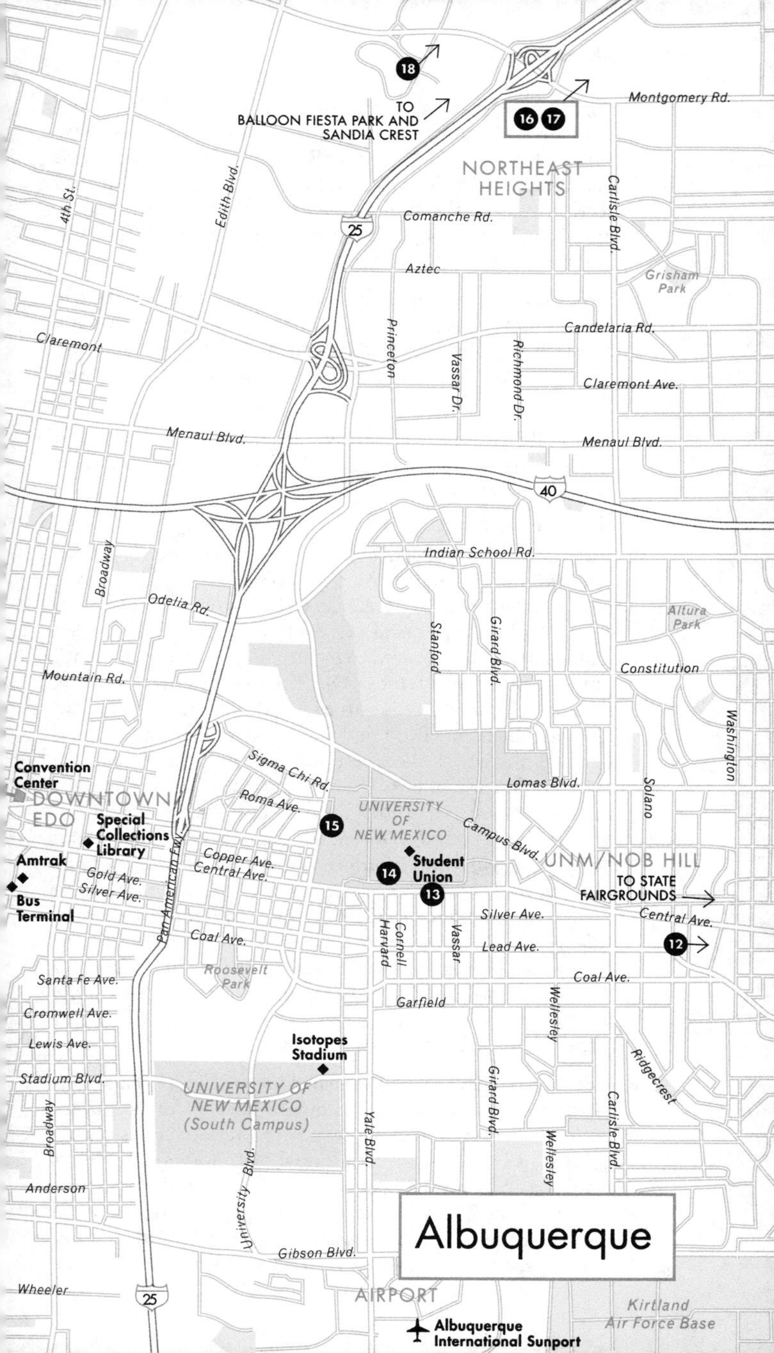

Albuquerque
18
TO BALLOON FIESTA PARK AND SANDIA CREST
16 17
Montgomery Rd.
NORTHEAST HEIGHTS
Carlisle Blvd.
4th St.
Edith Blvd.
25
Comanche Rd.
Aztec
Grisham Park
Candelaria Rd.
Claremont
Princeton
Vassar Dr.
Richmond Dr.
Claremont Ave.
Menaul Blvd.
Menaul Blvd.
40
Indian School Rd.
Broadway
Odelia Rd.
Altura Park
Stanford
Girard Blvd.
Mountain Rd.
Constitution
Washington
Sigma Chi Rd.
Convention Center
Lomas Blvd.
DOWNTOWN
EDO
Roma Ave.
Solano
UNIVERSITY OF NEW MEXICO
15
Special Collections Library
Campus Blvd.
UNM/NOB HILL
Amtrak
Copper Ave.
Central Ave.
Student Union
14
Gold Ave.
Silver Ave.
TO STATE FAIRGROUNDS
13
Bus Terminal
Pan American Fwy.
Silver Ave.
Central Ave.
Harvard
Cornell
Vassar
Lead Ave.
12
Coal Ave.
Roosevelt Park
Coal Ave.
Santa Fe Ave.
Garfield
Cromwell Ave.
Wellesley
Lewis Ave.
Isotopes Stadium
Ridgecrest
Stadium Blvd.
UNIVERSITY OF NEW MEXICO (South Campus)
Girard Blvd.
Broadway
Yale Blvd.
Wellesley
Carlisle Blvd.
University Blvd.
Anderson
Gibson Blvd.
Wheeler
25
AIRPORT
Kirtland Air Force Base
Albuquerque International Sunport

north and east of the plaza. In this area you'll also find a number of restaurants and scads of shops. The artsy Saw Mill and Wells Park/Mountain Road neighborhoods extend just east of Old Town's museum row; the Los Duranes section, where the Indian Pueblo Cultural Center commands attention, is just a bit beyond walking distance to the northeast of Old Town.

However, the IPCC runs an hourly courtesy shuttle (☎ *866/855–7902* ⊕ *www.indianpueblo.org*) from June through October on Fridays through Sundays, making for a pleasant 15-minute journey between Old Town and the museum.

From Old Town to Downtown, it's a rather drab (though quick) 1¼-mile bike ride, bus ride, walk, or drive southeast along Central Avenue.

TOP ATTRACTIONS

★ Fodor'sChoice **ABQ BioPark.** The city's foremost outdoor attraction and nature center, the park comprises Tingley Beach (and its trout-stocked ponds) as well as three distinct attractions: Aquarium, Botanic Garden, and Zoo. The garden and aquarium are located together (admission gets you into both facilities), just west of Old Town, off Central Avenue; the zoo is a short drive southeast, off 10th Street. You can also ride the scenic Rio Line vintage narrow-gauge railroad between the zoo and gardens and the aquarium complex; rides are free if you purchase a combination ticket to all of the park's facilities. ✉ *903 10th St. SW, Old Town, Albuquerque, USA* ☎ *505/764–6200* ⊕ *www.abqbiopark.com* 🎫 *Tingley Beach and grounds free, Aquarium and Botanic Garden $12.50 (includes both attractions), Zoo $12.50; combination ticket for all attractions, including unlimited rides on the Rio Line and the zoo loop Thunderbird Express trains $20. Free admission for all attractions for kids under 3* ⏲ *Aquarium, botanic garden, and zoo Sept.–May, daily 9–5; June–Aug., weekdays 9–5 and weekends 9–6. Tingley Beach daily sunrise–sunset. No trains Mon.*

FAMILY

★ Fodor'sChoice **Albuquerque Museum of Art and History.** This light-filled modern structure serves up a wealth of contemporary art, both from the museum's own Southwestern artists-centric collections and world-class touring shows. Additional exhibits display a collection of Spanish-colonial artifacts, the largest in the nation. The Common Ground galleries represent an important permanent collection of primarily 20th-century paintings, all by world-renowned artists with a New Mexico connection. The sculpture garden contains more than 50 contemporary works by Southwestern artists that include Glenna Goodacre, Michael Naranjo, and Luis Jiménez. Slate at the Museum, a casual eatery operated by Downtown's noted Slate Street Cafe, serves soups, salads, espresso drinks, desserts, and other tasty light fare. ✉ *2000 Mountain Rd. NW, Old Town, Albuquerque, USA* ☎ *505/243–7255 museum, 505/242–0434 shop, 505/242–5316 café* 🌐 *www.cabq.gov/museum* 🎟 *$4 (free Sun. 9–1)* ⏲ *Tues.–Sun. 9–5.*

FAMILY **American International Rattlesnake Museum.** Included in the largest collection of different species of living rattlers in the world are such rare and unusual specimens as an albino western diamondback. From the outside the museum looks like a plain old shop, but inside, the museum's exhibits, its engaging staff, and a video supply visitors with the lowdown on these venomous creatures—for instance, that they can't hear their own rattles and that the human death rate from rattlesnake bites is less than 1%. The mission here is to educate the public on the many positive benefits of rattlesnakes, and to contribute to their conservation. ✉ *202 San Felipe St. NW, just off the southeast corner of the plaza, Old Town, Albuquerque, USA* ☎ *505/242–6569* 🌐 *www.rattlesnakes.com* 🎟 *$5* ⏲ *June–Sept., Mon.–Sat. 10–6, Sun. 1–5; Oct.–May, weekdays 11:30–5:30, Sat. 10–6, Sun. 1–5.*

FAMILY **¡Explora!.** This imaginatively executed science museum—its driving concept is "Ideas You Can Touch"—is right across from the New Mexico Museum of Natural History and Science. ¡Explora! bills itself as an all-ages attraction (and enthralled adults abound), but there's no question that many of the innovative hands-on exhibits such as a high-wire bicycle and a kinetic sculpture display are geared to children. They offer big fun in addition to big science (and a good dose of art as well). While its colorful Bucky dome is immediately noticeable from the street, ¡Explora! also features a playground, theater, and a freestanding staircase that appears to "float" between floors. ✉ *1701 Mountain Rd. NW, Old Town, Albuquerque, USA* ☎ *505/224–8300* 🌐 *www.explora.us* 🎟 *$7* ⏲ *Mon.–Sat. 10–6, Sun. noon–6.*

FAMILY **New Mexico Museum of Natural History and Science.** The wonders at Albuquerque's most popular museum include a simulated volcano (with a river of bubbling hot lava flowing beneath the see-through glass floor), the frigid Ice Age cave, and "Dawn of the Dinosaurs." The only Triassic exhibit in North America, this permanent hall features some of the state's own rare finds. The Evolution Elevator (aka the Evolator) uses video, sound, and motion to whisk you through 35 million years of New Mexico's geological history. The Paul Allen–funded "Start-Up!" galleries explore the silicon age. Detailing the birth of the PC right here in the Duke City (bet you didn't know that Seattle was the *second* stop for Allen and a very young Bill Gates). These exhibitions are a fascinating tour through the early garage days of many such start-ups, including the Apple side of the story. Also here is, the LodeStar Science Center; the state-of-the-art planetarium is home to the wildly popular First Friday Fractals show (tickets available online only). ✉ *1801 Mountain Rd. NW, Old Town, Albuquerque, New Mexico, USA* ☎ *505/841–2800* 🌐 *www.nmnaturalhistory.org* 🎟 *Museum $7, DynaTheater $7, planetarium $7; combination ticket for any 2 attractions $12, for any 3 attractions $15* ⏲ *Daily 9–5.*

★ Fodor's Choice FAMILY **Old Town Plaza.** Tranquil, with the lovely 1793 San Felipe de Neri Catholic Church still presiding along the north side, Old Town Plaza is a pleasant place to sit on wrought-iron benches under shade trees. Roughly 200 shops, restaurants, cafés, galleries, and several cultural sites in *placitas* (small plazas) and lanes surround the plaza. During fiestas Old Town comes alive with mariachi bands and dancing señoritas; at Christmas time it is lit with luminarias. Mostly dating back to the late 1800s, styles from Queen Anne to Territorial and Pueblo Revival, and even Mediterranean, are apparent in the one- and two-story (almost all adobe) structures. ■ TIP → **An abundance of guided walks through Old Town are available** *(⇨ Albuquerque Planner, Guided Tours).* ✉ *Old Town, Albuquerque, New Mexico, USA.*

WORTH NOTING

FAMILY **Indian Pueblo Cultural Center.** The multilevel semicircular layout of this museum was inspired by Pueblo Bonito, the prehistoric ruin in northwestern New Mexico. Start by watching the museum's video about the region's Pueblo culture. Then move to the upper-level alcove, where changing exhibits feature aspects of the arts and crafts of each of the state's 19 Pueblos. Lower-level exhibits trace the history of the Pueblo people. Youngsters can touch Native American pottery, jewelry, weaving, tools, and dried corn at the Hands-On Corner, draw petroglyph designs, and design pots. Ceremonial dances are performed on weekends at 11 and 2, and there are arts-and-crafts demonstrations each weekend. The **Pueblo Harvest Café & Bakery** is a great

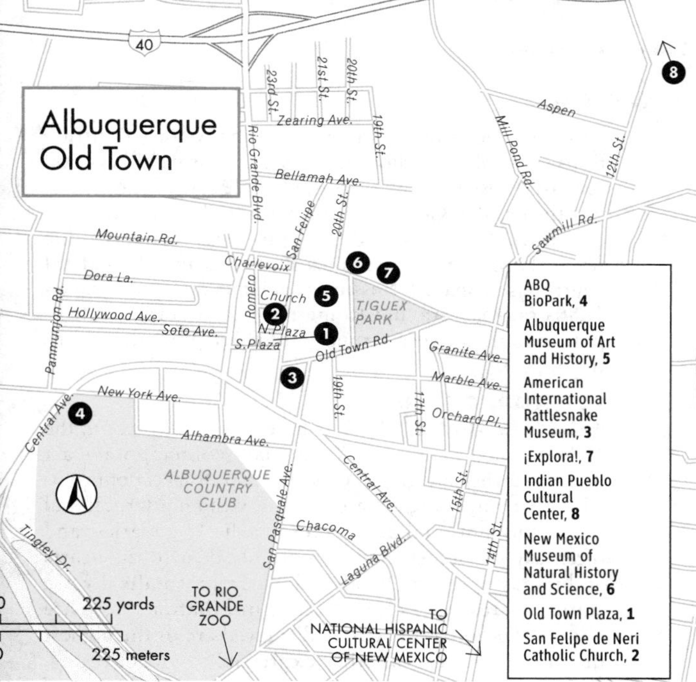

spot for breakfast, lunch, or dinner. Note: The museum lies a bit northeast of Old Town, in the Los Duranes neighborhood—a five-minute drive, or hop on their courtesy shuttle in summer months. ✉ *2401 12th St. NW, Old Town, Albuquerque, New Mexico, USA* ☎ *505/843–7270, 800/766–4405* 🌐 *www.indianpueblo.org* 💳 *$6* ⏲ *Daily 9–5.*

9

San Felipe de Neri Catholic Church. Well over two centuries after it first welcomed worshippers, this structure, erected in 1793, is still active. The building, which replaced Albuquerque's first Catholic church, has been expanded several times, but its adobe walls and other original features remain. Small gardens front and flank the church; the inside is a respite from the tourism bustle beyond its doorstep—the painting and iconography is simple, authentic, and lovely, the atmosphere hushed. Next to it is a shop and small museum that displays relics—vestments, paintings, carvings—dating from the 17th century. TIP→ **There's a hidden treasure behind the church: inside the gnarled tree is a statue that some speculate depicts the Virgin Mary.** ✉ *2005 Plaza NW, Old Town, Albuquerque, USA* ☎ *505/243–4628* 🌐 *www.sanfelipedeneri.org* ⏲ *Church open to public daily 8 am–dusk; museum Mon.–Sat. 9:30–5.*

DOWNTOWN

Although Downtown doesn't have many formal attractions short of its anchoring arts scene, this neighborhood rewards those who take a closer look. Along Central Avenue the parallel Gold Street there's a trail of architectural detail, from the Simms Building to the Venetian Gothic Revival Occidental Insurance Building, and the federal courthouse's Spanish Mission pile. Hints of Albuquerque's 1880s railroad-era and Route 66 past abound; contemporary murals and a strong Public Art presence add to the appeal.

TOP ATTRACTIONS

★ Fodor'sChoice **516 Arts.** 516 Arts holds a special place in the New Mexico art scene. World-class contemporary art dominates the changing shows at this multilevel nonprofit. Visually compelling collaborations with an international set of museums and artists cross media boundaries, and often explore issues that are not only dear to the hearts and minds of this multicultural, environmentally diverse state, but resonate globally. The installations here are always top-notch, the works displayed are of the highest quality, the ideas—whether expressed in video, prints, sculpture, diodes, or paint—provocative. ✉ *516 Central Ave. SW, Downtown, Albuquerque, USA* ☎ *505/242–1445* 🌐 *www.516arts.org.*

★ Fodor'sChoice **KiMo Theatre.** Decorated with light fixtures made from buffalo skulls (the eye sockets glow amber in the dark), Navajo symbols, and nine spectacular Western-themed wall murals by Carl Von Hassler, the KiMo represents Pueblo Deco at its apex. It's one of the few notable early-20th-century structures remaining in Downtown Albuquerque. The self-guided tour is fantastic (guided tours can also be arranged by appointment), or catch a film or a live performance. ✉ *423 Central Ave. NW, at 5th St., Downtown, Albuquerque, USA* ☎ *505/768–3522 theater, 505/768–3544 event info* 🌐 *www.cabq.gov/kimo* 🎟 *Free self-guided tours* ⏲ *Tues.–Fri. 8:30–4:30, Sat. 11–5.*

BARELAS/SOUTH VALLEY

The historic Barelas neighborhood, to the south of Old Town and Downtown, features the must-see National Hispanic Cultural Center. Otherwise it's mostly a residential neighborhood; bounded by the Bosque trails and a revitalizing railyard, it gradually gives way to the broad

South Valley, a rough-around-the-edges area that contains modest homes in some sections, and farmlands or light industry in others.

TOP ATTRACTIONS

★ Fodor'sChoice **National Hispanic Cultural Center.** A showpiece
FAMILY for the city, and a showcase for Hispanic culture in Albuquerque's historic Barelas neighborhood, this beautifully designed space contains a museum and art galleries, multiple performance venues, a restaurant, a 10,000-volume genealogical research center and library, and an education center. Its stunning and acoustically superb Roy E. Disney Center for Performing Arts and smaller Albuquerque Journal Theatre host ballet, flamenco dancing, bilingual theater, traditional Spanish and New Mexican music, the famous world music festival ¡Globalquerque!, and many other performances. Exhibits at its first-rate museum include dynamic displays of photography, paintings, sculpture, and traditional and contemporary craftwork by local artists as well as by internationally known names. There's a vintage WPA-era school that now contains the research library and **La Fonda del Bosque restaurant** ($$, no dinner), which serves tasty New Mexican fare indoors and out on the patio. ✉ *1701 4th St. SW, at Avenida César Chavez (Bridge Blvd.), Barelas, Albuquerque, New Mexico, USA* ☎ *505/246–2261 cultural center, 505/724–4771 box office* 🌐 *www.nhccnm.org* 🎫 *$3* ⏲ *Tues.–Sun. 10–5.*

UNM/NOB HILL

Established in 1889, the University of New Mexico (UNM) is the state's leading institution of higher education. Its many outstanding galleries and museums are open to the public free of charge. The university's Pueblo Revival–style architecture is noteworthy, particularly the beautifully preserved 1938 west wing of Zimmerman Library, which houses the superb Center for Southwest Research and changing historical exhibits, and the Alumni Chapel, both designed by John Gaw Meem, a Santa Fe–based architect whose mid-20th-century work became a template for new campus buildings for years to come. Newer structures, such as Antoine Predock's George Pearl Hall tip their hat to Meem, but are distinctive in their own right. Adorned in 2012 with Federico Muelas's mesmerizing Flor Azul/Blue Flower art work, the 900-square-foot LED and sound installation is best seen at night. It joins the numerous contemporary sculptures that make this campus worth a stroll;

Bruce Nauman's 1988 "The Center of the Universe" is a destination in itself. Stop at the campus Welcome Center (☎ *505/277–1989* ⊕ *www.unm.edu*) to pick up self-guided campus art and architecture tour maps.

UNM's campus easterly spread leads directly into the heart of Nob Hill and a quintessential assortment of Route 66 and Art Deco–era remnants. Vintage motels and gas stations with neon signage house cool galleries, microbreweries, cafés, upscale furnishing shops, and more. The circa 1947 Nob Hill Business Center sits right on old Route 66 (Central Avenue), sandwiched between Carlisle Boulevard and Amherst Drive SE, and is still the heart of this neighborhood. Anchored by the wonderful Mariposa Gallery and IMEC, Amherst Drive (just the one sweet block between Central and Silver) is the primo side street by far. Other noteworthy businesses—from some of the city's best restaurants, to offbeat shops, the Guild indie cinema, and a good mix of professional and student hangouts—run along Central, both a few block east of Carlisle, and to the west, back to UNM.

WORTH NOTING

Maxwell Museum of Anthropology. Tapping a vast collection of sublime Southwestern artifacts and archival photos, the Maxwell's superb shows encompass three fascinating fields: Archaeology, Cultural Anthropology, and Evolutionary Anthropology. As the first public museum in Albuquerque (established in 1932), its influence has grown over the years, but its compact space ensures that they scale their exhibits to the essentials. A viewer—whether of a permanent exhibit on peoples of the Southwest, or a shorter term one ("Curanderismo" and "Navajo Weavers in a Changing World" were featured in the mid-2010s)—will be intrigued and informed, but not overwhelmed. Of special note is their rare and substantial collection of Mimbres pottery from AD 800 to 1000. Parking permits for adjacent UNM lots are available inside the museum. ✉ *University of New Mexico, Redondo West Dr., west end of campus, UNM/Nob Hill, Albuquerque, New Mexico, USA* ☎ *505/277–4405* ⊕ *www.unm.edu/~maxwell* 🎟 *Free* ⏲ *Tues.–Sat. 10–4.*

Tamarind Institute. This world-famous institution played a major role in reviving the fine art of lithographic printing, which involves working with plates of traditional stone and modern metal. Tamarind certification is to a printer what a degree from Juilliard is to a musician. A small gallery within the modern facility exhibits prints and lithographs by well-known masters like Jim Dine, Kiki Smith, and Ed Ruscha, as well as up-and-comers in the craft. Guided tours (reservations essential) are conducted on the first Friday of each month at 1:30. ✉ *2500 Central Ave. SE, UNM/Nob Hill, Albuquerque, New Mexico, USA* ☎ *505/277–3901* 🌐 *tamarind.unm.edu* 🎟 *Free* ⏲ *Weekdays 9–5.*

★ Fodor's Choice **UNM Art Museum.** University Art Museum features magnificent 20th- and 21st-century prints, as well as photos and paintings that rival the finest collections throughout the Southwest. Changing exhibits cull from more than 30,000 archived works, which include groundbreaking works by modernist giants such as Bridget Riley, Richard Diebenkorn, and Elaine DeKooning. Photography—Ansel Adams, Beaumont Newhall—is a particular strength, and provocative shows have featured immense prints, complemented with video projections and a range of mixed-media installations. Transcendentalist master Raymond Jonson's work, along with landmark acquisitions he made, is displayed. Celebrating its 50th anniversary in 2013, a plan for a permanent collections gallery is afoot, which will allow more of their impressive holdings—a Picasso print, an O'Keeffe painting—to be seen regularly. Lectures and symposia, gallery talks, and guided tours are regularly scheduled. ✉ *University of New Mexico Center for the Arts, north of Central Ave. entrance opposite Cornell Dr. SE, UNM/Nob Hill, Albuquerque, New Mexico, USA* ☎ *505/277–4001* 🌐 *www.unmartmuseum.org* 🎟 *$5 donation suggested* ⏲ *Tues.–Fri. 10–4, weekends 1–4.*

LOS RANCHOS/NORTH VALLEY

Many attractions lie north of Downtown, Old Town, and the University of New Mexico. Quite a few, including the Casa Rondeña winery and the Rio Grande Nature Center, are clustered in a contiguous stretch that comprises two of the city's longest-settled areas: the lush cottonwood-lined North Valley and Los Ranchos de Albuquerque, along the Rio Grande. Early Spanish settlers made their homes here, building on top of even earlier Pueblo homesteads. Historic adobe houses abound. The Montaño Road Bridge crosses through the area, making a sublime gateway to the West Side.

TOP ATTRACTIONS

FAMILY **Anderson-Abruzzo International Balloon Museum.** This dramatic museum celebrates the city's legacy as the hot-air ballooning capital of the world. Albuquerque's high altitude, mild climate, and a fortuitous wind pattern known as the Albuquerque Box, make it an ideal destination for ballooning. The dashing, massive facility is named for Maxie Anderson and Ben Abruzzo, who pioneered ballooning here and were part of a team of three aviators who made the first manned hot-air balloon crossing of the Atlantic Ocean in 1978. Filling the airy museum space are several fully inflated historic balloons, and both large- and small-scale replicas of gas balloons and zeppelins. You'll also see vintage balloon baskets, china and flatware from the ill-fated *Hindenburg* and an engaging display on that tragic craft, and dynamic exhibits that trace the history of the sport, dating back to the first balloon ride, in 1783. Interactive stations are setup so kids can design their own balloons. ✉ *9201 Balloon Museum Dr. NE, off Alameda Blvd., Los Ranchos/North Valley, Albuquerque, New Mexico, USA* ☎ *505/768–6020* 🌐 *www.balloonmuseum.com* 🎟 *$4* ⏲ *Tues.–Sun. 9–5* ☞ *No food sold on-site.*

WORTH NOTING

FAMILY **Rio Grande Nature Center State Park.** Along the banks of the Rio Grande, this 270-acre refuge in a portion of the Bosque (about midway up on the Paseo del Bosque trail) is the nation's largest cottonwood forest. There are numerous walking and biking trails that wind into the 53-acre Aldo Leopold Forest and down to the river. Bird-watchers come to view all manner of birds and migratory waterfowl. Constructed half aboveground and half below the edge of a pond, the park's interpretive center has viewing windows and speakers that broadcast the sounds of the birds you're watching. You may see birds, frogs, ducks, and turtles. The park has active programs for adults and children. ✉ *2901 Candelaria Rd. NW, Los Ranchos/North Valley, Albuquerque, New Mexico, USA* ☎ *505/344–7240* 🌐 *www.nmparks.com* 🎟 *$3 per vehicle, grounds free* ⏲ *Nature center daily 10–5, park daily 8–5.*

NORTHEAST HEIGHTS

In the Northeast Heights you are approaching the foothills of the Sandia Mountains, in upscale neighborhoods that surprise you with the sudden appearance of piñon and ponderosa. Trips to this area can easily be combined with more north-central venues like the Balloon Museum and local microbreweries, or the National Museum of Nuclear Science & History, which, once you've made it into the foothills, is due south.

TOP ATTRACTIONS

Gruet Winery. It's hard to imagine a wine-tasting venue with less curb appeal. Behind the vaguely chalet-like exterior of an otherwise modern industrial building, you're afforded the chance to visit one of the nation's most acclaimed producers of sparkling wines (to see its actual vineyards you'll have to head south to Truth or Consequences). Gruet (pronounced *grew*-ay) had been famous in France since the 1950s for its Champagnes. In New Mexico, the Gruet family has been producing wine since 1984, and their winery has earned nationwide kudos for its Methode Champenoise (employing traditional Champagne-making methods for its sparkling wine), as well as for impressive Pinot Noirs, Syrahs, and Chardonnays. Most of the state's top restaurants carry Gruet vintages, as do many leading wine cellars around the country. Tastings include five wines and a souvenir glass. ✉ *8400 Pan American Freeway (I–25) NE, on the north frontage road for I–25, between Alameda Blvd. and Paseo del Norte, Northeast Heights, Albuquerque, New Mexico, USA* ☎ *505/821–0055, 888/857–9463* 🌐 *www.gruetwinery.com* 🎟 *Winery free, 5-wine tasting $6* ⏲ *Weekdays 10–5, Sat. noon–5; tours Mon.–Sat. at 2.*

★ Fodor's Choice | FAMILY **Sandia Peak Aerial Tramway.** Tramway cars climb 2.7 miles up the steep western face of the Sandias, giving you a close-up view of red rocks and tall trees—it's the world's longest aerial tramway. From the observation deck at the 10,378-foot summit you can see Santa Fe to the northeast and Los Alamos to the northwest—about 11,000 square miles of spectacular scenery. Tram cars leave from the base at regular intervals for the 15-minute ride to the top. You may see birds of prey soaring above or mountain lions roaming the cliff sides. An exhibit room at the top surveys the wildlife and landscape of the mountain. ■ TIP→ **It's much colder and windier at the summit than at the tram's base, so pack a jacket.** You can also use the tram as a way to reach the Sandia Peak ski and mountain-biking area. ✉ *10 Tramway Loop NE, Far Northeast Heights, Albuquerque, USA* ☎ *505/856–7325* 🌐 *www.sandiapeak.com* 🎟 *$20* ⏲ *Memorial Day–Labor Day, daily 9–9; Sept.–May, Wed.–Mon. 9–8, Tues. 5 pm–8 pm.*

EAST SIDE

South of I–40 and the Northeast Heights, the East Side bridges the older and historic parts of Route 66 with pockets of newer development of an upscale nature. Bicyclists frequent the nearby Tramway trails, and you might continue on into the mountains, but the area's charms are otherwise sparse—though you will want to make time for the destination-worthy National Museum of Nuclear Science & History.

TOP ATTRACTIONS

★ FAMILY Fodor'sChoice **National Museum of Nuclear Science & History.** Previously known simply as the National Atomic Museum, this brilliant Smithsonian Affiliate traces the history of the atomic age and how nuclear science has dramatically influenced the course of modern history. Exhibits include replicas of Little Boy and Fat Man (the bombs dropped on Japan at the end of World War II), a compelling display about the difficult decision to drop atomic bombs, and a look at how atomic culture has dovetailed with pop culture. There are also children's programs and an exhibit about X-ray technology. The campus also contains the 9-acre Heritage Park, which has a B-29 and other mega-airships, plus rockets, missiles, cannons, and even a nuclear sub sail. One highlight is the restored 1942 Plymouth that was used to transport the plutonium core of "the Gadget" (as that first weapon was known) down from Los Alamos to the Trinity Site for testing. ✉ *601 Eubank Blvd. SE, a few blocks south of I–40, Uptown/East Side, Albuquerque, New Mexico, USA* ☎ *505/245–2137* 🌐 *www.atomicmuseum.org* 🎟 *$8* ⏲ *Daily 9–5.*

WEST SIDE

The fastest-growing part of Albuquerque lies on a broad mesa high above the Rio Grande Valley. The West Side is primarily the domain of new suburban housing developments and strip malls, some designed more attractively than others. Somewhat controversially, growth on the West Side has seemed to occur below, above, and virtually all around the archaeologically critical Petroglyph National Monument. Allow a 20-minute drive from Old Town and the North Valley to reach the monument.

WORTH NOTING

FAMILY **Petroglyph National Monument.** Beneath the stumps of five extinct volcanoes, this park encompasses more than 25,000 ancient Native American rock drawings inscribed on the 17-mile-long West Mesa escarpment overlooking the Rio Grande Valley. For centuries, Native American hunting parties camped at the base, chipping and scribbling away. Archaeologists believe most of the petroglyphs were carved on the lava formations between 1100 and 1600, but some images at the park may date back as far as 1000 BC. A paved trail at **Boca Negra Canyon** (north of the visitor center on Unser Boulevard, beyond Montaño Road) leads past several dozen petroglyphs. A tad more remote is the sandy **Piedras Marcadas Canyon** trail, a few miles farther north. The trail at **Rinconado Canyon** (south of the visitor center on Unser) is unpaved. The rangers at the visitor center will supply maps and help you determine which trail is best for the time you have. ✉ *Visitor center, 6001 Unser Blvd. NW, at Western Trail Rd., 3 miles north of I–40 Exit 154, West Side, Albuquerque, USA* ☎ *505/899–0205* 🌐 *www.nps.gov/petr* 🎟 *$1 weekdays, $2 weekends for parking at Boca Negra Canyon; access to rest of monument is free* ⏲ *Daily 8–5.*

WHERE TO EAT

The Duke City has long been a place for hearty home-style cooking in big portions, and to this day, it's easy to find great steak-and-chops houses, retro diners, and authentic New Mexican restaurants. The trick is finding them amid Albuquerque's miles of chain options and legions of dives, but if you look, you'll be rewarded with innovative food, and generally at prices much lower than in Santa Fe or other major Southwestern cities.

9

In Nob Hill, Downtown, and Old Town many notable new restaurants have opened, offering swank decor and complex and artful variations on modern Southwest, Mediterranean, Asian, and other globally inspired cuisine. A significant Vietnamese population has made that cuisine a star, but Indian, Japanese, Thai, and South American traditions all have a presence, making this New Mexico's best destination for ethnic fare.

Prices in the restaurant reviews are the average cost of a main course at dinner or, if dinner is not served, at lunch; taxes and service charges are generally included.

BEST BETS: ALBUQUERQUE DINING

With hundreds of restaurants to choose from, how will you decide where to eat? Fodor's writers and editors have selected their favorite restaurants by cuisine in the Best Bets lists *below*. Find specific details about a restaurant in the full reviews.

Fodor's Choice ★
Barelas Coffee House $, Farina Pizzeria & Wine Bar $, The Grove Cafe & Market $, Jennifer James 101 $$$, Range Café $, Zacatecas $$

AMERICAN
Model Pharmacy $, Sophia's Place $, Standard Diner $$

CAFÉ
Flying Star $, Golden Crown Panaderia $, The Grove Café & Market $, Range Café $

CONTEMPORARY
Jennifer James 101 $$$, Nob Hill Bar and Grill $, Slate Street Cafe $$, Vinaigrette $$, Zinc Wine Bar & Bistro $$$

NEW MEXICAN
Barelas Coffee House $, Church Street Café $, Duran Central Pharmacy $, La Fonda del Bosque $$, Monica's El Portal $

BEST BURGER
Frontier Restaurant $, Range Café $, Standard Diner $$

BEST BREAKFAST
Barelas Coffee House $, Flying Star $, Frontier Restaurant $, La Fonda del Bosque $$, Range Café $, Sophia's Place $

CHILD-FRIENDLY
Flying Star $, Frontier Restaurant $, Golden Crown Panaderia $, Range Café $

OUTDOOR SEATING
Church Street Café $, Flying Star $, The Grove Café & Market $, Sophia's Place $

OLD TOWN

$$$ ✕ **Antiquity.** *American.* Within the thick adobe walls of this darkly lighted, romantic space off the plaza in Old Town, patrons have been feasting on rich, elegantly prepared American classics for more than 50 years. This isn't the edgy, contemporary restaurant to bring an adventuresome foodie—Antiquity specializes in classics, from starters of French onion soup and Alaskan King crabcakes with a perfectly piquant rémoulade sauce to main courses like Chicken Madagascar, Australian lobster tail with drawn butter, and black angus New York strip-loin steak with horseradish sauce. The place may be a bit on the timeworn

side itself, but the consistently well-prepared food and charming service still make it a winner. *Average main: $26 112 Romero St. NW, Old Town, Albuquerque, USA 505/247–3545 www.antiquityrestaurant.com Reservations essential No lunch.*

$ **Church Street Café.** *Latin American.* Built in the early 1700s, this structure is among the oldest in New Mexico. Renovations have preserved the original adobe bricks to ensure that this spacious eatery remains as authentic as its menu, which features family recipes spanning four generations—with fresh, local ingredients and spirits employed to satiate streams of hungry tourists and locals. Request the courtyard for alfresco dining amid trellises of sweet grapes and flowers, and where a classical and flamenco guitarist often performs. Buttery guacamole, with just a bit of bite, is the perfect appetizer to prep one's palate for tender carne asada, redolent and sumptuously spiced. Try the house specialty, chiles rellenos stuffed with beef and cheese, or a portobello-and-bell-pepper fajita. Traditional desserts and hearty breakfast choices are also offered. *Average main: $16 2111 Church St. NW, Old Town, Albuquerque, USA 505/247–8522 www.churchstreetcafe.com No dinner Sun.*

$ **Duran Central Pharmacy.** *Latin American.* This expanded Old Town lunch counter with a dozen tables and a tiny patio just might serve the best tortillas in town. A favorite of old-timers who know their way around a blue-corn enchilada, Duran's is an informal place whose patrons give their food the total attention it deserves. Be sure to leave some browsing time for the pharmacy's book section: Duran's has a good selection of not easily found history and coffeetable volumes covering the Duke City and its storied environs. *Average main: $9 1815 Central Ave. NW, Old Town, Albuquerque, USA 505/247–4141 www.durancentralpharmacy.com No credit cards Closed Sun. No dinner.*

9

$ **Golden Crown Panaderia.** *Bakery.* On the eastern fringe of
FAMILY Old Town, in a nascent arts district, this aromatic, down-home-style bakery is known for two things: the ability to custom-design and bake artful breads in the likeness of just about any person or place, and hearty green-chile bread (made with tomatoes, cilantro, Parmesan, green chile, and onions). You can order hot cocoa, cappuccino, *bizcochito* (the official state cookie, also known as New Mexican wedding cookies), pumpkin-filled empanadas, plenty of other sweets and sandwiches (ask what bread is fresh and

hot), and wonderfully spicy and aromatic pizzas made with green-chile crusts. There's seating on a small patio. *Average main: $9* *1103 Mountain Rd. NW, Old Town, Albuquerque, USA* *505/243–2424* *www.goldencrown.biz* *Closed Mon.*

$ **La Crepe Michel.** *French.* When red-or-green chile overload sets in, Old Town does offer an antidote: this tiny, French creperie tucked down a side alley, in what feels like a secret garden. Salads, steak frites, and a lovely dessert selection are foils for the nicely presented crepes, both *salées* (with salmon and aspargas) and *sucrées* (with chocolate). Is there a wine list? Mais oui! *Average main: $12* *400 San Felipe St. NW, Old Town, Albuquerque, New Mexico, USA* *505/242–1251* *www.lacrepemichel.com* *Closed Mon.*

$ **Monica's El Portal.** *Modern Mexican.* Locals in the know

FAMILY favor this authentic New Mexican restaurant on the west side of Old Town over the more famous, though less reliable, standbys around Old Town Plaza. Monica's has a prosaic dining room plus a cute tiled patio, and the service is friendly and unhurried. If you've never had *chicharrones* (fried pork skins), try them here with beans stuffed inside a flaky sopaipilla. Or consider the traditional blue-corn chicken or beef enchiladas, and the savory green-chile stew. This is honest, home-style food, and lunch here may just fill you up for the rest of the day. *Average main: $8* *321 Rio Grande Blvd. NW, Old Town, Albuquerque, USA* *505/247–9625* *Closed Mon. No dinner weekends.*

$$ **Seasons Rotisserie & Grill.** *Contemporary.* Upbeat yet elegant, this Old Town eatery is an easy place to have a business lunch or a dinner date, and oenophiles will revel in its well-chosen cellar. The kitchen serves innovative grills and pastas, such as wood-roasted duck breast with Gorgonzola–sweet-potato gratin and grilled Colorado lamb with Moroccan couscous, sautéed haricots verts, and cherry-mint demi-glace; great starters include pan-seared crab cakes with cilantro-lime aioli, and sweet-corn griddle cakes with marsala-fig chutney and almond-pepper tapenade. The rooftop patio and bar provides evening cocktails and lighter meals. *Average main: $18* *2031 Mountain Rd. NW, Old Town, Albuquerque, USA* *505/766–5100* *www.seasonsonthenet.com* *No lunch weekends.*

$$ **Vinaigrette.** *American.* This outpost of the popular Santa Fe establishment has been packed since it opened on the eastern reaches of Old Town in 2012. Salads are the thing, some more robust than others; carnivorous types are not ignored. Fresh greens and creative, though oddly bland, dressings

and sides (from scallops to flank steak) offer infinite, albeit somewhat pricey, possibilities. Soups and a sweet range of desserts round out the menu. Vinaigrette's industrial-style ceiling lends an airy feel—the place brims with natural light—but the unmuffled acoustics that result can make conversation a challenge. *Average main: $18 1828 Central Ave. SW, Old Town, Albuquerque, New Mexico, USA 505/842–5507 www.vinaigretteonline.com.*

DOWNTOWN

$$$ **Artichoke Café.** *Contemporary.* Locals praise the Artichoke for its service and French, American, and Italian dishes often prepared with organic ingredients. Specialties include house-made ravioli stuffed with ricotta and butternut squash with a white wine, sage, and butter sauce; and pan-seared sea scallops wrapped in prosciutto with red potatoes, haricots verts, and wax beans. The building is about a century old, in the historic Huning Highland district in the emerging EDo section of Downtown, but the decor is modern. *Average main: $22 424 Central Ave. SE, Downtown, Albuquerque, USA 505/243–0200 www.artichokecafe.com Reservations essential No lunch weekends.*

★ $ Fodor's Choice **Farina Pizzeria & Wine Bar.** *Pizza.* The team at the Artichoke Café, just across the street, has opened this stellar pizza lounge inside an ancient former grocery store with hardwood floors, exposed-brick walls, pressed-tin ceiling, and a couple of rows of wooden tables along with a long bar. This noisy, spirited place doles out exceptionally tasty pizzas with blistering-hot crusts and imaginative toppings; the Salsiccia, with sweet-fennel sausage, roasted onions, and mozzarella, has plenty of fans. Finish with rich butterscotch *budino* (Italian pudding), and take note of the extensive, fair-priced list of wines by the glass. *Average main: $16 510 Central Ave. SE, Downtown, Albuquerque, New Mexico, USA 505/243–0130 www.farinapizzeria.com No lunch weekends.*

★ $ Fodor's Choice **The Grove Café & Market.** *Café.* This airy, modern establishment is a local favorite that features locally grown, seasonal specials at reasonable prices. Enjoy such fresh, quality treats as Grove Pancakes with fresh fruit, crème fraîche, local honey, and real maple syrup; a Farmers Salad with roasted golden beets, Marcona almonds, goat cheese, and lemon-basil vinaigrette; or an aged Genoa salami sandwich with olive tapenade, arugula, and provolone on an artisanal sourdough bread. You can dine on the

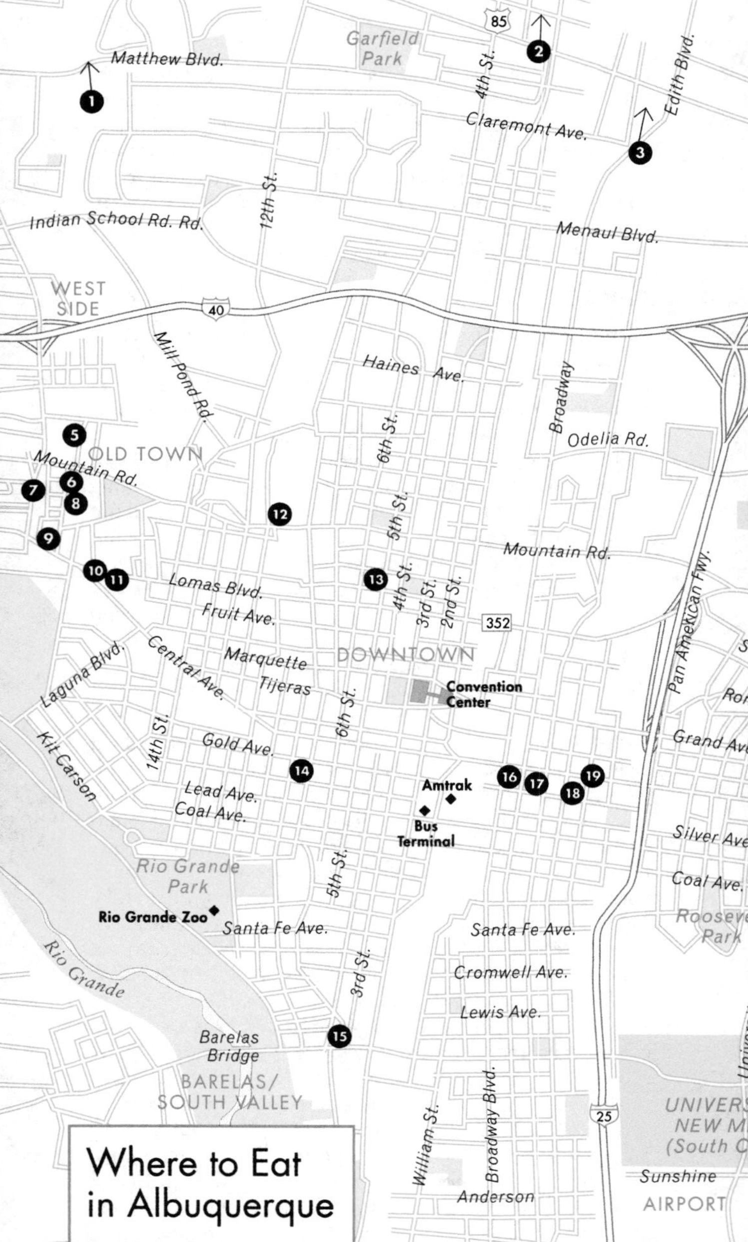
Where to Eat in Albuquerque
Matthew Blvd.
Garfield Park
85
4th St.
Claremont Ave.
Edith Blvd.
Indian School Rd. Rd.
12th St.
Menaul Blvd.
WEST SIDE
40
Mill Pond Rd.
Haines Ave.
Broadway
Odelia Rd.
OLD TOWN
Mountain Rd.
6th St.
5th St.
Mountain Rd.
Lomas Blvd.
Fruit Ave.
4th St.
3rd St.
2nd St.
352
Pan American Fwy.
Laguna Blvd.
Central Ave.
Marquette
Tijeras
DOWNTOWN
Convention Center
6th St.
Grand Ave.
Kit Carson
14th St.
Gold Ave.
Amtrak
Lead Ave.
Coal Ave.
Bus Terminal
Silver Ave.
Rio Grande Park
5th St.
Coal Ave.
Rio Grande Zoo
Santa Fe Ave.
Santa Fe Ave.
Rio Grande
3rd St.
Cromwell Ave.
Lewis Ave.
Barelas Bridge
BARELAS/ SOUTH VALLEY
Broadway Blvd.
William St.
25
Sunshine
Anderson
AIRPORT
Gibson Blvd.

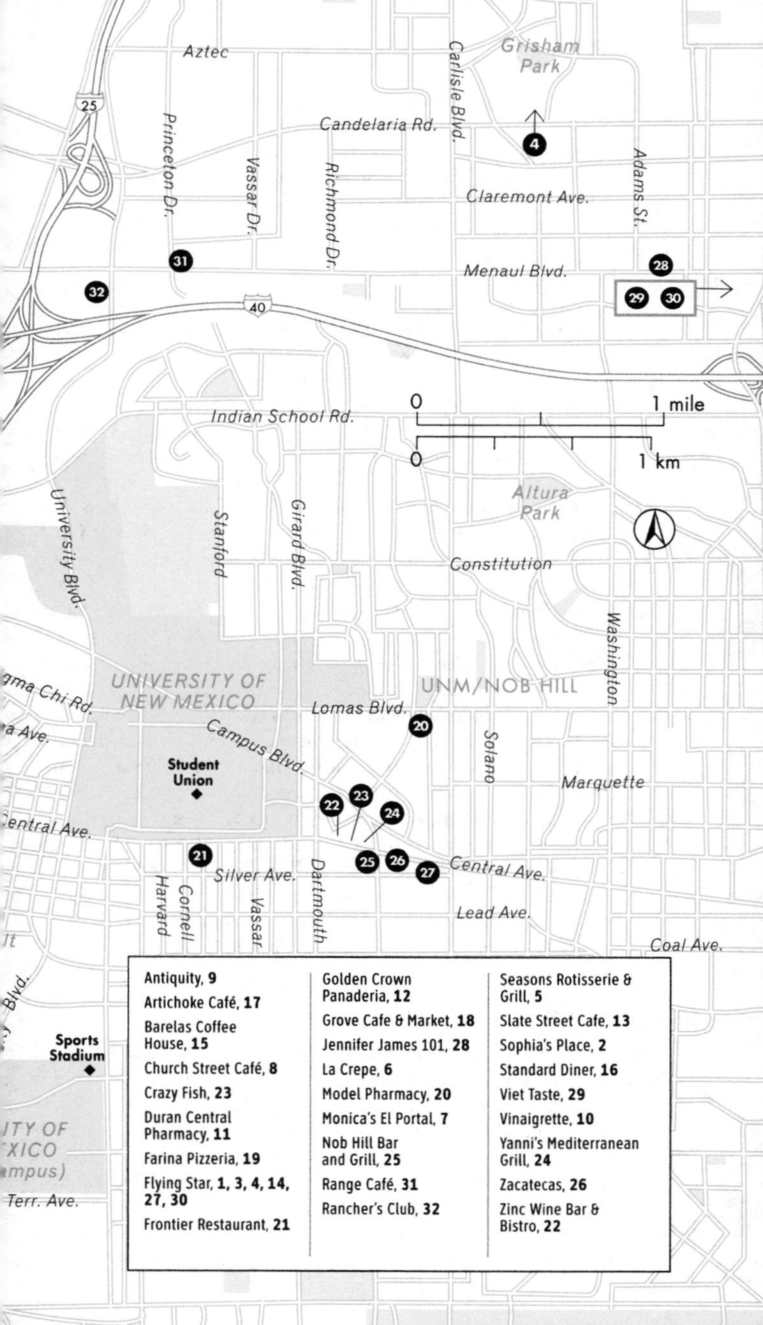

Aztec
Grisham Park
Carlisle Blvd.
Candelaria Rd.
Princeton Dr.
Vassar Dr.
Richmond Dr.
Claremont Ave.
Adams St.
Menaul Blvd.
Indian School Rd.
0
1 mile
0
1 km
Altura Park
University Blvd.
Stanford
Girard Blvd.
Constitution
Washington
UNIVERSITY OF NEW MEXICO
UNM/NOB HILL
Lomas Blvd.
Campus Blvd.
Solano
Student Union
Marquette
Central Ave.
Silver Ave.
Harvard
Cornell
Vassar
Dartmouth
Central Ave.
Lead Ave.
Coal Ave.
Sports Stadium
Terr. Ave.
Antiquity, **9**
Artichoke Café, **17**
Barelas Coffee House, **15**
Church Street Café, **8**
Crazy Fish, **23**
Duran Central Pharmacy, **11**
Farina Pizzeria, **19**
Flying Star, **1, 3, 4, 14, 27, 30**
Frontier Restaurant, **21**
Golden Crown Panaderia, **12**
Grove Cafe & Market, **18**
Jennifer James 101, **28**
La Crepe, **6**
Model Pharmacy, **20**
Monica's El Portal, **7**
Nob Hill Bar and Grill, **25**
Range Café, **31**
Rancher's Club, **32**
Seasons Rotisserie & Grill, **5**
Slate Street Cafe, **13**
Sophia's Place, **2**
Standard Diner, **16**
Viet Taste, **29**
Vinaigrette, **10**
Yanni's Mediterranean Grill, **24**
Zacatecas, **26**
Zinc Wine Bar & Bistro, **22**

arbored patio. Or come by for a loose-leaf tea or latte with a cupcake. The market sells an impressive mix of chocolates, cheeses, and gourmet foods. *Average main: $11* *600 Central Ave. SE, Downtown, Albuquerque, New Mexico, USA* *505/248–9800* *www.thegrovecafemarket.com* *Closed Mon. No dinner.*

$$ ✕ **Slate Street Cafe.** *Eclectic.* A high-energy, high-ceiling dining room with a semicircular, central wine bar and modern lighting, this stylish restaurant sits amid pawn shops and bail-bond outposts on a quiet, unprepossessing side street Downtown. But once inside, you'll find a sophisticated, colorful space serving memorable, modern renditions of classic American fare, such as fried chicken and meat loaf. The starters are notable, including grilled sesame-crusted ahi with wasabi cream, and bruschetta topped with honey-cured ham and Brie. Banana-stuffed brioche French toast is a favorite at breakfast and weekend brunch. More than 25 wines by the glass are served. *Average main: $18* *515 Slate St. NW, Downtown, Albuquerque, USA* *505/243–2210* *www.slatestreetcafe.com* *No dinner Sun.–Mon.*

$$ ✕ **Standard Diner.** *Contemporary.* The Standard occupies a 1930's Texaco station with high ceilings and massive plate-glass windows. It's a notch up from casual, serving upscale yet affordable takes on diner standbys. The extensive menu dabbles in meal-size salads (try the Southwestern cobb), burgers (including a terrific one topped with bourbon butter), sandwiches, and traditional diner entrées given nouvelle flourishes (country-fried tuna with green chile pesto, bacon-wrapped and porcini-crusted meat loaf). Kick everything up with a side of truffle-pecorino french fries, and save room for the fancy milk shakes in novel flavors such as cherry almond or Guinness. *Average main: $16* *320 Central Ave. SE, Downtown, Albuquerque, USA* *505/243–1440* *www.standarddiner.com* *No breakfast Mon.–Fri.*

BARELAS/SOUTH VALLEY

★ Fodor's Choice ✕ **Barelas Coffee House.** *Latin American.* Barelas
$ may look like a set in search of a script, but it's the real deal: diners come from all over the city to sup in this old-fashioned chile parlor in the Hispanic Historic Route 66 neighborhood south of Downtown. You may notice looks of quiet contentment on the faces of the many dedicated chile eaters as they dive into their bowls of Barelas's potent red. There's also tasty breakfast fare. The staff treats everybody like an old friend—indeed, many of the regulars who

come here have been fans of Barelas for decades. *Average main: $8 1502 4th St. SW, Barelas/South Valley, Albuquerque, New Mexico, USA 505/843–7577 Reservations not accepted Closed Sun. No dinner.*

UNM/NOB HILL

$ **Crazy Fish.** *Japanese.* A good bet for relatively straightforward sushi and sashimi, Crazy Fish is an attractive, upbeat storefront space with minimal fuss and gimmickry—just clean lines and a black-and-gray color scheme (and a subtle street-side sign one could easily miss). Friendly young servers whisk out plates of fresh food to a mix of students and yuppies. In addition to sushi, the kitchen prepares such favorites as crispy chicken, garlic-peppered beef, and seared-albacore salad with a ginger-soy dressing. Tempura-fried bananas with chocolate ice cream make for a sweet ending. *Average main: $16 3015 Central Ave. NE, UNM/Nob Hill, Albuquerque, New Mexico, USA 505/232–3474 www.crazyfishabq.com Closed Mon. No lunch weekends.*

$ **Flying Star.** *Café.* Flying Star has become a staple and miniphenom here, and although it's a chain, it's locally owned and—just as at its Satellite Coffee spots around town—each outpost offers something a little different. The cavernous Downtown branch is a favorite for its striking setting inside the historic Southern Union Gas Co. building and its unexpected modernist motif; the North Valley locale is notable for its shaded outdoor patio. At the original Nob Hill space, the crowd is youthful and bohemian, and the space tighter. The concept works on many levels: it's a newsstand, late-night coffeehouse (there's free Wi-Fi), and an order-at-the-counter restaurant serving a mix of creative Asian, American, and New Mexican dishes (plus several types of wine and beer). Options include Rosemary Chicken with Couscous Risotto, MOO-ve Over Meat Veggie Burger, Tossed Cobb salad with tangy tomatillo dressing, turkey-and-Jack-cheese-melt sandwiches, and an egg- and chile-packed "graburrito." Desserts change often, but count on a tantalizing array. For a winning pick-me-up, employ some strong hot coffee to wash down a tall slice of the fantastic coconut cream pie. *Average main: $11 3416 Central Ave. SE, UNM/Nob Hill, Albuquerque, New Mexico, USA 505/255–6633 www.flyingstarcafe.com.*

$ **Frontier Restaurant.** *Café.* This definitive student hangout across from UNM is open daily until 1 am for inexpensive diner-style American and New Mexican chow. A notch up from a fast-food joint, it's open later than most such spots in town, and the breakfast burritos are terrific. Featured along with the John Wayne and Elvis artwork in this sprawling '70s spot are oversize cinnamon buns. *Average main: $7 ✉ 2400 Central Ave. SE, at Cornell Dr. SE, UNM/Nob Hill, Albuquerque, New Mexico, USA ☎ 505/266–0550 ⊕ www.frontierrestaurant.com.*

★ Fodor's Choice ✕ **Jennifer James 101.** *Eclectic.* Helmed by and
$$$ named for one of New Mexico's most respected chefs, this small eatery is an imperative for foodies, locals, and fans of Jennifer James's previous restaurants around town. The menu is limited, and reservations are a must, but once you take your seat in the simple, high-ceilinged dining room in an unassuming shopping center, you're in for a treat. The menu changes seasonally; perhaps an appetizer of salt-cured foie gras with mâche and a balsamic-pomegranate reduction, or a main dish featuring wild boar braised with red wine and rosemary and served with polenta, grilled radicchio, and Gorgonzola. Thursday nights are even more special: a $25 multi-course menu is on offer as well. There's also a carefully considered wine list that includes several surprisingly affordable, good bottles. *Average main: $24 ✉ 4615 Menaul Blvd. NE, Uptown/East Side, Albuquerque, USA ☎ 505/884–3860 ⊕ www.jenniferjames101.com ⚠ Reservations essential ⊗ No lunch Sun. and Mon.*

$ ✕ **Model Pharmacy.** *American.* Forget the ersatz Route 66–
FAMILY blazoned diners down on Central Avenue—a short hop north gets you an experience that's a cut above. Soda fountain, check; custom grilled-to-order sandwiches, check; friendly, speedy service, check. Model has been at this location since the '80s, but it first opened across the street in 1947, and it's still got the spirit, and the goods: Milk shakes, egg creams, rickeys, fresh fruit cobblers. The compact lunchroom serves until 3 pm or so. Enjoy the delightful mobiles that swirl high above; high-end personal care items and fine-art cards and stationery complete the scene. *Average main: $9 ✉ 3636 Monte Vista Blvd NE, UNM/Nob Hill, Albuquerque, New Mexico, USA ☎ 505/255–8686 ⊕ modelpharmacy.com ⊗ No dinner.*

$ ✕ **Nob Hill Bar and Grill.** *American.* The dapper and nearly always packed Nob Hill Bar and Grill is a draw for its delicious modern takes on American classics. While the staff's youthful and energetic personality can be rough on the edges, and they don't always have the wine you chose on hand, the dining room and bar's swanky yet still unfussy decor are big plusses. Tuck into a plate of applewood-smoked chicken wings with Coca-Cola barbecue sauce, or nachos topped with ahi tuna, before feasting on hearty mains like steak-frites with garlic-parsley fries, and a terrific veggie burger fashioned out of *edamame* (green soy beans) and wild mushrooms, and served with ginger-lime mayo. *Average main: $16 3128 Central Ave. SE, UNM/Nob Hill, Albuquerque, New Mexico, USA 505/266–4455 www.upscalejoint.com Closed Mon.*

$$$$ **Rancher's Club.** *Steakhouse.* This clubby, old-world steak house in the Crowne Plaza Hotel (formerly the Albuquerque Hilton) is popular with deep-pocketed carnivores for its aged steaks and ribs. It may not be as stellar as it once was, but it's still the best in town of its type. The dining room is hung with saddles, mounted bison heads, and ranching-related art. If you want to impress a date or clients, order the fillet of Wagyu Kobe beef with creamed spinach, lobster-mashed potatoes, and morel-mushroom jus. Other standouts include elk chops, Alaskan wild salmon, and porterhouse steak. *Average main: $28 Crowne Plaza, 1901 University Blvd. NE, UNM/Nob Hill, Albuquerque, New Mexico, USA 505/889–8071 therancherscluboffnm.com No lunch.*

★ Fodor's Choice **Range Café.** *American.* A local standby for
$ any meal, the Range Cafe has a high-comfort quotient with
FAMILY hearty dishes like their spinach enchiladas, Matt's Hoosier Tenderloin Plate, and the generously plated salmon-berry salad. Breakfast, served until 3 pm, has fans for its house-made green-chile turkey sausage and the huevos rancheros. The food is fresh and well made, with dessert options heavy on pie. This University-area location takes its cues from the Bernalillo original, with roadtrip-wise decor, local art, and comfy booths. *Average main: $14 2200 Menaul Blvd. NE, UNM/Nob Hill, Albuquerque, New Mexico, USA 505/888–1660 www.rangecafe.com.*

9

$ **Viet Taste.** *Vietnamese.* Come here for another side of spicy hot. Excellent, authentic Vietnamese food is served up in this compact, modern, bamboo-accented restaurant. Ignore the fact that it's within one of Albuquerque's ubiquitous strip malls. Consider the popular *pho* (noodle soup) variations, order the tofu (or chicken or shrimp) spring rolls with tangy peanut sauce, dig into the spicy lemongrass with chicken, and all will be well. *Average main: $9 5721 Menaul Blvd. NE, UNM/Nob Hill, Albuquerque, New Mexico, USA 505/888–0101 Closed Sun.*

$$ **Yanni's Mediterranean Grill.** *Greek.* Yanni's is a convivial place where the food can run second to its refreshing azure-tiled ambience. Serving marinated grilled lamb chops with lemon and oregano, grilled yellowfin sole encrusted with Parmesan, *pastitsio* (a Greek version of mac and cheese), and spinach, feta, and roasted garlic pizzas, Yanni's also offers a vegetarian plate with good meatless moussaka, tabbouleh, spanakopita, and stuffed grape leaves. There's a huge patio off the main dining room, and next door you can sip cocktails and mingle with locals at their Lemoni Lounge. *Average main: $20 ✉ 3109 Central Ave. NE, UNM/Nob Hill, Albuquerque, New Mexico, USA ☎ 505/268–9250 www.yannisandlemoni.com.*

★ $$ Fodor's Choice × **Zacatecas.** *Mexican.* With the vibrant Zacatecas, The Compound's Mark Kiffin introduces an exciting New Mexican restaurant to the Albuquerque scene. Its blue facade and simple white walls inside—brightened by an array of festive Day-of-the-Dead papier-mâché masks—make sitting by one of the large open windows feel like a day on the zócalo. Chef Danny Marquez's creative offerings—*empanada de hongos* with *queso fresca* (tortillas with fresh mushrooms and cheese), tacos of slow-braised cochinita de pibil, serrano-spiked shrimp, and a complex chicken mole come to mind—are complemented by a range of tequilas, mezcals, and beer not readily found elsewhere in the state. *Average main: $15 ✉ 3423 Central Ave. NE, UNM/Nob Hill, Albuquerque, New Mexico, USA ☎ 505/255–8226 zacatecastacos.com.*

$$$ × **Zinc Wine Bar & Bistro.** *Contemporary.* A snazzy spot in lower Nob Hill, fairly close to UNM, Zinc captures the essence of a San Francisco neighborhood bistro with its high ceilings, hardwood floors, and white tablecloths and dark-wood straight-back café chairs. You can sample wine from the long list or listen to live music downstairs in the Cellar Bar. Consider the starter of crispy duck-confit eggrolls with curry-chile-lime dipping sauce; or the main dish of seared scallops with wild-rice–cranberry pilaf and a tarragon-crayfish beurre blanc. The kitchen uses organic ingredients whenever available. Don't miss the exceptional weekend brunch. *Average main: $22 ✉ 3009 Central Ave. NE, UNM/Nob Hill, Albuquerque, New Mexico, USA ☎ 505/254–9462 www.zincabq.com.*

LOS RANCHOS/NORTH VALLEY

$ × **Sophia's Place.** *Café.* Devotees can't get enough of the *muy buenos* berry pancakes with real maple syrup, breakfast burritos (with the *papas*—or potatoes—inside, so ask if you'd like them out instead), enchiladas sprinkled with *cotija* (a mild, crumbly cow's milk cheese), and just about anything the kitchen whips up. Dishes range from creative and generous salads and chipotle-chile bacon cheeseburgers to udon noodles and fish tacos. In Los Ranchos de Albuquerque, in the heart of the North Valley, Sophia's (named after the Alice Waters–trained chef-owner's daughter) is a simple neighborhood spot, yet one that people drive out of their way for—especially for the weekend brunch. Everything is fresh, often organic, prettily presented, and always made-to-order. *Average main: $10 ✉ 6313 4th St. NW, Los Ranchos/North Valley, Albuquerque, New Mexico, USA ☎ 505/345–3935 Reservations not accepted ⊙ No dinner Sun.*

WHERE TO STAY

With a few notable independently owned exceptions—Hotel Albuquerque, Hotel Andaluz, and Hotel Parq Central—Albuquerque's lodging options fall into two categories: modern chain hotels and motels, and distinctive and typically historic inns and B&Bs.

If you are seeking charm and history, both Los Poblanos Inn in the North Valley and the Hotel Parq Central in EDo are tops; many others in this realm are described below. In Old Town, the Best Western Rio Grande Inn has a real Southwest feel and is very fairly priced to boot. And the Nativo Lodge makes a stay along the chain-strewn north Interstate 25 corridor a more memorable experience. If you need to be near the airport, there's no shortage of economical, plain-Jane, franchise hotels there, though the Sheraton Airport is by far the nicest of the lot. But keep in mind that it's barely a 15-minute ride from the airport to the more interesting neighborhoods and lodging opportunities covered here. And, wherever you stay in Albuquerque, you can generally count on finding rates considerably lower than the national average, and much cheaper than those in Santa Fe.

Prices in the hotel reviews are the lowest cost of a standard double room in high season, excluding taxes, service charges, and meal plans. For expanded reviews, facilities, and current deals, visit Fodors.com.

OLD TOWN

$$ **Best Western Rio Grande Inn.** *Hotel.* Although part of the Best Western chain, this contemporary four-story low-rise just off Interstate 40—a 10-minute walk from Old Town's plaza—has an attractive Southwestern design and furnishings, plus such modern touches as free Wi-Fi. **Pros:** free

BEST BETS: ALBUQUERQUE LODGINGS

Fodor's offers a selective listing of quality lodging experiences in every price range, from the city's best budget beds to its most sophisticated luxury hotels. Here, we've compiled our top recommendations by experience. Properties that provide a particularly remarkable experience in their price range are designated with the Fodor's Choice logo.

Fodor's Choice ★

Hotel Parq Central $$, Los Poblanos Inn $$$, Mauger Estate B&B Inn $$,

BEST HOTEL BAR

Hotel Albuquerque at Old Town $$$, Hotel Andaluz $$, Hotel Parq Central $$, Sheraton Albuquerque Airport Hotel $

BEST FOR KIDS

Best Western Rio Grande Inn $$, Embassy Suites Hotel Albuquerque $$, Hotel Albuquerque at Old Town $$$

ROMANTIC

Downtown Historic Bed & Breakfasts of Albuquerque $$, Hotel Andaluz $$, Los Poblanos Inn $$$, Mauger Estate B&B Inn $$

BEST SERVICE

Böttger Mansion of Old Town $$, Cinnamon Morning B&B $$, Hotel Parq Central $$, Los Poblanos Inn $$$, Mauger Estate B&B Inn $$

BEST VIEWS

Hotel Albuquerque at Old Town $$$, Hotel Parq Central $$, Hyatt Regency Albuquerque $$, Los Poblanos Inn $$$, Sheraton Albuquerque Airport Hotel $

shuttle to airport and around town within 1-mile radius; excellent value. **Cons:** it's a hike from the rear rooms to the front desk; a bit close to the interstate. *Rooms from: $160 ✉ 1015 Rio Grande Blvd. NW, Old Town, Albuquerque, USA ☎ 505/843–9500, 800/959–4726 🌐 www.riograndeinn.com ⇨ 173 rooms.*

$$ **Böttger Mansion of Old Town.** *B&B/Inn.* The current owners of Böttger Mansion, a National Register property built in 1912, have thoughtfully refurbished the rooms, emphasizing fine woodwork and other details—a clawfoot tub, a lovely mural by the original owner's grandson, or a pressed-tin ceiling. **Pros:** tour packages are available; close to dining and attractions. **Cons:** stair-access only to the upper rooms. *Rooms from: $160 110 San Felipe St. NW, Old Town, Albuquerque, USA 505/243–3639, 800/758–3639 www.bottger.com 7 rooms, 1 2-bedroom suite Breakfast.*

$$ **Casas de Sueños.** *B&B/Inn.* This historic compound (it's a National Register property) of 1930s- and '40s-era adobe casitas is perfect if you're seeking seclusion and quiet, yet desire proximity to museums, restaurants, and shops. **Pros:** charming and tucked away; some private patios. **Cons:** rooms vary greatly in amenities and configuration—some are more enchanting than others. *Rooms from: $200 310 Rio Grande Blvd. SW, on the south side of Central Ave., Old Town, Albuquerque, USA 505/247–4560, 800/665–7002 www.casasdesuenos.com 21 casitas Breakfast.*

$$$ **Hotel Albuquerque at Old Town.** *Hotel.* This 11-story Southwestern-style hotel rises distinctly above Old Town's ancient structures. **Pros:** the high-ceiling, rustically furnished, Territorial-style lobby is a comfy place to hang out, as are the lovely gardens and pool patio out back. **Cons:** no seating provided for the room balconies; a/c units are loud. *Rooms from: $290 800 Rio Grande Blvd. NW, Old Town, Albuquerque, USA 505/843–6300, 877/901–7666 www.hhandr.com/albuquerque 168 rooms, 20 suites No meals.*

9

DOWNTOWN

$$ **DoubleTree Hotel.** *Hotel.* A cool, mellow palette distinguishes the sleek, contemporary lobby of this 15-story Downtown hotel, with attractive, pale-gold rooms that contain mid-20th-century-inspired furnishings and art. **Pros:** shuttle service to the airport and destinations in a 3-mile radius is available; nicely updated rooms and amenities; free Wi-Fi. **Cons:** not all rooms have mountain views; parking has daily fee. *Rooms from: $140 201 Marquette Ave. NW, Downtown, Albuquerque, USA 505/247–3344, 800/222–8733 www.doubletree.com 295 rooms No meals.*

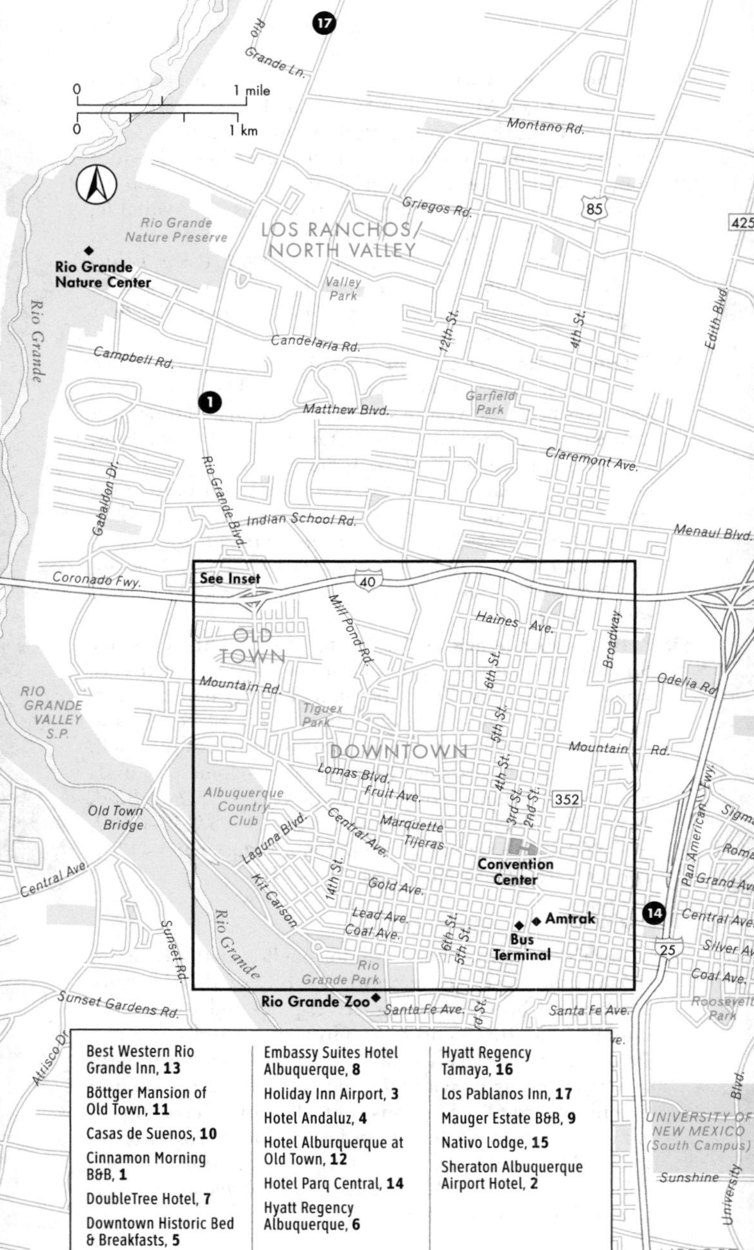

0
1 mile
0
1 km
Rio Grande Ln.
Montano Rd.
Griegos Rd.
85
425
Rio Grande Nature Preserve
LOS RANCHOS/ NORTH VALLEY
Rio Grande Nature Center
Valley Park
Rio Grande
12th St.
4th St.
Edith Blvd.
Candelaria Rd.
Campbell Rd.
Matthew Blvd.
Garfield Park
Claremont Ave.
Rio Grande Blvd.
Gabaldon Dr.
Indian School Rd.
Menaul Blvd.
Coronado Fwy.
See Inset
40
Mill Pond Rd.
Haines Ave.
Broadway
OLD TOWN
6th St.
Odelia Rd.
Mountain Rd.
RIO GRANDE VALLEY S.P.
Tiguex Park
5th St.
DOWNTOWN
Mountain Rd.
Lomas Blvd.
4th St.
Fruit Ave.
Albuquerque Country Club
352
Old Town Bridge
Laguna Blvd.
Central Ave.
Marquette
Tijeras
3rd St.
2nd St.
Pan American Fwy.
Sigma
Roma
Central Ave.
14th St.
Convention Center
Grand Ave.
Kit Carson
Gold Ave.
Sunset Rd.
Lead Ave.
Amtrak
Central Ave.
Coal Ave.
Bus Terminal
Silver Ave.
Rio Grande
6th St.
5th St.
25
Coal Ave.
Rio Grande Park
Rio Grande Zoo
Santa Fe Ave.
Santa Fe Ave.
Roosevelt Park
Sunset Gardens Rd.
Atrisco Dr.
Best Western Rio Grande Inn, 13
Böttger Mansion of Old Town, 11
Casas de Suenos, 10
Cinnamon Morning B&B, 1
DoubleTree Hotel, 7
Downtown Historic Bed & Breakfasts, 5
Embassy Suites Hotel Albuquerque, 8
Holiday Inn Airport, 3
Hotel Andaluz, 4
Hotel Alburquerque at Old Town, 12
Hotel Parq Central, 14
Hyatt Regency Albuquerque, 6
Hyatt Regency Tamaya, 16
Los Pablanos Inn, 17
Mauger Estate B&B, 9
Nativo Lodge, 15
Sheraton Albuquerque Airport Hotel, 2
UNIVERSITY OF NEW MEXICO (South Campus)
University Blvd.
Sunshine
AIRPORT

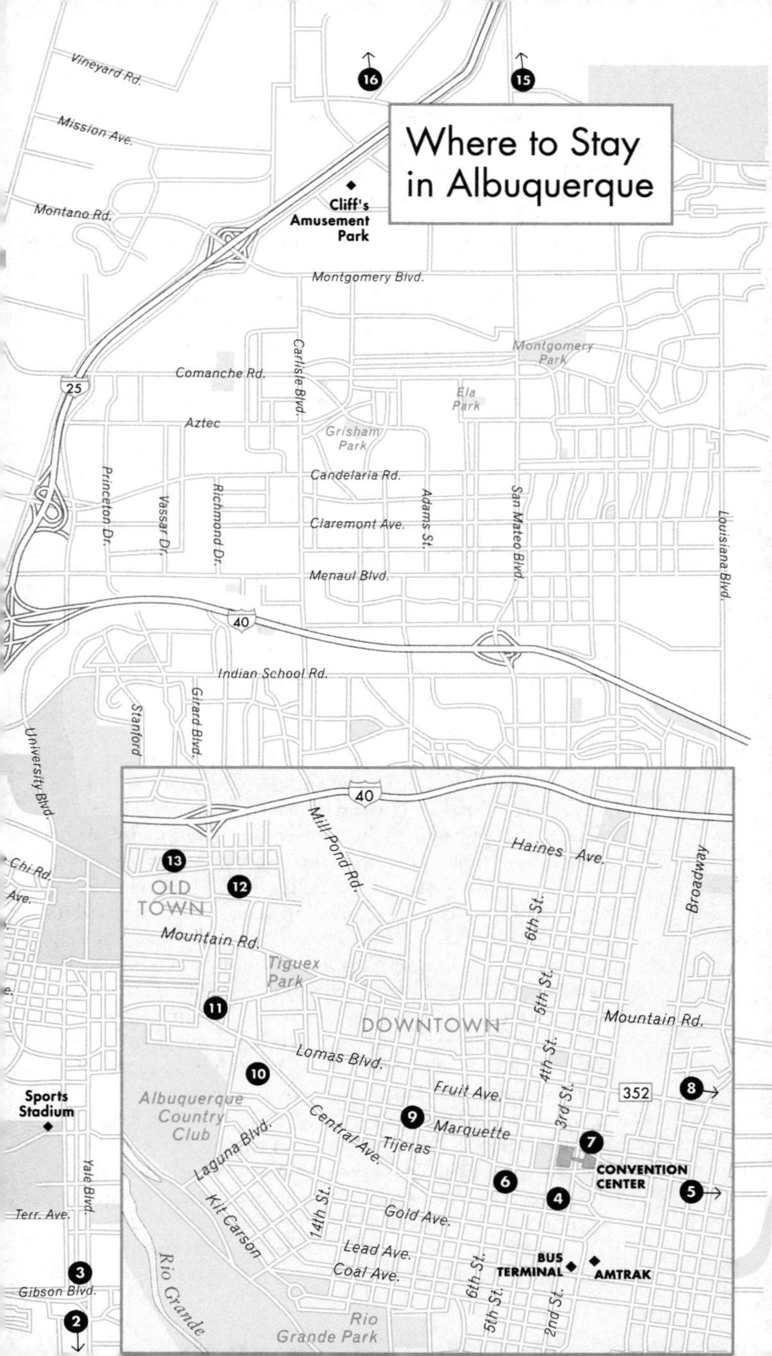

Where to Stay in Albuquerque
Vineyard Rd.
Mission Ave.
Montano Rd.
Cliff's Amusement Park
Montgomery Blvd.
Montgomery Park
Comanche Rd.
Carlisle Blvd.
25
Ela Park
Aztec
Grisham Park
Candelaria Rd.
Princeton Dr.
Vassar Dr.
Richmond Dr.
Claremont Ave.
Adams St.
San Mateo Blvd.
Louisiana Blvd.
Menaul Blvd.
40
Indian School Rd.
Stanford
Girard Blvd.
University Blvd.
Mill Pond Rd.
Haines Ave.
OLD TOWN
Broadway
6th St.
Mountain Rd.
Tiguex Park
5th St.
DOWNTOWN
Mountain Rd.
4th St.
Lomas Blvd.
3rd St.
Fruit Ave.
352
Sports Stadium
Albuquerque Country Club
Central Ave.
Marquette
Tijeras
Laguna Blvd.
CONVENTION CENTER
Yale Blvd.
Kit Carson
14th St.
Gold Ave.
Lead Ave.
Coal Ave.
BUS TERMINAL
AMTRAK
Gibson Blvd.
Rio Grande
6th St.
5th St.
2nd St.
Rio Grande Park

$$ **Downtown Historic Bed & Breakfasts of Albuquerque.** *B&B/Inn.* Comprising a pair of grand early-20th-century homes as well as a private carriage house and one other cottage in the Huning Highland Historic District, this stunning property exudes romance. **Pros:** exquisite furnishings; intimate property but where guests have plenty of privacy and independence; central Downtown location. **Cons:** some may find the decor to be excessively antique. *Rooms from: $140 ✉ 207 High St., Downtown, Albuquerque, USA ☎ 505/842–0223, 888/342–0223 🌐 www.albuquerquebedandbreakfasts.com ⇨ 8 rooms, 2 cottages.*

$$ **Embassy Suites Hotel Albuquerque.** *Hotel.* This all-suites
FAMILY high-rise with a striking contemporary design sits on a bluff alongside Interstate 25, affording guests fabulous views of the Downtown skyline and vast desert mesas to the west, and the verdant Sandia Mountains to the east. **Pros:** quiet but convenient location adjacent to Interstate 25 and just south of Interstate 40; congenial staff. **Cons:** suites attract families in addition to business travelers; the occasional child run rampant may not appeal to all. *Rooms from: $200 ✉ 1000 Woodward Pl. NE, Downtown, Albuquerque, USA ☎ 505/245–7100, 800/362–2779 🌐 www.embassysuitesalbuquerque.com ⇨ 261 suites 🍽 Breakfast.*

$$ **Hotel Andaluz.** *Hotel.* Opened in 1939 by Conrad Hilton (who honeymooned here with Zsa Zsa Gabor), this glamorous 10-story hotel on the National Register of Historic Places was known as La Posada de Albuquerque until it was reinvented as a high-end boutique hotel in 2009. **Pros:** historic cachet aesthetic but with plenty of modern perks. **Cons:** street noise can carry into rooms; may be too dark and moody for some; fitness center access is across street. *Rooms from: $250 ✉ 125 2nd St. NW, Downtown, Albuquerque, USA ☎ 505/242–9090, 800/777–5732 🌐 www.hotelandaluz.com ⇨ 107 rooms, 7 suites 🍽 No meals.*

★ Fodor's Choice **Hotel Parq Central.** *Hotel.* One of the more
$$ imaginative adaptations of a disused building, the landmark Parq Central occupies a striking three-story former AT & SF Railroad employees' hospital that dates to 1926. **Pros:** wonderfully landscaped historic building; smartly designed rooms are very quiet, thanks to sound-blocking windows; free shuttle to airport and within 3 miles of hotel; hip clientele. **Cons:** desks in rooms are smallish secretary types (though hotel will provide a larger one on request). *Rooms from: $200 ✉ 806 Central Ave. SE, Downtown, Albuquerque, USA ☎ 505/242–0040 🌐 www.hotelparqcentral.com ⇨ 56 rooms, 18 suites 🍽 Breakfast.*

$$ **Hyatt Regency Albuquerque.** *Hotel.* Adjacent to the Albuquerque Convention Center, this upscale high-rise comprises a pair of soaring, desert-color towers that figure prominently in the city's skyline. **Pros:** easy walking distance from the KiMo Theatre and Downtown's art galleries and restaurants, and a quick cab (or bus) ride elsewhere; the views, lap pool, and well-equipped 24/7 fitness center. **Cons:** until you get your bearings the layout can seem somewhat mazelike; no views on lower floors. *Rooms from: $180* *330 Tijeras Ave. NW, Downtown, Albuquerque, USA* *505/842–1234, 800/233–1234* *www.albuquerque.hyatt.com* *395 rooms, 14 suites* *No meals.*

★ **$$** Fodor's Choice **Mauger Estate B&B Inn.** *B&B/Inn.* This well-run B&B has retained many of its original 1897 Queen Anne–style architectural elements, including oval windows with beveled and "feather-pattern" glass, hardwood floors, high ceilings, a redbrick exterior, and a front veranda. **Pros:** pleasant common room, with a library and a late-afternoon cookies-and-wine spread; responsive and informed innkeeper; good breakfasts, which they will pack to go on request. **Cons:** at night, on the western fringe of Downtown, it can feel a bit sketchy for walking, but parking is secure. *Rooms from: $130* *701 Roma Ave. NW, Downtown, Albuquerque, USA* *505/242–8755, 800/719–9189* *www.maugerbb.com* *8 rooms, 1 2-bedroom town house* *Breakfast.*

LOS RANCHOS/NORTH VALLEY

$$ **Cinnamon Morning B&B.** *B&B/Inn.* A private, beautifully maintained, pet-friendly compound set back from the road and a 10-minute drive north of Old Town, Cinnamon Morning is just south of Rio Grande Nature Center State Park and a perfect roost if you want to be close to the city's wineries and the launching areas used by most hot-air-ballooning companies. **Pros:** host will gladly help with travel ideas and planning. **Cons:** cancellations must be made 14 days ahead; you need a car to get around town from here. *Rooms from: $130* *2700 Rio Grande Blvd. NW, Los Ranchos/North Valley, Albuquerque, New Mexico, USA* *505/345–3541, 800/214–9481* *www.cinnamonmorning.com* *3 rooms, 1 casita, 1 guesthouse* *Breakfast.*

★ Fodor's Choice Hotel **Hyatt Regency Tamaya.** This spectacular large-
$$$ scale resort, on more than 500 acres on the Santa Ana
RESORT Pueblo (just outside Bernalillo), includes the superb Twin Warriors Golf Course, the 12,000-square-foot Tamaya Mist Spa & Salon, and a cultural museum and learning center. **Pros:** this is the place to come to get away; it's in the direction of Santa Fe, making it a good base for day trips to that area. **Cons:** it's way out there—factor in a 30-minute drive from Albuquerque. *Rooms from: $189 ✉ 1300 Tuyuna Trail, Santa Ana Pueblo, USA ☎ 505/867–1234, 800/633–7313 ⊕ www.tamaya.hyatt.com 327 rooms, 23 suites.*

★ Fodor's Choice Hotel **Los Poblanos Historic Inn & Organic Farm.** *B&B/*
$$$ *Inn.* Designed in the 1930s by the renowned Pueblo Revival architect John Gaw Meem for a local political power couple, Los Poblanos stands today as a quintessential element of Albuquerque's North Valley and its pastoral soul. **Pros:** seasonal farm-to-fork dining; fine bedding and linens; day spa service available. **Cons:** peacocks may let out an occasional (and short) screech-like sound; dinner service is not always available; spa service is off-site, a short drive away. *Rooms from: $200 ✉ 4803 Rio Grande Blvd. NW, Los Ranchos/North Valley, Albuquerque, New Mexico, USA ☎ 505/344–9297, 866/344–9297 ⎙ 505/342–1302 ⊕ www.lospoblanos.com 14 guest rooms, 7 suites 🍽 Breakfast.*

NORTHEAST HEIGHTS

$ Hotel **Nativo Lodge.** *Hotel.* This five-story Heritage Hotels & Resorts property exudes character, especially in the expansive public areas, bar, and its Spirit Winds Cafe, which have an attractive Southwestern motif that includes hand-carved panels depicting symbols from Native American lore and river-rock walls. **Pros:** fitness center and year-round pool; perfect location for Balloon Fiesta, or when en route to Santa Fe. **Cons:** if your primary business is Downtown, this is a bit far north. *Rooms from: $80 ✉ 6000 Pan American Freeway NE, Northeast Heights, Albuquerque, USA ☎ 505/798–4300, 888/628–4861 ⊕ www.nativolodge.com 146 rooms, 2 suites 🍽 No meals.*

AIRPORT

$ **Holiday Inn Hotel & Suites Albuquerque Airport.** *Hotel.* Just west of the airport, this upscale, four-story hotel sits high on a bluff, affording nice views of Downtown and the western mesa as well as the Sandia Mountains. **Pros:** work areas are well lit, a plus for the business traveler. **Cons:** bland neighborhood—you'll need to drive or take cab to get to Downtown or Nob Hill. *Rooms from: $135 ✉ 1501 Sunport Pl. SE, Airport, Albuquerque, USA ☎ 505/944–2255, 800/465–4329 ⊕ www.holidayinnabq.com ⇨ 110 rooms, 20 suites ǀ⊙ǀ No meals.*

$ **Sheraton Albuquerque Airport Hotel.** *Hotel.* Only 200 yards from the airport, this 15-story hotel sits up high on a mesa with vast views of the Sandia Mountains to the east and Downtown Albuquerque to the northwest. **Pros:** short walk from airport (but they offer 24-hour free shuttle service too); sleek, appealing room decor. **Cons:** bland neighborhood—you'll need to drive or take cab to get Downtown or to Nob Hill, about 15 minutes away. *Rooms from: $130 ✉ 2910 Yale Blvd. SE, Airport, Albuquerque, USA ☎ 505/843–7000, 888/325–3535 ⊕ sheratonalbuquerqueairport.com ⇨ 276 rooms, 2 suites ǀ⊙ǀ No meals.*

NIGHTLIFE AND THE ARTS

For the 411 on arts and nightlife, consult the freebie weeklies Local IQ (⊕ *www.local-IQ.com*) and Alibi (⊕ *www.alibi.com*), and the monthly abqARTS & Entertainment paper (⊕ *www.abqarts.org*). For highlights on some of the best live music programming in town, go to ⊕ *ampconcerts.org*. The *Albuquerque Journal*'s (⊕ *www.abqjournal.com*) Friday "Venue" section provides listings as well.

NIGHTLIFE

BARS AND LOUNGES

Dirty Bourbon Dance Hall & Saloon. Two-step the night away, join the line dancers, or just show up for some free-range carousing. Live music fills the place Thursday through Sunday nights, where the crowd is eclectic, as is the musical line-up (from A Hawk and a Hacksaw or Fanfare Ciacarlia, to cowboy hat–wearing rockers like Dierks Bentley). It's today's version of *Urban Cowboy* nightlife, complete with a 1,300-square-foot dance floor. *✉ 9800 Montgomery Blvd. NE, Northeast Heights, Albuquerque, New Mexico, USA ☎ 505/296–2726 ⊕ www.thedirtybourbon.com.*

Effex. Albuquerque's sizable gay and lesbian community—and anyone else who had been seeking a jumping dance scene—rejoiced with the 2010 opening of Effex, a vibrant, centrally located, two-level nightclub with a huge rooftop bar and an even larger downstairs dance floor. ✉ *100 5th St. NW, UNM/Nob Hill, Albuquerque, New Mexico, USA* ☎ *505/842–8870* 🌐 *www.effexnightclub.com.*

O'Niell's Pub. O'Niell's Pub serves up the Irish comfort food you'd expect, along with a touch of Cajun and Mexican for variety, and presents jazz, bebop, and other music. The expansive patio is perfect for afternoon beer and snacks. ✉ *4310 Central Ave. SE, UNM/Nob Hill, Albuquerque, New Mexico, USA* ☎ *505/256–0564* 🌐 *www.oniells.com.*

BREWPUBS

The art of craft beer brewing is hardly new to Albuquerque—credit relative long-timers like Marble Brewery, Tractor Brewing, and Chama River Brewing for setting the bar. Award-winners abound, and the area now has at least a dozen microbreweries, with hoppy, big IPAs representing about 50% of the lot. But half the fun is trying out their seasonal beers. In addition to an annual bounty of brew fests (🌐 *www.nmbeer.org*), a few favored hangouts include:

Bosque Brewing Co. Striking nature photographs line this well-appointed classic pub, which offers their memorable Brewers' Boot Amber Ale year-round and seasonal specialties like Doppelbier, a double German ale—and savory repasts to accompany them. ✉ *8900 San Mateo Blvd., Northeast Heights, Albuquerque, New Mexico, USA* ☎ *505/750–7596* 🌐 *www.bosquebrewing.com.*

I.V.B. Canteen. Music, beer, eats (bratwurst to veggie wrap)—not necessarily in that order—are generously offered here. Picture cut-offs, casual picnic seating, and a cold 2012 NM State Fair Gold Medal–winning "Pigtail Pilsner." ✉ *2381 Aztec Rd. NE, University of New Mexico, Albuquerque, New Mexico, USA* ☎ *505/881-2737* 🌐 *www.ilvicino.com/brewery.*

★ Fodor's Choice **La Cumbre Brewing Co.** La Cumbre's Elevated IPA took home gold in the 2011 Great American Brew Fest and Bronze in the 2012 World Beer Cup; its Malpais Stout caught silver that year. Food trucks await outside their taproom. ✉ *3313 Girard Blvd. NE, University of New Mexico, Albuquerque, New Mexico, USA* ☎ *505/917–4467* 🌐 *www.lacumbrebrewing.com.*

Marble Brewery. Distinctive craft brews like hoppy Imperial Red and rich Oatmeal Stout draw fans of artisan beer to Downtown's Marble Brewery. The elegant tasting room and pub, with an expansive outdoor patio, contains a beautiful 40-foot bar and serves tasty apps and sandwiches—there's live music some evenings, and the owners have opened a taproom on the Plaza in Santa Fe, too. ✉ *111 Marble Ave. NW, Downtown, Albuquerque, USA* ☎ *505/243–2739* 🌐 *www.marblebrewery.com.*

LIVE MUSIC

★ Fodor'sChoice **¡Globalquerque!.** Held at the National Hispanic Cultural Center, ¡Globalquerque! is a dazzling two-day world-music festival that puts Albuquerque on the global music map. In addition to three evening performances, a full day is devoted to (free) kids' programming. The festival's producer AMP Concerts is also the organization that lures acts like Lucinda Williams, Vieux Farka Toure, David Byrne, Philip Glass, and Richard Thompson to intimate venues all around town. ✉ *Albuquerque, USA* 🌐 *www.globalquerque.com.*

FAMILY

Outpost Performance Space. Outpost Performance Space programs an inspired, eclectic slate, from local *nuevo*-folk to techno, jazz, and traveling East Indian ethnic. Some big names—especially in the jazz world—show up at this special small venue, which is a key player in bringing the stellar New Mexico Jazz Festival to the state every July. ✉ *210 Yale Blvd. SE, UNM/Nob Hill, Albuquerque, New Mexico, USA* ☎ *505/268–0044* 🌐 *www.outpostspace.org.*

THE ARTS

Albuquerque has a remarkable wealth of local talent, but it also draws a surprising number of world-class stage performers from just about every discipline imaginable. Check the listings mentioned at the introduction to this section for everything from poetry readings, impromptu chamber music recitals, folk, jazz, and blues festivals, and formal symphony performances to film festivals, Flamenco Internacional, and theater.

MUSIC

★ Fodor'sChoice **Chatter Sunday.** Holding sway at 10:30 Sunday mornings, the Chatter chamber ensemble's classical music program draws a devoted crowd of regulars. Free cappuccino and a spoken word performance round out the one-hour shows. Expect the crème of local and guest performers—Santa Fe Opera stars often pop in during the season. Arrive early—seating (140 spots) and parking can get scarce. Tickets are $15 and available at the door only. ✉ *Kosmos @ Factory on 5th Art Space, 1715 5th St. NW, Downtown, Albuquerque, New Mexico, USA* 🌐 *www.chatterchamber.org.*

PERFORMING ARTS CENTERS

★ Fodor'sChoice **KiMo Theatre.** The stunning KiMo Theatre, an extravagantly ornamented 650-seat Pueblo Deco movie palace, is one of the best places in town to see anything. Jazz, dance, blues, film—everything from traveling road shows to an inspired city-sponsored film series (Hitchcock pre-Hollywood, for example)—might turn up here. Former Albuquerque resident Vivian Vance of *I Love Lucy* fame once performed on the stage; today you're more likely to see Laurie Anderson, Wilco, or a film-festival screening. ✉ *423 Central Ave. NW, Downtown, Albuquerque, USA* ☎ *505/768–3544* 🌐 *www.cabq.gov/kimo.*

Popejoy Hall. Popejoy Hall presents blockbuster Broadway touring shows, dance performances, concerts, from rock and pop to mariachi and classical, plus comedy acts, and lectures. **Rodey Theatre,** a smaller, 400-seat house in the same complex, stages experimental and niche works throughout the year. **Keller Hall,** also in the Center for the Arts, is a small venue with fine acoustics, a perfect home for the university's excellent chamber music program. ✉ *University of New Mexico Center for the Arts, North of Central Ave. entrance opposite Cornell Dr. SE, UNM/Nob Hill, Albuquerque, New Mexico, USA* ☎ *505/925–5858, 877/664–8661* 🌐 *www.popejoyhall.com.*

THEATER

Albuquerque Little Theatre. Albuquerque Little Theatre is a nonprofit community troupe that's been going strong since 1930. Its staff of professionals teams up with local volunteer talent to produce comedies, dramas, musicals, and mysteries. The company theater, across the street from Old Town, was built in 1936 and designed by John Gaw Meem. It contains an art gallery, a large lobby, and a cocktail lounge. ✉ *224 San Pasquale Ave. SW, Old Town, Albuquerque, USA* ☎ *505/242–4750* 🌐 *www.albuquerquelittletheatre.org.*

Tricklock Company. In January and February, theater fans of the fresh and new flock to the Revolutions International Theatre Festival, presented by the Tricklock Company. Recognized internationally, Tricklock's productions tour regularly and emphasize works that take it—and the audience—to the edge of theatrical possibility. ✉ *110 Gold Ave. SW, Downtown, Albuquerque, New Mexico, USA* ☎ *505/254–8393* 🌐 *www.tricklock.com.*

SHOPPING

Albuquerque's shopping strengths include a handful of cool retail districts, such as Nob Hill, Old Town, Downtown/EDo, and the North Valley. These are good neighborhoods for galleries; antiques; Native American arts; Old West finds and apparel; Mexican crafts; textiles, jewelry, pottery, glass, and other fine handicrafts by nationally acclaimed local artists; and home-furnishing shops; bookstores; and offbeat gift shops. Indoor flea markets are quite popular all around town, and everyone knows that museum gift shops are always worth a look-see—Albuquerque's are no exception.

ART GALLERIES

In addition to 516 Arts *(⇨ Downtown section in Exploring Albuquerque, above)*, and Tamarind Institute at UNM *(⇨ UNM/Nob Hill section in Exploring Albuquerque, above)*, Albuquerque has a solid and growing gallery scene. For comprehensive gallery listings, turn to the *Collector's Guide* (🌐 *www.collectorsguide.com*); Albuquerque ARTScrawl listings are online (🌐 *artscrawlabq.org*) as well as in the *abqARTS* monthly.

DSG. DSG, owned by John Cacciatore, handles works of paint, tapestry, sculpture, and photography by leading regional artists, including Frank McCulloch, Carol Hoy, Leo Neufeld, Larry Bell, Angus Macpherson, Jim Bagley, Nancy Kozikowski, and photographer Nathan Small. ✉ *510 14th St. SW, Old Town, Albuquerque, USA* ☎ *505/266–7751, 800/474–7751* 🌐 *www.dsg-art.com* ⏲ *By appointment only.*

Harwood Art Center. Harwood Art Center, on the fringe of Downtown and Old Town in the historic Sawmill/Wells Park neighborhood, is a remarkable city resource for its working-artist studios, classes, and as a gallery in its own right. Shows—predominantly of New Mexico–based artists working in nontraditional forms—take place in their historic brick school building and change monthly. ✉ *1114 7th St. NW, off Mountain Rd., Old Town, Albuquerque, USA* ☎ *505/242–6367* 🌐 *www.harwoodartcenter.org.*

9

IMEC. A sliver of a shop that's really a gallery, IMEC (International Metalsmith Exhibition Center) carries a superb range of work by a nationally renowned group of metal- and glass-work artisans. Many are New Mexico–based, like Luis Mojica, who does stunning work in sterling, resin, and mother-of-pearl, and Mary Kanda, whose intricate glass-bead pieces are richly colored. ✉ *101 Amherst Dr. SE, Nob Hill, Albuquerque, New Mexico, USA* ☎ *505/265–8352.*

Mariposa Gallery. Mariposa Gallery sells contemporary fine crafts, including jewelry, sculptural glass, works in mixed media and clay, and fiber arts. The changing exhibits focus on established and upcoming artists; its buyer's sharp eyes can result in real finds for the serious browser. ✉ *3500 Central Ave. SE, UNM/Nob Hill, Albuquerque, New Mexico, USA* ☎ *505/268–6828* 🌐 *www.mariposa-gallery.com.*

Matrix Fine Art. A 2,000-square-foot space specializing in works by some of the state's most acclaimed current artists, Matrix Fine Art carries an impressive collection of paintings and photography. ✉ *3812 Central Ave. SE, UNM/Nob Hill, Albuquerque, New Mexico, USA* ☎ *505/268–8952* 🌐 *www.matrixfineart.com.*

Richard Levy Gallery. A stellar roster of artists with an international following show at this shoebox-shaped gallery that would be right at home on either coast. Its clean lines are perfect for displaying pieces from photographers (Natsumi Hayashi, Hiroshi Sugimoto), multimedia artists (Eric Tillinghast, John Baldessari), and printmakers (Alex Katz, Ed Ruscha), as well as works from special global initiatives like ISEA 2012: Machine Wilderness and 2009's LAND/ART New Mexico. ✉ *514 Central Ave. SW, Downtown, Albuquerque, New Mexico, USA* ☎ *505/766–9888* 🌐 *www.levygallery.com* ⏲ *Sun.–Mon.*

Weyrich Gallery. Weyrich Gallery carries distinctive jewelry, fine art, Japanese tea bowls, woodblocks, hand-colored photography, and other largely Asian-inspired pieces, all at prices that are very reasonable. ✉ *2935–D Louisiana Blvd. NE, Uptown/East Side, Albuquerque, USA* ☎ *505/883–7410* 🌐 *www.weyrichgallery.com.*

SHOPS

BOOKS

Bookworks. One of the last of the great independents, Bookworks, maintains an eclectic stock of regional coffee-table books, a well-culled selection of modern fiction and nonfiction, architecture and design titles, and a (small) playground's worth of kids' books. Regular signings and readings draw some very big guns to this tiny treasure. ✉ *4022 Rio Grande Blvd. NW, Los Ranchos/North Valley, Albuquerque, New Mexico, USA* ☎ *505/344–8139* 🌐 *www.bkwrks.com.*

CLOTHING AND ACCESSORIES

★ Fodor's Choice **The Man's Hat Shop.** The Man's Hat Shop has been a mainstay on Central Avenue since 1946. Anyone, man or woman, who needs just the right hat, with just the right fit, will find what they're looking for—fedora, porkpie, cossack-style, or coonskin, and of course top-of-the-line western felt or straw. Owner Stuart Dunlap clearly loves his business and will help guide you among some 4,000 styles to a new chapeau that suits, or modify one you already have. ✉ *511 Central Ave. NW, Downtown, Albuquerque, New Mexico, USA* ☎ *505/247–9605* 🌐 *www.manshatshop.com.*

GIFTS, FOOD, AND TOYS

Beeps. Beeps, a Nob Hill favorite, carries cards, T-shirts, and amusing retro novelties. ✉ *Nob Hill Shopping Center, 3500 Central Ave. SE, UNM/Nob Hill, Albuquerque, New Mexico, USA* ☎ *505/262–1900.*

Candy Lady. Candy Lady is known for adult novelty candies, its tasty red- and green-chile brittle, its *Breaking Bad* "Blue Meth" rock candy, and a global assortment of licorice. Their homemade version is soft and delicious. Also on hand is fudge, chocolate truffles, and piñon caramels. ✉ *Romero St. NW, Old Town, Albuquerque, USA* ☎ *505/224–9837, 800/214–7731* 🌐 *www.thecandylady.com.*

★ Fodor's Choice FAMILY **The Farm Shop at Los Poblanos.** The Farm Shop at Los Poblanos, beside the beautiful country inn of the same name, carries books, culinary gadgets, the same housemade lavender lotions and soaps inn guests receive, and a considerable variety of artisan jams, vinegars, sauces, and gourmet goodies. A crew of well-cared-for pigs, goats, and ponies will entertain the kids while you shop. ✉ *4803 Rio Grande Blvd. NW, Los Ranchos/North Valley, Albuquerque, New Mexico, USA* ☎ *505/344–9297, 866/344–9297* 🌐 *www.lospoblanos.com.*

HISPANIC IMPORTS AND TRADITIONS

Casa Talavera. Peruse a wide selection of hand-painted Mexican Talavera tiles at this Old Town stalwart that's been in business since 1970. Prices are reasonable, making the colorful geometrics, florals, mural patterns, and solids, close to irresistible. Tin lighting fixtures as well as ceramic sink and cabinet knobs fill in the rest of the space in this DIY-inspiring shop. ✉ *621 Rio Grande Blvd., Old Town, Albuquerque, USA* ☎ *505/243–2413* 🌐 *www.casatalavera.com.*

Hispaniae. Sure it has every permutation of Our Lady of Guadalupe imaginable (on switch plates, tin tokens, etc.), but Nuestra Señora is just the tip of it. This long narrow space is well laid-out, yet packed with cleverly selected finds of the Latino craft kind, from cheery chickens formed from colorful recycled metal parts, to tile Christmas ornaments and hand-carved hardwood furnishings. ✉ *410 Romero St. NW, Old Town, Albuquerque, USA* ☎ *505/244–1533* 🌐 *www.hispaniae.com.*

NATIVE AMERICAN ARTS AND CRAFTS

Andrews Pueblo Pottery & Art Gallery. Andrews Pueblo Pottery carries a very special selection of Pueblo pottery, fetishes, kachina dolls, and baskets, as well as some contemporary and vintage Native jewelry, for the beginning and seasoned collector. Relocated in 2013 back to their original Old Town location, this shop is a well-respected stalwart in its field, and presents work from all 19 Pueblos as well as some Hopi and Navajo pieces. ✉ *400 San Felipe St. NW, Ste. 8, Old Town, Albuquerque, USA* ☎ *505/243–0414, 877/606–0543* 🌐 *www.andrewspp.com.*

Bien Mur Indian Market Center. Bien Mur Indian Market Center in Sandia Pueblo showcases the best of regional Native American rugs, jewelry, and crafts of all kinds. You can feel very secure about what you purchase at this trading post, and prices are fair. ✉ *100 Bien Mur Dr. NE, off Tramway Rd. NE east of I–25, Northeast Heights, Albuquerque, USA* ☎ *505/821–5400, 800/365–5400* 🌐 *www.sandiapueblo.nsn.us.*

SPORTS AND THE OUTDOORS

Albuquerque is blessed with an exceptional setting for outdoor sports, backed by a favorable, if sometimes unpredictable, climate. Biking and hiking are year-round activities here. Usually 10°F warmer than Santa Fe's, Albuquerque's winter days are often mild enough for most outdoor activities. The Sandias tempt you with challenging mountain adventures; the Rio Grande and its cottonwood forest, the Bosque, provide settings for additional outdoors pursuits.

BALLOONING

If you've never been ballooning, you may picture a bumpy ride, where changes in altitude produce the queasy feeling you get in a tiny propeller plane. But the experience is far calmer than that. The balloons are flown by licensed pilots (don't call them operators) who deftly turn propane-fueled flames on and off, climbing and descending to find winds blowing the way they want to go—there's no real steering involved, which makes the pilots' control that much more admirable. Pilots generally land balloons where the wind dictates, so chase vehicles pick you up and return you to your departure point, but particularly skilled pilots can use conditions created by the Box to land precisely where you started. Even without door-to-door service, many visitors rank a balloon ride over the Rio Grande Valley as their most memorable experience.

Several reliable companies around Albuquerque offer tours. A ride costs about $150 to $200 per person.

Rainbow Ryders. One of the best balloon tours is with Rainbow Ryders, an official ride concession for the Albuquerque International Balloon Fiesta. As part of the fun, you get to help inflate and pack away the balloon. In case you missed breakfast prior to your flight, a Continental breakfast and glass of champagne await your return. ✉ *Albuquerque, New Mexico, USA* ☎ *505/823–1111, 800/725–2477* 🌐 *www.rainbowryders.com.*

9

BICYCLING

With the creation of many lanes, trails, and dedicated bike paths (by 2013 an impressive 400 miles of designated bikeways were in place), Albuquerque's city leaders are recognized for their bike-friendly efforts—a serious challenge given the committed car culture of its residents.

Albuquerque Bicycle Map. The city's public works department produces the detailed Albuquerque Bicycle Map, which can be obtained free at most bike shops or viewed on their website. ✉ *Albuquerque, USA* ☎ *505/768–3550* 🌐 *www.cabq.gov/bike.*

Paseo del Bosque Recreation Trail. The Paseo del Bosque Recreation Trail, which follows along the Rio Grande Valley and runs flat for most of its 16-mile run, is one of the loveliest rides in town. ✉ *Albuquerque, USA* 🌐 *www.cabq.gov.*

RENTALS

Bike rental shops have clustered in that area, though rentals can be found closer to the mountains and at the Sandia Peak Ski Area as well.

The Bike Smith. The accommodating proprietors at The Bike Smith can sell you a new bike or fix you up with a rental (and any accessories needed) from an excellent selection of well-maintained mountain, road, and commuter bikes ($35–$50/day). ✉ *Rio Grande Plaza Center, 901 Rio Grande Blvd. NW, Suite D124, Old Town, Albuquerque, New Mexico, USA* ☎ *505/242–9253* 🌐 *thebikesmithllc.com.*

Routes. Tours—by bike and snowshoe—dominate the Routes shop, but straight rentals are also available, by the hour or day. They include, on the bike side, cruisers, mountain bikes, kids bikes, and tandems ($15/hr to $50/day). ✉ *1102 Mountain Rd. NW, Old Town, Albuquerque, New Mexico, USA* ☎ *505/933–5667* 🌐 *www.routesrentals.com.*

BIRD-WATCHING

The Rio Grande Valley, one of the continent's major flyways, attracts many migratory bird species.

★ Fodor's Choice **Open Space Visitor Center.** Sandhill cranes make their winter home here, or stop for a snack en route to the Bosque del Apache, just south, in Socorro. Albuquerque is right in their flyway, and the Open Space center, which is replete with trails heading down to the shores of the Rio Grande, provides a most hospitable setting for them. The outdoor viewing station is complemented inside the Visitors Center with changing art exhibits and well-informed guides. ✉ *6500 Coors Blvd. NW, West Side, Albuquerque, New Mexico, USA* ☎ *505/897–8831* 🌐 *www.cabq.gov/openspace.*

Rio Grande Nature Center State Park. Good bird-viewing locales include the Rio Grande Nature Center State Park (⇨ *Exploring, North Valley, above*). ✉ *2901 Candelaria Rd. NW, Los Ranchos/North Valley, Albuquerque, New Mexico, USA* ☎ *505/344–7240* 🌐 *www.nmparks.com.*

GOLF

Most of the better courses in the region—and there are some outstanding ones—are just outside town. The four courses operated by the city of Albuquerque have their charms, and the rates are reasonable. Each course has a clubhouse and pro shop, where clubs and other equipment can be rented. Weekday play is first-come, first-served, but reservations are taken for weekends.

Golf Management Office. Contact the Golf Management Office for details. ✉ *Albuquerque, USA* ☎ *505/888–8115* 🌐 *www.cabq.gov/golf.*

HIKING

In the foothills in Albuquerque's Northeast Heights, you'll find great hiking in Cibola National Forest (🌐 *www.fs.usda.gov/cibola*), which can be accessed from Tramway Boulevard Northeast, about 4 miles east of Interstate 25 or 2 miles north of Paseo del Norte. Just follow the road into the hillside, and you'll find several parking areas (there's a daily parking fee of $3). This is where you'll find the trailhead for the steep and challenging La Luz Trail (🌐 *www.laluztrail.com*), which rises for some 9 miles (an elevation gain of more than 3,000 feet) to the top of Sandia Crest. You can take the Sandia Peak Aerial Tram (⇨ *Exploring Albuquerque, above*) to the top and then hike down the trail, or vice versa (keep in mind that it can take up to six hours to hike up the trail, and four to five hours to hike down). Spectacular views of Albuquerque and many miles of desert and mountain beyond that are had from the trail. You can also enjoy a hike here without going the whole way—if your energy and time are limited, just hike a mile or two and back. Or enjoy one of the shorter trails that emanate from the Elena Gallegos Picnic Area (🌐 *www.cabq.gov/openspace*), just a few miles south along Tramway. No matter how far you hike, however, pack plenty of water.

For lovely but even less rugged terrain, the Aldo Leopold Forest and trails at the Open Space Visitor Center on the West Side will be of interest.

KAYAKING

Quiet Waters Paddling Adventures. The Rio at sunset (or just about any time) is best seen from a kayak or canoe and this reliable outfit offers rentals as well as guided and self-guided tours to help you do just that. A 15-minute drive from Downtown, then you are set for floating down the calm waters of the middle Rio Grande. ✉ *105D Pleasant View Dr., Los Ranchos/North Valley, Bernalillo, New Mexico, USA* ☎ *877/453–5628* 🌐 *www.quietwaterspaddling.com*.

TAOS

10

Updated by Andrew Collins

Taos casts a lingering spell. Set on an undulating mesa at the base of the Sangre de Cristo Mountains, it's a place of piercing light and spectacular views, where the desert palette changes almost hourly as the sun moves across the sky. Adobe buildings—some of them centuries old—lie nestled amid pine trees and scrub, some in the shadow of majestic Wheeler Peak, the state's highest point, at just over 13,000 feet. The smell of piñon-wood smoke rises from the valley from early autumn through late spring; during the warmer months, the air smells of fragrant sage.

The earliest residents, members of the Taos-Tiwa tribe, have inhabited this breathtaking valley for more than a millennium; their descendants still live and maintain a traditional way of life at Taos Pueblo, a 95,000-acre reserve 4 miles northeast of Taos Plaza. Spanish settlers arrived in the 1500s, bringing both farming and Catholicism to the area; their influence remains most pronounced in the diminutive village of Ranchos de Taos, 4 miles south of town, where the massive adobe walls and *camposanto* (graveyard) of San Francisco de Asís Church have been attracting photographers for generations.

In the early 20th century, another population—artists—discovered Taos and began making the pilgrimage here to write, paint, and take photographs. The early adopters of this movement, painters Bert Phillips and Ernest Blumenschein stopped here in 1898 quite by chance to repair a wagon wheel while en route from Denver to Mexico in 1898. Enthralled with the earthy beauty of the region, they abandoned their intended plan, settled near the plaza, and in 1915 formed the Taos Society of Artists. In later years, many illustrious artists—including Georgia O'Keeffe, Ansel Adams, and D. H. Lawrence—frequented the area, helping cement a vaunted arts tradition that thrives to this day. The steadily emerging bohemian spirit has continued to attract hippies, counterculturalists, New Agers, gays and lesbians, and free spirits. Downtown—along with some outlying villages to the south and north, such as Ranchos de Taos and Arroyo Seco—now support a rich abundance of galleries and design-driven shops. Whereas Santa Fe, Aspen, Scottsdale, and other gallery hubs in the West tend toward pricey work, much of it by artists living elsewhere, Taos remains very much an ardent hub of local arts and crafts production and sales. A half-dozen excellent museums here also document the town's esteemed artistic history.

About 5,600 people live year-round within Taos town limits, but another 28,000 reside in the surrounding county, much of which is unincorporated, and quite a few others live here seasonally. This means that in summer and, to a lesser extent, during the winter ski season, the town can feel much larger and busier than you might expect, with a considerable supply of shops, restaurants, and accommodations. Still, overall, the valley and soaring mountains of Taos enjoy relative isolation, low population-density, and magnificent scenery, parts of which you can access by visiting Rio Grande del Norte National Monument, one of the park service's newest properties—it's was designated in March 2013. These elements combine to make Taos an ideal retreat for those aiming to escape, slow down, and embrace a distinct regional blend of art, cuisine, outdoor recreation, and natural beauty.

ORIENTATION AND PLANNING

GETTING ORIENTED

Taos is small and resolutely rustic, but for the prosaic stretch of chain motels and strip malls that greet you as you approach from the south. Persevere to the central plaza, and you'll find several pedestrian-friendly blocks of galleries, shops, restaurants, and art museums. Easygoing Taoseños are a welcoming lot, and if you ever lose your orientation, you'll find locals happy to point you where you need to go. It's difficult to reach Taos without a car, and you'll need one to reach those attractions and businesses outside the village center (the Rio Grande Gorge, Millicent Rogers Museum, and the area's best skiing and hiking). The narrow, historic streets near the plaza can be choked with traffic in the peak summer and winter seasons, especially on weekends—ask locals about the several shortcuts for avoiding traffic jams, and try walking when exploring the blocks around the plaza.

TAOS NEIGHBORHOODS

Plaza and Vicinity. More than four centuries after it was laid out, the Taos Plaza and adjacent streets remain the community's hub of commercial and social activity. Dozens of independent shops and galleries, along with several notable restaurants, hotels, and museums, thrive here. The plaza itself is a bit overrun with mediocre souvenir shops, but you only need to walk a block in any direction—especially north and east—to find better offerings.

TOP REASONS TO GO

Small-town sophistication. For a tiny, remote community, Taos supports a richly urbane culinary scene, a fantastic bounty of galleries and design shops, and plenty of stylish B&Bs and inns.

Indigenous and artistic roots. The Taos Pueblo and its inhabitants have lived in this region for centuries and continue to play a vital role the community. And few U.S. towns this size have a better crop of first-rate art museums, which document the history of one of the West's most prolific arts colonies.

Desert solitaire. Few panoramas in the Southwest can compare with that of the 13,000-foot Sangre de Cristo Mountains soaring over the adobe homes of Taos, and beyond that, the endless high-desert mesa that extends for miles to the west.

South Side. The first Spanish settlers were agrarian, and many families continue to till the fertile land south of Taos, an area anchored by tiny Ranchos de Taos, which is home to iconic San Francisco de Asís Church, memorialized by Georgia O'Keeffe and photographer Ansel Adams. The main approach road into Taos from the south, NM 68, is lined with gas stations, convenience stores, and chain motels.

Taos Pueblo. The Pueblo is the ancient beating heart of the entire valley, the historic and architectural basis for everything that Taos has become. A small, unmemorable casino aside, this area a short drive northeast of the plaza has been spared commercial development and remains a neighborhood of modest homes and farms. The Pueblo itself is the sole draw for visitors and worth a visit.

El Prado. As you drive north from Taos toward Arroyo Seco and points north or west, you'll first take the main thoroughfare, Paseo del Pueblo Norte (U.S. 64) through the small village of El Prado, a mostly agrarian area that's notable for having several of the area's best restaurants, B&Bs, and shops.

West Side. Taos is hemmed in by the Sangre de Cristo mountains on the east, but to the west, extending from downtown clear across the precipitously deep Rio Grande Gorge (and the famous bridge that crosses it), the landscape is dominated by sweeping, high-desert scrub and wide-open spaces. The west side is mostly residential and makes for a scenic shortcut around the sometimes traffic-clogged plaza (from Ranchos de Taos, just follow NM 240 to Blueberry Hill Road to complete this bypass).

Arroyo Seco. Set on a high mesa north of Taos, this funky, hip village and arts center is an ideal spot to browse galleries, grab a meal at one of a handful of excellent restaurants, or simply pause to admire the dramatic views before driving on to the Enchanted Circle or Taos Ski Valley. You'll find a few excellent B&Bs here as well.

TAOS PLANNER

WHEN TO GO

With more than 300 days of sunshine annually, Taos typically yields good—if sometimes chilly—weather year-round. The summer high season brings warm days (upper 80s) and cool nights (low 50s), as well as frequent afternoon thunderstorms. A packed arts and festival schedule in summer means hotels and B&Bs sometimes book well in advance, lodging rates are high, restaurants are jammed, and traffic anywhere near the plaza can slow to a standstill. Spring and fall are stunning and favor mild days and cool nights, fewer visitors, and reasonable hotel prices. In winter, especially during big years for snowfall, skiers arrive en masse but tend to stay close to the slopes and only venture into town for an occasional meal or shopping raid.

GETTING HERE AND AROUND

AIRPORTS

Albuquerque International Sunport, about 130 miles away and a 2½-hour drive, is the nearest major airport to Taos. The small Santa Fe Municipal Airport, a 90-minute drive, also has daily service from Dallas, Denver, Los Angeles, and Phoenix. Alternatively, as Taos is one of the gateway towns to New Mexico if coming from Colorado, some visitors fly into Denver (five hours north) or Colorado Springs (four hours). Taos Municipal Airport, 12 miles west of town, serves only charters and private planes.

Airports **Albuquerque International Sunport** (*ABQ*). ☎ *505/244–7700* 🌐 *www.cabq.gov/airport.* **Santa Fe Municipal Airport** (*SAF*). ☎ *505/955–2900* 🌐 *www.santafenm.gov/?nid=171.*

TRANSFERS

From Santa Fe, your best bet is renting a car. Taos Express provides bus service between Taos and Santa Fe, including a stop at Santa Fe's train station, from which you can catch the New Mexico Rail Runner train to Albuquerque (and then a free bus to the airport). The fare is just $10 round-trip, but service is offered only on weekends (one Friday evening run, and two Saturday and Sunday runs, one in the morning, one in the evening). Twin Hearts Express has shuttle service four times daily between Taos and Albuquerque Sunport ($95 round-trip), but they don't stop in Santa Fe. Additionally, during the ski season (late fall–early spring), Taos Ski Valley operates a daily shuttle between the airports in Albuquerque ($85 round-trip) and Santa Fe ($65 round-trip) and the ski valley; once at the ski valley, you have to take a taxi ($35 one-way) or the local Chili Line Shuttle bus ($2 round-trip) into Taos. Unless you're coming to Taos just for skiing, this is a pretty cumbersome and expensive option. It's possible to rent a car in Taos once you arrive—Cottam Walker Ford and Enterprise are two local options.

Shuttle Contacts **Taos Express** ☎ *575/751-4459* ⊕ *www.taos-express.com.* **Taos Ski Valley Airport Shuttle** ☎ *800/776-1111* ⊕ *www.skitaos.org.* **Twin Hearts Express** ☎ *575/751-1201* ⊕ *www.twinheartsexpresstransportation.com.*

CAR TRAVEL

A car is your most practical means both for reaching and getting around Taos. The main route from Santa Fe is via U.S. 285 north to NM 68 north, also known as the Low Road, which winds between the Rio Grande and red-rock cliffs before rising to a spectacular view of the mesa and river gorge. You can also take the spectacular and vertiginous High Road to Taos, which takes longer but offers a wonderfully scenic ride—many visitors come to Taos via the Low Road, which is more dramatic when driven south to north, and then return to Santa Fe via the High Road, which has better views as you drive south. From Denver, it's a five-hour drive south via I–25, U.S. 160 west (at Walsenburg), and CO 159 to NM 522—the stretch from Walsenburg into Taos is quite scenic.

TAXI TRAVEL

Taxi service in Taos is sparse, but Taos Cab serves the area. Rates are about $5–$7 within town, $20–$25 to Arroyo Seco, and $35 to Taos Ski Valley, plus $1 per each additional person.

Taxi Contacts **Taos Cab** ☎ *505/901–7604* ⊕ *www.taoscab.com.*

VISITOR INFORMATION

Taos Ski Valley Chamber of Commerce ☎ *575/776–1413, 800/517–9816* ⊕ *www.taosskivalley.com.*

Taos Visitor Center ✉ *1139 Paseo del Pueblo Sur* ☎ *505/758–3873, 800/587–9007* ⊕ *www.taos.org.*

PLANNING YOUR TIME

Whether you've got an afternoon or a week in the area, begin by strolling around Taos Plaza and along Bent Street, taking in the galleries, Native American crafts shops, and eclectic clothing stores, plus nearby museums, including the Harwood, Kit Carson Home, and Taos Art Museum. A few of the must-see attractions in the area are a bit farther afield, and you need at least two days and ideally three or four to take in everything. Among the top outlying attractions, it's possible to visit Taos Pueblo, the magnificent Millicent Rogers Museum, the village of Arroyo Seco, and the Rio Grande Gorge Bridge all in one day—you can connect them to make one loop to the north and west of the city. If you're headed south, stop at La Hacienda de los Martínez to gain an appreciation of early Spanish life in Taos and then to Ranchos de Taos to see the stunning San Francisco de Asís Church. If you approach Taos from the south, as most visitors do, you could also visit both these attractions on your way into town, assuming you arrive by early afternoon.

EXPLORING

The Museum Association of Taos includes five properties: the Harwood Museum, Taos Art Museum, Millicent Rogers Museum, E. L. Blumenschein Home and Museum, and La Hacienda de los Martínez. These museums charge $8–$10 admission individually, but you can buy a combination ticket—$25 for all five, valid for one year.

PLAZA AND VICINITY

TOP ATTRACTIONS

★ Fodor'sChoice **Harwood Museum.** The Pueblo Revival former home of Burritt Elihu "Burt" Harwood, a dedicated painter who studied in France before moving to Taos in 1916, is adjacent to a museum dedicated to the works of local artists. Traditional Hispanic northern New Mexican artists, early art-colony painters, post–World War II modernists, and contemporary artists such as Larry Bell, Agnes Martin, Ken Price, and Earl Stroh are represented. Mabel Dodge Luhan, a major arts patron, bequeathed many of the 19th- and early-20th-century works in the Harwoods' collection, including *retablos* (painted wood representations of Catholic saints) and *bultos* (three-dimensional carvings of the saints). In the Hispanic Traditions Gallery upstairs are 19th-century tinwork, furniture, and sculpture. Downstairs, among early-20th-century art-colony holdings, look for E. Martin Hennings's *Chamisa in Bloom,* which captures the Taos landscape particularly beautifully. A tour of the ground-floor galleries shows that Taos painters of the era, notably Oscar Berninghaus, Ernest Blumenschein, Victor Higgins, Walter Ufer, Marsden Hartley, and John Marin, were fascinated by the land and the people linked to it. ✉ *238 Ledoux St., Plaza and Vicinity* ☎ *575/758–9826* 🌐 *www.harwoodmuseum.org* 🎫 *$10; 5-museum Museum Association of Taos combination ticket, $25* ⏲ *Mon.–Sat. 10–5, Sun. noon–5 (Closed Mon. Nov.–Mar.).*

★ Fodor'sChoice **Taos Art Museum and Fechin House.** The interior of this extraordinary adobe house, built between 1927 and 1933 by Russian émigré and artist Nicolai Fechin, is a marvel of carved Russian-style woodwork and furniture. Fechin constructed it to showcase his daringly colorful paintings. The house now contains the Taos Art Museum, which showcases a rotating collection of some 600 paintings by more than 50 Taos artists, including founders of the original Taos Society of Artists, among them Joseph Sharp, Ernest Blumenschein, Bert Phillips, E. I. Couse, and Oscar Berninghaus. ✉ *227 Paseo del Pueblo Norte, Plaza and Vicinity* ☎ *575/758–2690* 🌐 *www.taosartmuseum.org* 🎫 *$8; 5-museum Museum Association of Taos combination ticket, $25* ⏲ *Tues.–Sun. 10–5 (reduced hrs in winter; call first).*

A GOOD WALK: TAOS PLAZA

Begin at the gazebo in the middle of **Taos Plaza**. After exploring the plaza, head south from its western edge down the small, unmarked alley (its name is West Plaza Drive), crossing Camino de la Placita, to where West Plaza Drive becomes Ledoux Street. Continue south to the **E. L. Blumenschein Home and Museum** and, a few doors farther south, the **Harwood Museum**. (Parking for the Harwood Foundation is at Ledoux and Ranchitos Road.)

Walk back to the plaza, and stroll east across Paseo del Pueblo Norte (NM 68) to visit the **Kit Carson Home and Museum**. Then head back to Paseo del Pueblo Norte, turn right (north) and go past the Taos Inn, to reach the **Taos Art Museum and Fechin House**.

TIMING

The entire walk can be done in five hours, but allow about eight hours if you stop for lunch along the way and browse in the shops and galleries. You can tour each of the museums in 45 minutes to an hour.

WORTH NOTING

E. L. Blumenschein Home and Museum. For an introduction to the history of the Taos art scene, start with Ernest L. Blumenschein's residence, which provides a glimpse into the cosmopolitan lives led by the members of the Taos Society of Artists, of which Blumenschein was a founding member. One of the rooms in the adobe-style structure dates from 1797. On display are the art, antiques, and other personal possessions of Blumenschein and his wife, Mary Greene Blumenschein, who also painted, as did their daughter Helen. Several of Ernest Blumenschein's vivid oil paintings hang in his former studio, and works by other early Taos artists are also on display. ✉ *222 Ledoux St., Plaza and Vicinity* ☎ *575/758–0505* 🌐 *www.taoshistoricmuseums.org* 🎫 *$8; 5-museum Museum Association of Taos combination ticket, $25* ⏲ *Apr.–Oct., Mon.–Sat. 10–5, Sun. noon–5; Nov.–Mar., Mon., Tues., and Thurs.–Sat. 10–4, Sun. noon–4.*

10

FAMILY **Kit Carson Home and Museum.** Kit Carson bought this low-slung 12-room adobe home in 1843 for his wife, Josefa Jaramillo, the daughter of a powerful, politically influential Spanish family. Three of the museum's rooms are furnished, as they were when the Carson family lived here. The rest of the museum is devoted to gun and moun-

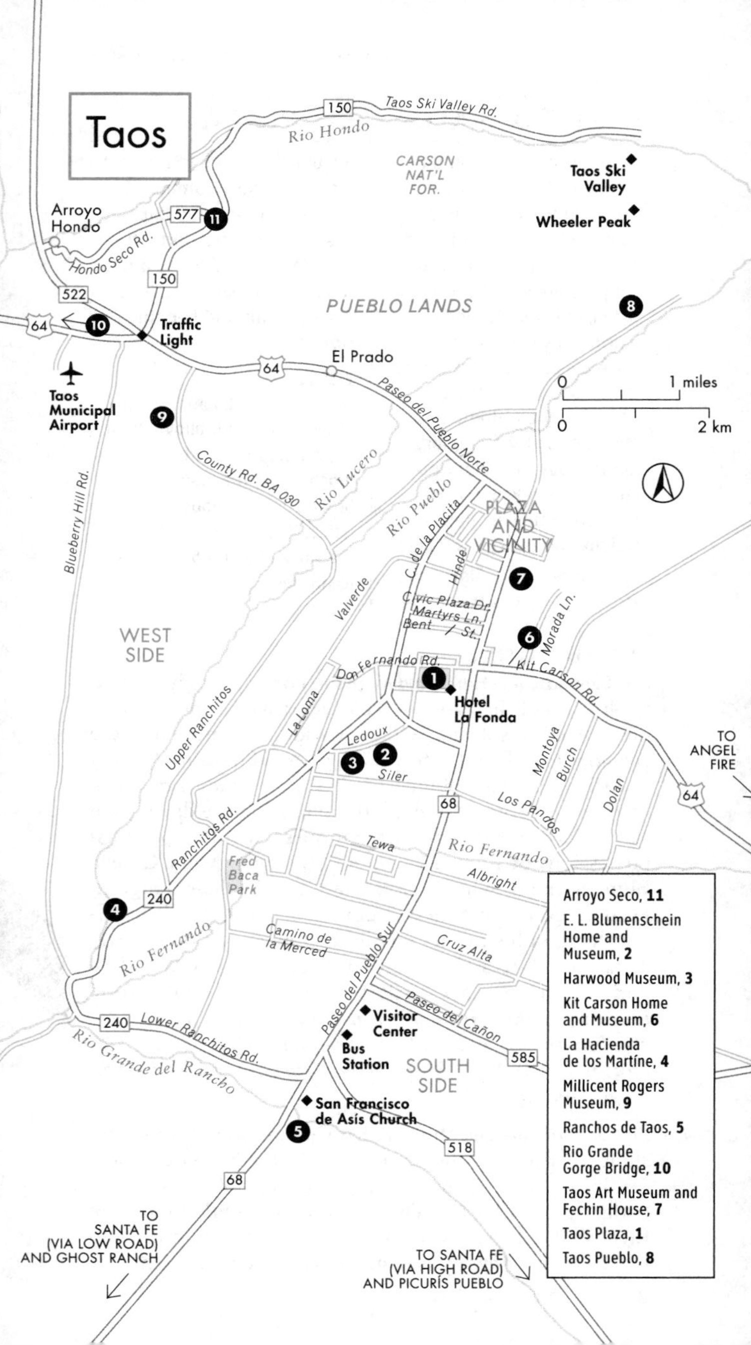
Taos
Taos Ski Valley Rd.
Rio Hondo
CARSON NAT'L FOR.
Taos Ski Valley
Wheeler Peak
Arroyo Hondo
Hondo Seco Rd.
PUEBLO LANDS
Traffic Light
El Prado
Taos Municipal Airport
Paseo del Pueblo Norte
County Rd. BA 030
Rio Lucero
Rio Pueblo
Blueberry Hill Rd.
C. de la Placita
PLAZA AND VICINITY
Hinde
Valverde
Civic Plaza Dr.
Martyrs Ln.
Bent St.
Morada Ln.
WEST SIDE
Don Fernando Rd.
Kit Carson Rd.
Hotel La Fonda
La Loma
Upper Ranchitos
Ledoux
Siler
Montoya
Burch
Dolan
Los Pandos
TO ANGEL FIRE
Ranchitos Rd.
Tewa
Rio Fernando
Fred Baca Park
Albright
Camino de la Merced
Cruz Alta
Rio Fernando
Paseo del Pueblo Sur
Paseo del Cañon
Visitor Center
Bus Station
Lower Ranchitos Rd.
Rio Grande del Rancho
SOUTH SIDE
San Francisco de Asís Church
TO SANTA FE (VIA LOW ROAD) AND GHOST RANCH
TO SANTA FE (VIA HIGH ROAD) AND PICURÍS PUEBLO
0 1 miles
0 2 km
Arroyo Seco, 11
E. L. Blumenschein Home and Museum, 2
Harwood Museum, 3
Kit Carson Home and Museum, 6
La Hacienda de los Martíne, 4
Millicent Rogers Museum, 9
Ranchos de Taos, 5
Rio Grande Gorge Bridge, 10
Taos Art Museum and Fechin House, 7
Taos Plaza, 1
Taos Pueblo, 8

tain-man exhibits, such as rugged leather clothing and Kit's own Spencer carbine rifle with its beaded leather carrying case, and early Taos antiques, artifacts, and manuscripts. ✉ *113 Kit Carson Rd., Plaza and Vicinity* ☎ *575/758–0505* 🌐 *www.kitcarsonhomeandmuseum.com* 🎫 *$5* ⏲ *Daily 10–5:30.*

Taos Plaza. The first European explorers of the Taos Valley came here with Captain Hernando de Alvarado, a member of Francisco Vásquez de Coronado's expedition of 1540. Basque explorer Don Juan de Oñate arrived in Taos in July 1598 and established a mission and trading arrangements with residents of Taos Pueblo. The settlement developed into two plazas: the plaza at the heart of the town became a thriving business district for the early colony, and a walled residential plaza was constructed a few hundred yards behind. It remains active today, home to a throng of shlocky gift shops, plus a few more-noteworthy galleries and boutiques. On the southeastern corner of Taos Plaza is the Hotel La Fonda de Taos. Some infamous erotic paintings by D. H. Lawrence that were naughty in his day but are quite tame by present standards can be viewed in the Karavas Conference Room. ✉ *Plaza and Vicinity.*

SOUTH SIDE

WORTH NOTING

La Hacienda de los Martínez. Spare and fortlike, this adobe structure built between 1804 and 1827 on the bank of the Rio Pueblo served as a community refuge during Comanche and Apache raids. Its thick walls, which have few windows, surround two central courtyards. Don Antonio Severino Martínez was a farmer and trader; the hacienda was the final stop along El Camino Real (the Royal Road), the trade route the Spanish established between Mexico City and New Mexico. The restored period rooms here contain textiles, foods, and crafts of the early 19th century. There's a working blacksmith's shop, usually open to visitors on Saturday, and weavers create beautiful textiles on reconstructed period looms. ✉ *708 Hacienda Rd., off Ranchitos Rd. (NM 240), South Side* ☎ *575/758–1000* 🌐 *www.taoshistoricmuseums.org* 🎫 *$8; 5-museum Museum Association of Taos combination ticket, $25* ⏲ *Apr.–Oct., Mon.–Sat. 10–5, Sun. noon–5; Nov.–Mar., Mon., Tues., and Thurs.–Sat. 10–4, Sun. noon–4.*

Ranchos de Taos. A few minutes' drive south of the center of Taos, this village still retains some of its rural atmosphere despite the highway traffic passing through. Huddled around its famous adobe church and dusty plaza are cheerful, remodeled shops and galleries standing shoulder to shoulder with crumbling adobe shells. This ranching, farming, and budding small-business community was an early home to Taos Native Americans before being settled by Spaniards in 1716. Several of the ancient adobe dwellings contain shops, galleries, and restaurants. ✉ *South Side.*

TAOS PUEBLO

★ Fodor'sChoice FAMILY For nearly 1,000 years the mud-and-straw adobe walls of Taos Pueblo have sheltered Tiwa-speaking Native Americans. A United Nations World Heritage Site, this is the largest collection of multistory pueblo dwellings in the United States. The pueblo's main buildings, Hlauuma (north house) and Hlaukwima (south house), are separated by a creek. These structures are believed to be of a similar age, probably built between 1000 and 1450. The dwellings have common walls but no connecting doorways—the Tiwas gained access only from the top, via ladders that were retrieved after entering. Small buildings and corrals are scattered about.

The pueblo today appears much as it did when the first Spanish explorers arrived in New Mexico in 1540. The adobe walls glistening with mica caused the conquistadors to believe they had discovered one of the fabled Seven Cities of Gold. The outside surfaces are continuously maintained by replastering with thin layers of mud, and the interior walls are frequently coated with thin washes of white clay. Some walls are several feet thick in places. The roofs of each of the five-story structures are supported by large timbers, or vigas, hauled down from the mountain forests. Pine or aspen *latillas* (smaller pieces of wood) are placed side by side between the vigas; the entire roof is then packed with dirt.

Even after 400 years of Spanish and Anglo presence in Taos, inside the pueblo the traditional Native American way of life has endured. Tribal custom allows no electricity or running water in Hlauuma and Hlaukwima, where varying numbers (usually fewer than 150) of Taos Native Americans live full-time. About 1,900 others live in conventional homes on the pueblo's 95,000 acres. The crystal-clear Rio

Pueblo de Taos, originating high above in the mountains at the sacred Blue Lake, is the primary source of water for drinking and irrigating. Bread is still baked in *hornos* (outdoor domed ovens). Artisans of the Taos Pueblo produce and sell (tax-free) traditionally handcrafted wares, such as mica-flecked pottery and silver jewelry. Great hunters, the Taos Native Americans are also known for their work with animal skins and their excellent moccasins, boots, and drums.

Although the population is predominantly Catholic, the people of Taos Pueblo, like most Pueblo Native Americans, also maintain their native religious traditions. At Christmas and other sacred holidays, for instance, immediately after Mass, dancers dressed in seasonal sacred garb proceed down the aisle of St. Jerome Chapel, drums beating and rattles shaking, to begin other religious rites.

The pueblo **Church of San Geronimo,** or St. Jerome, the patron saint of Taos Pueblo, was completed in 1850 to replace the one destroyed by the U.S. Army in 1847 during the Mexican War. With its smooth symmetry, stepped portal, and twin bell towers, the church is a popular subject for photographers and artists.

The public is invited to certain ceremonial dances held throughout the year (a full list of these is posted on the pueblo Web site's Events page): highlights include the Feast of Santa Cruz (May 3); Taos Pueblo Pow Wow (mid-July); Santiago and Santa Ana Feast Days (July 25 and 26), San Geronimo Days (September 29 and 30); Procession of the Virgin Mary (December 24); and Deer Dance or Matachines Dance (December 25). While you're at the pueblo, respect all rules and customs, which are posted prominently. There are some restrictions, which are posted, on personal photography. ✉ *Off Paseo del Pueblo Norte, turn right just north of Kachina Lodge Hotel, Taos Pueblo* ☎ *575/758–1028* 🌐 *www.taospueblo.com* 🎟 *$16* ⏲ *Mon.–Sat. 8–4:30, Sun. 8:30–4:30. Tours by appointment. Closed for funerals, religious ceremonies, and for 10-week quiet time in late winter or early spring, and last part of Aug.; call ahead to confirm hrs.*

WEST SIDE

TOP ATTRACTIONS

★ Fodor'sChoice **Millicent Rogers Museum.** More than 5,000 pieces of spectacular Native American and Hispanic art, many of them from the private collection of the late Standard Oil heiress Millicent Rogers, are on display here. Among the pieces are baskets, blankets, rugs, kachina dolls, carvings, paintings, rare religious artifacts, and, most significantly, jewelry (Rogers, a fashion icon in her day, was one of the first Americans to appreciate the turquoise-and-silver artistry of Native American jewelers). Other important works include the pottery and ceramics of Maria Martinez and other potters from San Ildefonso Pueblo (north of Santa Fe). Docents conduct guided tours by appointment, and the museum hosts lectures, films, workshops, and demonstrations. The two-room gift shop has exceptional jewelry, rugs, books, and pottery. ✉ *1504 Millicent Rogers Rd., off Paseo del Pueblo Norte, about 4½ miles north of Plaza* ☎ *575/758–2462* 🌐 *www.millicentrogers.org* 🎫 *$10; 5-museum Museum Association of Taos combination ticket, $25* ⏲ *Daily 10–5; closed Mon. Nov.–Mar.*

FAMILY **Rio Grande Gorge Bridge.** It's a dizzying experience to see the Rio Grande 650 feet underfoot, where it flows at the bottom of an immense, steep rock canyon. In summer the reddish rocks dotted with green scrub contrast brilliantly with the blue sky, where you might see a hawk lazily floating in circles. The bridge is the second-highest suspension bridge in the country. Hold on to your camera and eyeglasses when looking down. Shortly after daybreak, hot-air balloons fly above and even inside the gorge. There's a campground with picnic shelters and basic restrooms on the west side of the bridge. ✉ *U.S. 64, 8 miles west of Jct. with NM 522 and NM 150, West Side.*

ARROYO SECO

★ Fodor'sChoice Established in 1834 by local Spanish farmers and ranchers, this charming village has today become a secluded, artsy escape from the sometimes daunting summer crowds and commercialism of the Taos Plaza—famous residents include actress Julia Roberts and former U.S. Defense Secretary Donald Rumsfeld, who own ranches adjacent to one another. You reach the tiny commercial district along NM 150, about 5 miles north of the intersection with U.S. 64 and NM 522 (it's about 9 miles north of the plaza). The drive is part of the joy of visiting, as NM 150 rises steadily above the Taos Valley, offering panoramic views of the Sangre de Cristos—you pass through Arroyo Seco en route to the Taos Ski Valley.

Arroyo Seco is without any formal attractions or museums, and that's partly its charm. The main reasons for making the trip here are to behold the dramatic scenery, grab a bite at one of the handful of excellent restaurants (ice cream from **Taos Cow Cafe** and tamales from **Abe's Cantina** are both revered by locals), and browse the several galleries and boutiques, whose wares tend to be a little more idiosyncratic but no less accomplished than those sold in Taos proper. ✉ *Arroyo Seco* 🌐 *www.visitseco.com.*

WHERE TO EAT

For a relatively small, remote town, Taos has a sophisticated and eclectic dining scene. It's a fine destination for authentic New Mexican fare, but you'll also find several upscale spots serving creative regional fare utilizing mostly local ingredients, a smattering of excellent Asian and Middle Eastern spots, and several very good cafés and coffeehouses perfect for light but bountiful breakfast and lunch fare.

Prices in the restaurant reviews are the average cost of a main course at dinner or, if dinner is not served, at lunch; taxes and service charges are generally included.

PLAZA AND VICINITY

$$ ✕ **Antonio's.** *Mexican.* Chef Antonio Matus has been delighting discerning diners in the Taos area for many years. In this rambling, art-filled adobe compound with a redbrick courtyard, Matus focuses more on regional Mexican than New Mexican fare. Specialties include *chile en nogada* (poblano peppers stuffed with pork, pears, and raisins and topped with a walnut-cream sauce) and *tortas de jaiba* (blue crab cakes with roasted tomatillo and chile *de árbol* sauce), plus a fantastic *tres leches* (three milks) cake and a rich chipotle-chocolate cake. Local favorites such as pork-stuffed sopaipillas are also served. Try the ceviche, which is made daily. $ *Average main: $17* ✉ *122 Dona Luz St., Plaza and Vicinity* ☎ *575/751–4800* 🌐 *www.antoniosoftaos.com* ⏲ *Closed Sun.*

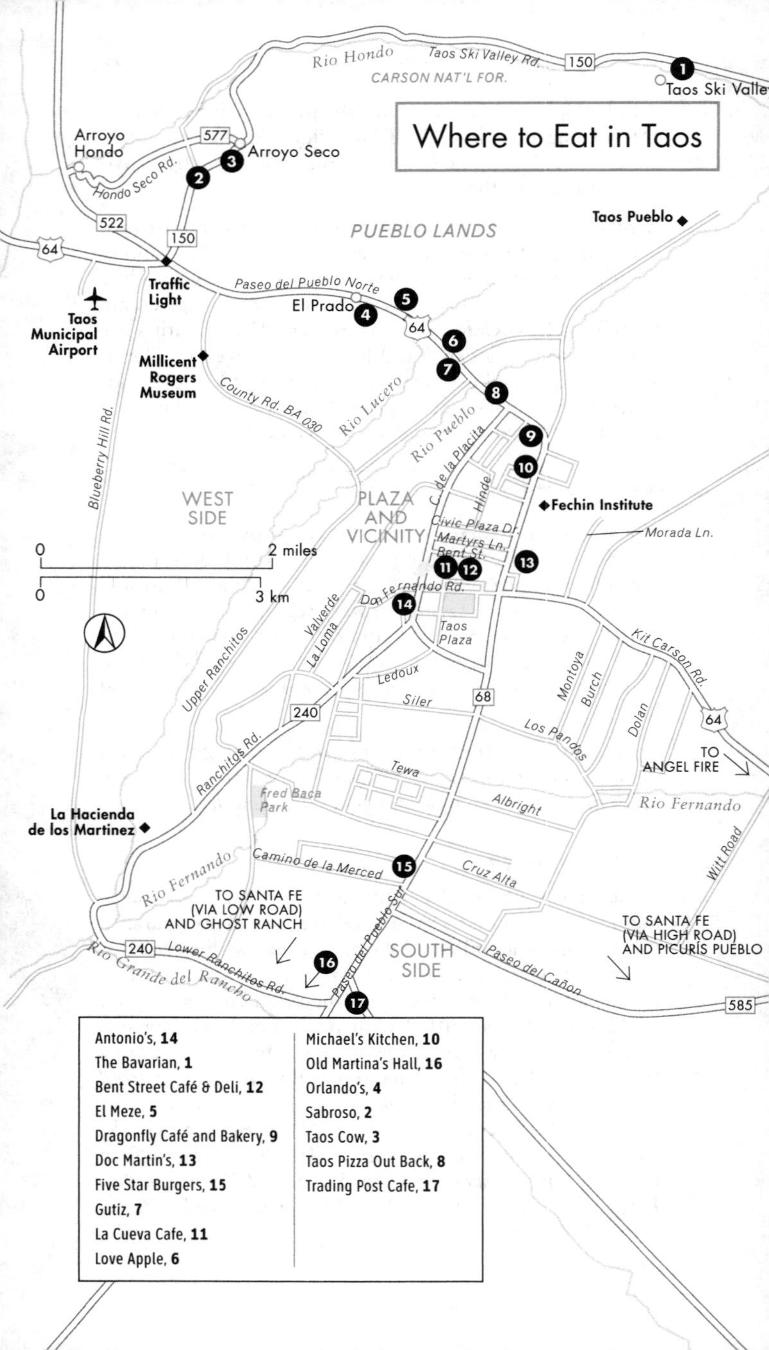
Where to Eat in Taos
Rio Hondo
Taos Ski Valley Rd.
150
CARSON NAT'L FOR.
Taos Ski Valley
Arroyo Hondo
577
Arroyo Seco
Hondo Seco Rd.
522
150
64
PUEBLO LANDS
Taos Pueblo
Traffic Light
Taos Municipal Airport
Paseo del Pueblo Norte
El Prado
64
Millicent Rogers Museum
County Rd. BA 030
Rio Lucero
Rio Pueblo
C. de la Placita
Hinde
Fechin Institute
Morada Ln.
WEST SIDE
PLAZA AND VICINITY
Blueberry Hill Rd.
Civic Plaza Dr.
Martyrs Ln.
Bent St.
0
2 miles
0
3 km
Don Fernando Rd.
Valverde
La Loma
Taos Plaza
Kit Carson Rd.
Upper Ranchitos
Ledoux
Siler
68
Montoya
Burch
Dolan
64
240
Los Pandos
TO ANGEL FIRE
Ranchitos Rd.
Tewa
Fred Baca Park
Albright
Rio Fernando
La Hacienda de los Martinez
Witt Road
Camino de la Merced
Cruz Alta
Rio Fernando
TO SANTA FE (VIA LOW ROAD) AND GHOST RANCH
Paseo del Pueblo Sur
TO SANTA FE (VIA HIGH ROAD) AND PICURÍS PUEBLO
240
Lower Ranchitos Rd.
SOUTH SIDE
Rio Grande del Rancho
Paseo del Cañon
585
Antonio's, 14
The Bavarian, 1
Bent Street Café & Deli, 12
El Meze, 5
Dragonfly Café and Bakery, 9
Doc Martin's, 13
Five Star Burgers, 15
Gutiz, 7
La Cueva Cafe, 11
Love Apple, 6
Michael's Kitchen, 10
Old Martina's Hall, 16
Orlando's, 4
Sabroso, 2
Taos Cow, 3
Taos Pizza Out Back, 8
Trading Post Cafe, 17

$ ✕ **Bent Street Café & Deli.** *American.* Try for a seat on the cheery, covered outdoor patio next to giant sunflowers, as the interior of this often-packed spot can feel a bit cramped, although service is friendly and helpful wherever you sit. Enjoy breakfast burritos, eggs Benedict with green chile, homemade granola, fresh-baked goods, dozens of deli sandwiches, tortilla soup, and homemade stews. You might finish your meal with a chocolate-nut brownie. Beer, wine, and gourmet coffees are also served. *Average main: $10* ✉ *120-M Bent St., Plaza and Vicinity* ☎ *575/758–5787* *www.bentstreetdeli.com* *No dinner.*

★ $$ Fodor's Choice ✕ **Doc Martin's.** *Southwestern.* The stylish restaurant of the Historic Taos Inn takes its name from the building's original owner, a local physician who saw patients in the rooms that are now the dining areas. The creative menu hews toward innovative takes on comforting classics, with an emphasis on sustainable ingredients—try the curious but quite tasty rattlesnake-rabbit sausage with ancho chile–cherry sauce among the starters. Entrées of note include local lamb shank with horseradish-mashed potatoes, and a juicy elk burger with crisp fries. There's an extensive wine list, and the adjoining Adobe Bar serves up some of the best margaritas in town. In winter ask for a table near the cozy kiva fireplace. *Average main: $22* ✉ *Historic Taos Inn, 125 Paseo del Pueblo Norte, Plaza and Vicinity* ☎ *575/758–1977* *www.taosinn.com.*

$$ ✕ **Dragonfly Café and Bakery.** *Eclectic.* This charming café bakes its own bread and serves a variety of ethnic specialties including organic kale salad with grapes and hazelnuts; Middle Eastern lamb with a Greek salad, hummus, and pita bread; curried chicken salad; bison burgers; and Vietnamese chicken salad; plus a separate menu of East Indian dishes. You can sit out front of this 1920s adobe cottage on a shaded outdoor patio with a fountain when it's warm and watch the tourists go by. Wine and beer are served. *Average main: $19* ✉ *402 Paseo del Pueblo Norte, Plaza and Vicinity* ☎ *575/737–5859* *www.dragonflytaos.com* *No dinner Sun.*

10

★ $ Fodor's Choice ✕ **Gutiz.** *Eclectic.* This ambitious and consistently terrific favorite for lunch and breakfast (served all day) blends French, Spanish, and South American culinary influences. Best bets in the morning include cinnamon French toast made with thick homemade bread and a baked omelet topped with a green tapenade. Lunch specialties include a warm salade Niçoise; steamed clams with garlic, paprika, and white wine; and *chicharon de pollo*—fried chicken tenders topped with hot *ají* Amarillo sauce. Meals are served on a gravel patio with lovely mountain panoramas or inside the small lilac-hued dining room that overlooks the open kitchen. *Average main: $10* *812B Paseo del Pueblo Norte, El Prado* *575/758–1226* *www.gutiztaos.com* *Reservations not accepted* *Closed Mon. No dinner.*

La Cueva Cafe. *Modern Mexican.* This casual eatery in an 1850s building was opened in 2012 by Mexico-born couple Juana and Horacio Zarazua, who have worked at a number of the best restaurants in town, including the defunct Rellenos, which used to occupy this space. Their specialty is regional Mexican food, including *camarones al mojo de ajo*, ceviche, chipotle shrimp tacos, and several other seafood dishes, plus chiles rellenos, chicken mole enchiladas, and some familiar New Mexico–style standbys. There's a good selection of vegetarian items, too, and everything at La Cueva is gluten-free. Breakfast is served daily, and there's a cheery patio out back. *Average main: $11* *135 Paseo del Pueblo Sur, Plaza and Vicinity* *575/758–7001* *www.lacuevacafe.com* *Reservations not accepted.*

$ **Michael's Kitchen.** *American.* This casual, homey restaurant
FAMILY serves up a bit of everything—you can have a hamburger while your friend who can't get enough chile sauce can order up vegetarian cheese enchiladas garnished with lettuce and tomatoes. Brunch is popular with the locals (dig into a plate of strawberry-banana-pecan pancakes), and amusing asides to the waitstaff over the intercom contribute to the energetic buzz. Dinner is served Friday through Sunday, but just until 8. *Average main: $8* *304 Paseo del Pueblo Norte, Plaza and Vicinity* *575/758–4178* *www.michaelskitchen.com* *Reservations not accepted* *No dinner Mon.–Thurs.*

SOUTH SIDE

$ **Five Star Burgers.** *Burger.* A standout amid the strip of mostly unmemorable fast-food restaurants along Paseo del Pueblo on the south side of town, this airy, high-ceiling contemporary space—part of a regional chain with locations in Santa Fe and Albuquerque as well—serves stellar burgers using hormone-free Angus beef from respected Harris Ranch; turkey, veggie, Colorado lamb, bison, and salmon burgers are also available, and you can choose from an assortment of novel toppings, including fried eggs, wild mushrooms, caramelized onions, and applewood-smoked bacon. Beer and wine are also served. *Average main: $10*

1032 Paseo del Pueblo Sur, South Side ☎ *575/758–8484* ⊕ *www.5starburgers.com.*

★ Fodor's Choice ✕ **Old Martina's Hall.** *Modern American.* Although this enchanting restaurant is new, the building it's in has a long, storied history. This restored Pueblo Revival building with thick adobe walls and sturdy viga-and-latilla ceilings is across the road from the famed San Francisco de Asís Church and was run as a rowdy dance hall for generations by the town's iconic Martinez family (former resident and late actor Dennis Hopper used to party here). It's no less convivial today, as both an inviting spot for cocktails and happy-hour snacks as for dining, in one of the beautiful salons with modern spherical chandeliers and local artwork. Come early for crab eggs Benedict or steak and eggs for breakfast, or flaky tart from the French bakery in the evening. The wild salmon with baby bok choy and truffle-chive beurre blanc is quite good. *Average main: $19* *4140 NM 68, South Side, Ranchos de Taos* ☎ *575/758–3003* ⊕ *www.oldmartinashall.com* *Closed Tues.*

$$ ✕ **Trading Post Cafe.** *Italian.* Local hipsters outnumber tourists at this casual spot serving mostly modern Italian fare with regional accents. Intelligent and attentive service along with well-presented contemporary Southwestern art make any meal a pleasure. For starters try the signature noodle soup or minestrone with smoked ham before moving on to an oven-roasted duck with seasonal vegetables and creamy mashed potatoes or any of the traditional pasta dishes, such as penne Arrabbiata (with spicy Italian sausage). Superb desserts include a coconut-cream pie and rich strawberry shortcake. Parking is just around the back, off NM 518. *Average main: $19* *4179 Paseo del Pueblo Sur, Ranchos de Taos* ☎ *575/758–5089* ⊕ *www.tradingpostcafe.com* *Closed Sun.–Mon.*

EL PRADO

$$ ✕ **El Meze.** *Spanish.* Set back from NM 68 in tiny El Prado, this 1840s adobe house with an expansive back patio affords unobstructed views of the Sangre de Cristo Mountains. Tightly spaced tables, polished-wood floors, and bright red adobe walls make it easy to imagine you're tucked away inside a small café in the southern Spain countryside, and indeed, El Meze specializes in the flavorful cuisine and wine of this region (along with some more regionally inspired fare). Andalusian-style *chicharrones* (fried pork rinds) and buffalo short ribs *adovada* (marinated in red chile) make terrific starters, while duck

confit with slow-braised collard greens, smoked bacon, preserved lemon, and hot-pepper vinegar is a perfectly prepared larger plate. The well-chosen wine list includes Torrontes, Albarino, and fine Rioja blends from throughout Spain. *Average main: $21 ✉ 1017 Paseo del Pueblo Norte, El Prado ☎ 575/751–3337 ⊕ www.elmeze.com ⊗ Closed Sun.–Mon. No lunch.*

★ Fodor's Choice ✕ **Love Apple.** *Eclectic.* It's easy to drive by the small adobe former chapel that houses this delightful restaurant a short drive north of Taos Plaza, just beyond the driveway for Hacienda del Sol B&B. But slow down—you don't want to miss the culinary magic inside. Chef Andrea Meyer uses organic, mostly local ingredients in the preparation of simple yet sophisticated farm-to-table creations like homemade sweet-corn tamales with red-chile mole, a fried egg, and crème fraîche, and tacos (using homemade tortillas) filled with grilled antelope, potato-gruyère gratin, and parsley gremolata. The price is right, too—just remember it's cash-only. *Average main: $15 ✉ 803 Paseo del Pueblo Norte ☎ 575/751–0050 ⊕ www.theloveapple.net ▭ No credit cards ⊗ No lunch.*
$$

★ Fodor's Choice ✕ **Orlando's.** *Southwestern.* This family-run local favorite is likely to be packed during peak hours, while guests wait patiently to devour perfectly seasoned favorites such as *carne adovada* (red chile–marinated pork), blue-corn enchiladas, and scrumptious shrimp burritos. You can eat in the cozy dining room, outside on the umbrella-shaded front patio, or call ahead for takeout if you'd rather avoid the crowds. Margaritas here are potent. *Average main: $9 ✉ 114 Don Juan Valdez La., off Paseo del Pueblo Norte, El Prado ☎ 575/751–1450 ⊕ www.orlandostaos.com.*
$

$ ✕ **Taos Pizza Out Back.** *Pizza.* Set in a funky timber-frame shack of a building with a large tree-shaded patio hemmed in with coyote fencing, this venerable pizza joint has cultivated a loyal following over the years for its thick-crust, creatively topped pies (plus very good pastas and salads). Distinctive pizza combos include the Ranchero, with Italian sausage, sundried tomatoes, smoked cheddar, and green onions; and the classic white pizza with fresh tomato, basil, ricotta, Parmesan, and mozzarella. Everything is available by the slice (they're massive), or in several pie sizes. Organic ingredients are favored, and there's a good list of beers and wines. *Average main: $11 ✉ 712 Paseo del Pueblo Norte, El Prado ☎ 575/758–3112 ⊕ www.taospizzaoutback.com.*
FAMILY

ARROYO SECO

★ Fodor's Choice ✕ **Sabroso.** *Modern American.* Reasonably
$$$ priced, innovative cuisine and outstanding wines are served in this 150-year-old adobe hacienda, where you can also relax in lounge chairs near the bar, or on a delightful patio surrounded by plum trees. The Mediterranean-influenced contemporary American menu changes regularly, but an evening's entrée might be pan-seared sea scallops, risotto cakes, and ratatouille, or rib-eye steak topped with a slice of Stilton cheese. There's live jazz and cabaret in the piano bar several nights a week. Order from the simpler bar menu if you're seeking something light—the antipasto plate and white-truffle-oil fries are both delicious. *Average main: $28 ✉ 470 NM 150 (Taos Ski Valley Rd.), Arroyo Seco ☎ 575/776–3333 🌐 www.sabrosotaos.com ⊗ No lunch.*

★ Fodor's Choice ✕ **Taos Cow.** *Café.* Locals, hikers, and skiers
$ headed up to Taos Ski Valley, and visitors to funky Arroyo
FAMILY Seco flock to this cozy storefront café operated by the famed Taos Cow ice-cream company. This isn't merely a place to sample amazing homemade ice cream (including such innovative flavors as piñon-caramel, lavender, and Chocolate Rio Grande—chocolate ice cream packed with cinnamon-chocolate chunks). You can also nosh on French toast, omelets, turkey-and-Brie sandwiches, black-bean-and-brown-rice bowls, organic teas and coffees, natural sodas, homemade granola, and more. *Average main: $8 ✉ 485 NM 150, Arroyo Seco ☎ 575/776–5640 🌐 www.taoscow.com ⊗ No dinner.*

TAOS SKI VALLEY

★ Fodor's Choice ✕ **The Bavarian.** *German.* The restaurant inside
$$$ the romantic, magically situated alpine lodge, which also offers Taos Ski Valley's most luxurious accommodations, serves outstanding contemporary Bavarian-inspired cuisine, such as baked artichokes and Gruyère, and braised local lamb shank with mashed potatoes and red wine–roasted garlic-thyme jus. Lunch is more casual and less expensive, with burgers and salads available. Bavarian is an excellent spot to fuel up before attempting an ambitious hike, as the restaurant is steps from the trailhead for Wheeler Peak and other popular mountains. There's an extensive wine list, plus a nice range of beers imported from Spaten Brewery in Munich, and traditional Swiss fondue is served Tuesday nights in winter. *Average main: $28 ✉ 100 Kachina Rd., Taos Ski Valley ☎ 575/776–8020 🌐 www.thebavarian.net ⊗ Closed for a few weeks in spring and fall and Tues.–Wed. in summer; call to confirm hrs outside ski season.*

WHERE TO STAY

The hotels and motels along NM 68 (Paseo del Pueblo), most of them on the south side of town, suit every need and budget; rates vary little between big-name chains and smaller establishments—Hampton Inn is the best maintained of the chains. Make advance reservations and expect higher rates during ski season (usually from late December to early April, and especially for lodgings on the north side of town, closer to the ski area) and in the summer. The Taos Ski Valley has a number of condo and rental units, but there's little reason to stay up here unless you're in town expressly for skiing—it's too far from Taos proper to be a convenient base for exploring the rest of the area. The area's many B&Bs offer some of the best values, when you factor in typically hearty full breakfasts, personal service, and, often, roomy casitas with private entrances.

Prices in the hotel reviews are the lowest cost of a standard double room in high season, excluding taxes, service charges, and meal plans. For expanded reviews, facilities, and current deals, visit Fodors.com.

PLAZA AND VICINITY

$ **Adobe & Pines Inn.** *B&B/Inn.* Native American and Mexican artifacts decorate the main house of this B&B, which has expansive mountain views. **Pros:** quiet rural location; fantastic views; beautiful gardens. **Cons:** a bit of a drive south of Plaza; least expensive rooms are a bit small. *Rooms from: $109* *4107 NM 68, South Side, Ranchos de Taos* *575/751–0947, 800/723–8267* *www.adobepines.com* *4 rooms, 2 suites, 2 casitas* *Breakfast.*

★ Fodor'sChoice **Casa Europa.** *B&B/Inn.* The main part of this
$ exquisite 18th-century adobe estate has been tastefully expanded to create an unforgettable B&B with old-world romance. **Pros:** attentive service; memorable setting and sophisticated style; smallest rooms are very affordable. **Cons:** short drive or leisurely stroll to town. *Rooms from: $115* *840 Upper Ranchitos Rd., Plaza and Vicinity* *575/758–9798* *www.casaeuropanm.com* *5 rooms, 2 suites* *Breakfast.*

$$$ **El Monte Sagrado.** *Resort.* Although rates have been lowered considerably in recent years, this posh, eco-minded, and decidedly quirky boutique resort—part of Marriott's distinctive, high-end Autograph Collection brand—is still among the priciest properties in the state. **Pros:** eco-friendly; imaginative

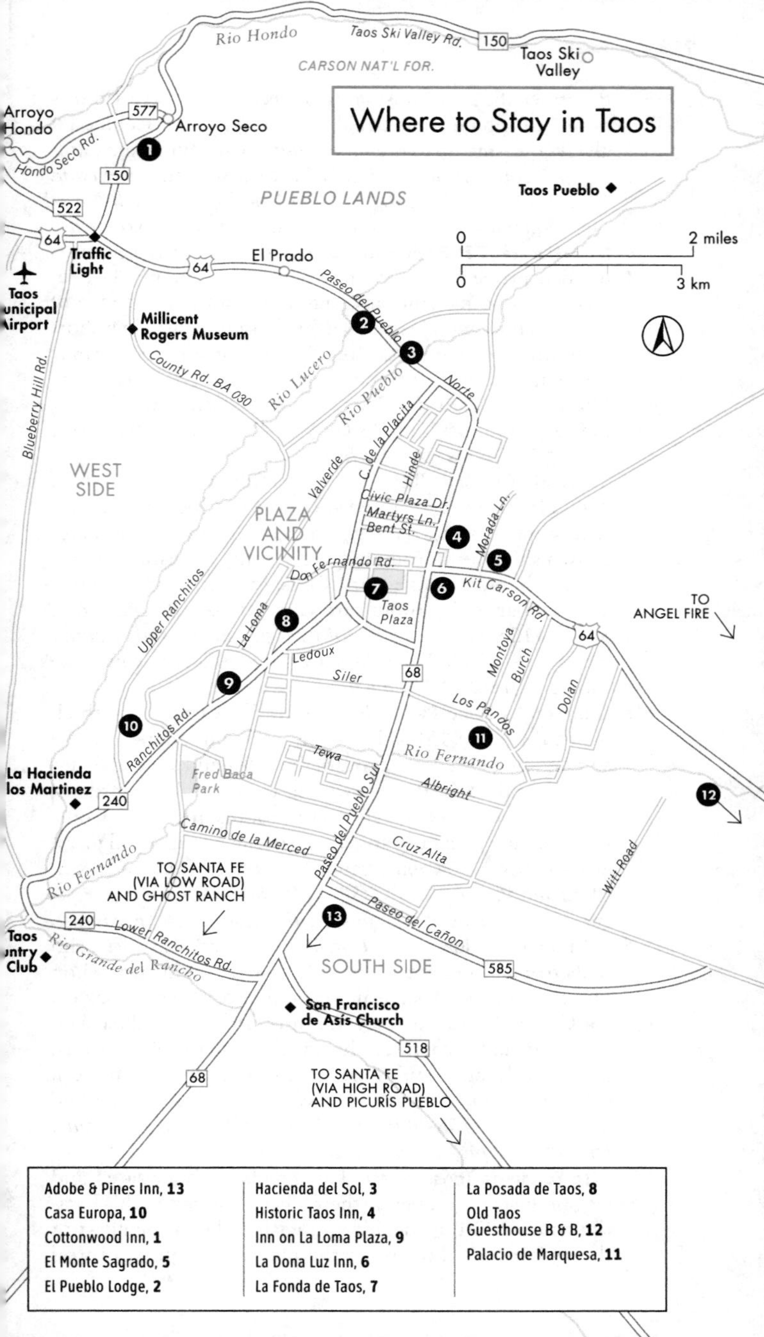

Where to Stay in Taos
Rio Hondo
Taos Ski Valley Rd.
150
CARSON NAT'L FOR.
Taos Ski Valley
Arroyo Hondo
577
Arroyo Seco
Hondo Seco Rd.
150
522
PUEBLO LANDS
Taos Pueblo
64
Traffic Light
Taos Municipal Airport
64
El Prado
0
2 miles
0
3 km
Paseo del Pueblo
Millicent Rogers Museum
County Rd. BA 030
Rio Lucero
Rio Pueblo
Norte
Blueberry Hill Rd.
C. de la Placita
Hinde
WEST SIDE
Valverde
Civic Plaza Dr.
Martyrs Ln.
Bent St.
Morada Ln.
PLAZA AND VICINITY
Don Fernando Rd.
Kit Carson Rd.
Taos Plaza
TO ANGEL FIRE
64
Upper Ranchitos
La Loma
Ledoux
Montoya
Burch
Siler
68
Los Pandos
Dolan
Ranchitos Rd.
Tewa
Rio Fernando
La Hacienda los Martinez
Fred Baca Park
Albright
240
Paseo del Pueblo Sur
Camino de la Merced
Cruz Alta
Witt Road
Rio Fernando
TO SANTA FE (VIA LOW ROAD) AND GHOST RANCH
240
Paseo del Cañon
Lower Ranchitos Rd.
Taos Country Club
Rio Grande del Rancho
SOUTH SIDE
585
San Francisco de Asís Church
518
68
TO SANTA FE (VIA HIGH ROAD) AND PICURÍS PUEBLO
Adobe & Pines Inn, 13
Casa Europa, 10
Cottonwood Inn, 1
El Monte Sagrado, 5
El Pueblo Lodge, 2
Hacienda del Sol, 3
Historic Taos Inn, 4
Inn on La Loma Plaza, 9
La Dona Luz Inn, 6
La Fonda de Taos, 7
La Posada de Taos, 8
Old Taos Guesthouse B & B, 12
Palacio de Marquesa, 11

decor; terrific spa. **Cons:** unusual decor isn't to everybody's taste and some rooms could use updating; service doesn't always measure up to premium rates; fee for Wi-Fi and parking. *Rooms from: $224 ✉ 317 Kit Carson Rd., Plaza and Vicinity ☎ 575/758–3502, 888/213–4419 ⊕ www.elmontesagrado.com ⇨ 48 rooms, 6 casitas, 30 suites 🍽 No meals.*

★ Fodor's Choice **El Pueblo Lodge.** *Hotel.* Among the budget-
$ minded properties in town, this well-maintained adobe-style hotel with a fun retro sign out front and the vibe of an old-school motel is a real gem. **Pros:** terrific value; short walk north of the plaza; free Wi-Fi. **Cons:** nothing fancy (but still bright decor and clean rooms). *Rooms from: $92 ✉ 412 Paseo del Pueblo Norte, Plaza and Vicinity ☎ 575/758–8700, 800/433–9612 ⊕ www.elpueblolodge.com ⇨ 50 rooms 🍽 Breakfast.*

$$ **Historic Taos Inn.** *B&B/Inn.* A 10-minute walk north of Taos Plaza, this celebrated property is a local landmark, with some devotees having been regulars here for decades. **Pros:** a short walk from the plaza; lushly furnished rooms, exudes character and history. **Cons:** noise from street traffic and the bar; some rooms are very small. *Rooms from: $140 ✉ 125 Paseo del Pueblo Norte, Plaza and Vicinity ☎ 575/758–2233, 888/518–8267 ⊕ www.taosinn.com ⇨ 40 rooms, 4 suites 🍽 No meals.*

$$$ **Inn on La Loma Plaza.** *B&B/Inn.* Surrounded by thick walls, this early 1800s Pueblo Revival building—and the surrounding gardens—capture the spirit and style of Spanish-colonial Taos. **Pros:** towering trees and lush gardens; inspiring views; extremely comfy rooms and beds. **Cons:** lots of stairs; on a busy street; one of the pricier small properties in town. *Rooms from: $200 ✉ 315 Ranchitos Rd., Plaza and Vicinity ☎ 575/758–1717, 800/530–3040 ⊕ www.vacationtaos.com ⇨ 5 rooms, 1 suite, 2 studios 🍽 Breakfast.*

$ **La Dona Luz Inn.** *B&B/Inn.* Paul "Paco" Castillo, who hails from a long line of local Taos artists and curio-shop owners, runs this festive and friendly B&B just a block off Kit Carson Road and a few minutes' stroll from the plaza. **Pros:** affordable rooms; a short walk from the plaza. **Cons:** in a slightly busy and noisy area (especially in summer). *Rooms from: $94 ✉ 114C Kit Carson Rd., Plaza and Vicinity ☎ 575/758–9000, 888/758–9060 ⊕ www.ladonaluz.com ⇨ 4 rooms, 3 suites 🍽 Breakfast.*

$$ **La Fonda de Taos.** *Hotel.* This handsomely updated and elegant historic property (there's been a hotel on this location since 1820) is ideal if you wish to be in the heart of the action—it's directly on the plaza. **Pros:** great central

location; the building has a great history. **Cons:** less than ideal if you're seeking peace and quiet. *Rooms from: $139 108 S. Plaza, Plaza and Vicinity 575/758–2211, 800/833–2211 www.lafondataos.com 19 rooms, 5 suites, 1 penthouse No meals.*

$$ **La Posada de Taos.** *B&B/Inn.* A couple of blocks from Taos Plaza, this family-friendly 100-year-old inn—the former home of early Taos Society artist Burt Phillips—has beam ceilings, a decorative arched doorway, and the intimacy of a private hacienda. **Pros:** a few blocks from the plaza; historic building; fantastic breakfasts. **Cons:** somewhat small rooms; not much privacy in the main house. *Rooms from: $139 309 Juanita La., Plaza and Vicinity 575/758–8164, 800/645–4803 www.laposadadetaos.com 5 rooms, 1 cottage Breakfast.*

★ **$$$** Fodor'sChoice **Palacio de Marquesa.** *B&B/Inn.* Tile hearths, French doors, and traditional viga ceilings grace this sophisticated inn. **Pros:** tranquil and secluded setting; on-site spa; walking distance from plaza. **Cons:** one of the higher-priced B&Bs in town. *Rooms from: $190 405 Cordoba Rd., Plaza and Vicinity 575/758–4777, 855/846–8267 www.marquesataos.com 6 rooms, 2 suites No meals.*

SOUTH SIDE

★ **$** FAMILY Fodor'sChoice **Old Taos Guesthouse B&B.** *B&B/Inn.* Once a ramshackle 180-year-old adobe hacienda, this homey B&B on 7½ verdant acres has been completely outfitted with the owners' hand-carved doors and furniture, Western artifacts, and antiques—all have private entrances, and some have fireplaces. **Pros:** beautifully appointed; private entrance to each room; serene setting. **Cons:** small bathrooms; some rooms are dark; a short drive from town. *Rooms from: $120 1028 Witt Rd., South Side 575/758–5448, 800/758–5448 www.oldtaos.com 7 rooms, 2 suites Breakfast.*

EL PRADO

★ **$$** Fodor'sChoice **Hacienda del Sol.** *B&B/Inn.* Art patron Mabel Dodge Luhan bought this house about a mile north of Taos Plaza in the 1920s and lived here with her husband, Tony Luhan, while building their main house. **Pros:** cozy public rooms; private setting; some excellent restaurants within walking distance. **Cons:** traffic noise; some rooms are less private than others. *Rooms from: $155 109 Mabel Dodge La., El Prado 575/758–0287, 866/333–4459 www.taoshaciendadelsol.com 11 rooms Breakfast.*

10

ARROYO SECO

$$ **Cottonwood Inn.** *B&B/Inn.* This rambling, two-story adobe house with 11 fireplaces and such classic regional architectural details as *bancos, nichos,* and high latilla-and-viga ceilings is right along the road to the ski valley, just a couple of miles south of Arroyo Seco's quaint village center. **Pros:** closer to Taos than most accommodations in Arroyo Seco; some of the largest and fanciest bathrooms of any B&Bs in Taos; great views of mesa and mountains. **Cons:** not within walking distance of any restaurants, one of the few accommodations close to Arroyo Seco. *Rooms from: $135 ✉ NM 230, just beyond junction with NM 150 ☎ 575/776–5826, 800/324–7120 ⊕ www.taos-cottonwood.com ⇒ 8 rooms 🍽 Breakfast.*

NIGHTLIFE AND THE ARTS

Evening entertainment is modest in Taos, but a few cool and distinctive nightspots keep things interesting for night owls. In addition to the bars listed here, note that a few restaurants in town are fun for bar options, too, including Old Martina's Hall in Ranchos de Taos and Sabroso in Arroyo Seco.

NIGHTLIFE

★ Fodor's Choice **Adobe Bar.** This local meet-and-greet spot, often dubbed "Taos's living room," books talented acts, from solo guitarists to small folk groups and, two or three nights a week, jazz musicians. It's a favorite spot for happy hour—there's a great menu of appetizers and cocktails, and the patio is a lovely hangout on warm evenings. *✉ Taos Inn, 125 Paseo del Pueblo Norte ☎ 575/758–2233 ⊕ www.taosinn.com/adobe_bar.html.*

Alley Cantina. Housed in the oldest structure in downtown Taos, this friendly spot has jazz, folk, and blues—as well as shuffleboard, pool, and board games for those not moved to dance. It's also one of the few places in town for a late-night bite. *✉ 121 Teresina La. ☎ 575/758–2121 ⊕ www.alleycantina.com.*

★ Fodor's Choice **KTAOS Solar Bar.** A fun place to cap off a day of exploring Arroyo Seco or playing outside in Taos Ski Valley, this bar and restaurant is part of the KTAOS Solar Center, home to the world-celebrated and solar-powered KTAOS (101.9 FM) radio station. It's a first-rate live-music venue that brings in all types of great rock, blues, folk, and indie bands. You can dine and drink in the festive bar or out on a sprawling green lawn with stunning views of the Sangre de Cristos. ✉ *9 NM 150, just east of Jct. with U.S. 64, El Prado* ☎ *575/758–5826* 🌐 *www.ktaos.com/StationBar.*

Taos Mesa Brewing. It's worth the 15-minute drive northwest of Taos Plaza to reach this fabulously bizarre looking pub and microbrewery near the airport, just a few miles east of the Rio Grande Gorge Bridge. In a high-ceilinged, eco-friendly building with soaring windows, sample exceptionally well-crafted Scottish Ale, Black Widow Porter, and Kolsch 45. Live music and entertainment is presented on indoor and outdoor stages—the latter has amazing mountain and mesa views. Tasty tapas and bar snacks are served, too. ✉ *20 ABC Mesa Rd., West Side* ☎ *575/758–1900* 🌐 *www.taosmesabrewing.com.*

THE ARTS

Long a beacon for visual artists, Taos has also become a magnet for touring musicians, especially in summer, when performers and audiences are drawn to the heady high-desert atmosphere. Festivals celebrate the visual arts, music, poetry, and film.

MUSIC

★ Fodor's Choice **Taos School of Music Program and Festival.** From mid-June to early August the Taos School of Music fills the evenings with the sounds of chamber music at the Taos School of Music Program and Festival. Running strong since 1963, this is America's oldest chamber music summer program and possibly the largest assembly of top string quartets in the country. Concerts are presented a couple of times a week from mid-June through early August, at the Taos Community Auditorium and at Taos Ski Valley. Tickets cost $20. The events at Taos Ski Valley are free. ☎ *575/776–2388* 🌐 *www.taosschoolofmusic.com.*

★ Fodor's Choice **Taos Solar Music Festival.** Solar energy was pioneered in this land of sunshine, and each year in late June the flag of sustainability is raised at the three-day Taos Solar Music Festival. Top-name acts appear, and booths promote alternative energy, permaculture, and other eco-friendly technologies. ✉ *Kit Carson Park, 113 Kit Carson Rd.* 🌐 *www.solarmusicfest.com.*

SHOPPING

Retail options on Taos Plaza consist mostly of T-shirt emporiums and souvenir shops that are easily bypassed, though a few stores carry quality Native American artifacts and jewelry. The more distinctive galleries and boutiques begin barely a block north on Bent Street, including the John Dunn House Shops, and extend just east on Kit Carson Road (U.S. 64). You'll find another notable cluster of galleries and shops, along with a few good restaurants, up north in Arroyo Seco.

ART GALLERIES

Inger Jirby Gallery. This popular gallery displays Jirby's whimsical, brightly colored landscape paintings. Be sure to stroll through the lovely sculpture garden. ✉ *207 Ledoux St.* ☎ *575/758–7333* 🌐 *www.jirby.com.*

Michael McCormick Gallery. This esteemed gallery is home to the sensual, stylized female portraits of Miguel Martinez and the iconic portraits of Malcolm Furlow. The gallery also has an extensive collection of Rembrandt etchings. ✉ *106-C Paseo del Pueblo Norte* ☎ *575/758–1372, 800/279–0879* 🌐 *www.mccormickgallery.com.*

★ Fodor'sChoice **Mission Gallery.** Set inside the historic former home of painter Joseph H. Sharp, Mission Gallery carries the works of early Taos artists, early New Mexico modernists, and important contemporary artists. ✉ *138 E. Kit Carson Rd.* ☎ *575/758–2861.*

Navajo Gallery. Here you can view and purchase the works of the internationally renowned Navajo painter and sculptor R. C. Gorman, known for his ethereal imagery—especially his portraits of Native American women. ✉ *210 Ledoux St.* ☎ *575/758–3250* 🌐 *www.rcgormangallery.com.*

★ Fodor'sChoice **Parks Gallery.** The works of the late and critically acclaimed mixed-media artist Melissa Zink are shown at this gallery specializing in contemporary paintings, sculptures, and prints, as are the acclaimed paintings by Jim Wagner. ✉ *127-A Bent St.* ☎ *575/751–0343* 🌐 *www.parksgallery.com.*

★ Fodor'sChoice **Robert L. Parsons Fine Art.** This is one of the best sources of early Taos art-colony paintings, antiques, and authentic antique Navajo blankets. Inside you'll find originals by such luminaries as Ernest Blumenschein, Bert Geer

Phillips, Oscar Berninghaus, Joseph Bakos, and Nicolai Fechin. ✉ *131 Bent St.* ☎ *575/751–0159, 800/613–5091* 🌐 *www.parsonsart.com.*

Studio de Colores Gallery. This El Prado art space shows the work of husband and wife Ann Huston and Ed Sandoval, who have extremely distinctive styles. Sandoval is known for his trademark *Viejito* (Old Man) images and swirling, vibrantly colored landscapes; Ann specializes in soft-hue still lifes and scenes of remarkable stillness. ✉ *119 Quesnel St., El Prado* ☎ *575/751–3502, 888/751–3502* 🌐 *www.decoloresgallery.com.*

★ Fodor's Choice **Total Arts Gallery.** If you have time for just one contemporary gallery, make a point of stopping in this building displaying works by some of the area's most celebrated artists, including Barbara Zaring, David Hettinger, Doug Dawson, and Ken Elliott. Themes vary greatly from abstract paintings and sculptures to more traditional landscapes and regional works. ✉ *122-A Kit Carson Rd.* ☎ *575/758–4667* 🌐 *www.totalartsgallery.com.*

SHOPS

BOOKS

Brodsky Bookshop. This venerable shop specializes in new and used books—contemporary literature, Southwestern classics, children's titles. Amiable proprietor Rick Smith can help you sort among the hundreds of titles. ✉ *226-A Paseo del Pueblo Norte* ☎ *575/758–9468.*

Moby Dickens. This full-service bookstore specializes in rare and out-of-print books and carries a wide selection of contemporary fiction and nonfiction. It's one of the finest independent bookshops in the state. ✉ *John Dunn House, 124-A Bent St.* ☎ *575/758–3050* 🌐 *www.mobydickens.com.*

CLOTHING

Artemisia. Look to this boutique for its wide selection of one-of-a-kind wearable art by local artist Annette Randell. Many of her creations incorporate Native American designs. The store also carries jewelry, bags, and accessories by several local artists. ✉ *117 Bent St.* ☎ *575/737–9800* 🌐 *www.artemisiataos.com.*

Francesca's. Long a fixture among the cluster of hip boutiques and galleries in Arroyo Seco, Francesca's is inside the former post office. The store specializes in reasonably priced, fanciful, and stylish threads with materials and design inspirations from India, Nepal, and Southeast Asia. ✉ *492 NM 150, Arroyo Seco* ☎ *575/776–8776* 🌐 *www.styleintaos.com.*

★ Fodor'sChoice **Overland Sheepskin Company.** This spacious store carries high-quality sheepskin coats, hats, mittens, and slippers, many with Taos beadwork. This is the original location of what has become a network of about a dozen stores, mostly in the West, and the setting—in the shadows of the Sangre de Cristos, amid a complex of several other shops along with a great little café for breakfast and lunch, is itself a reason for a visit. ✉ *Overland Ranch, 1405 Paseo del Pueblo Norte, El Prado* ☎ *575/758–8820, 888/754–8352* 🌐 *www.overland.com.*

COLLECTIBLES AND GIFTS

★ Fodor'sChoice **Arroyo Seco Mercantile.** Packed to the rafters with a varied assortment of 1930s linens, handmade quilts, candles, organic soaps, vintage cookware, hand-thrown pottery, decorated crosses, and souvenirs, this colorful shop is a highlight of shopping in the charming village of Arroyo Seco. ✉ *488 NM 150, Arroyo Seco* ☎ *575/776–8806* 🌐 *www.secomerc.com.*

Taos Drums. This is the factory outlet for the Taos Drum Factory. The store, 5 miles south of Taos Plaza (look for the large tepee), stocks handmade Pueblo log drums, leather lampshades, and wrought-iron and Southwestern furniture. ✉ *3956 NM 68, South Side, Ranchos de Taos* ☎ *575/758–9844, 800/424–3786* 🌐 *www.taosdrums.com.*

HOME FURNISHINGS

Antiquarius Imports. At this eclectic shop, you'll find rare Indian, Afghan, and African antiques and furniture along with contemporary, naturally dyed carpets made in Pakistan. There's a newer branch in Santa Fe, too. ✉ *487 NM 150, Arroyo Seco* ☎ *575/776–8381* 🌐 *www.antiquariusimports.com.*

Country Furnishings of Taos. Set inside a rambling, picturesque adobe house, Country Furnishings of Taos sells folk art from northern New Mexico, handmade furniture, metalwork lamps and beds, and colorful accessories. ✉ *534 Paseo del Pueblo Norte* ☎ *575/758–4633* 🌐 *www.cftaos.com.*

Taos Tin Works. This colorful gallery and studio in El Prado sells handcrafted tinwork, such as wall sconces, mirrors, lamps, and table ornaments by Marion Moore. ✉ *1204-D Paseo del Pueblo Norte, El Prado* ☎ *575/758–9724* 🌐 *www.taostinworks.com.*

NATIVE AMERICAN ARTS AND CRAFTS

Buffalo Dancer. This shop on the Plaza buys, sells, and trades Native American arts and crafts, including pottery, belts, kachina dolls, hides, and silver-coin jewelry. ✉ *103-A E. Plaza* ☎ *575/758–8718* 🌐 *www.buffalodancer.com.*

SPORTING GOODS

★ Fodor's Choice **Cottam's Ski & Outdoor.** This is your one-stop for hiking and backpacking gear, maps, fishing licenses and supplies, and ski and snowboard equipment and rentals, along with related clothing and accessories. There are also branches near the ski lifts at Taos Ski Valley and Angel Fire, and near the ski area in Santa Fe. ✉ *207-A Paseo del Pueblo Sur* ☎ *575/758–2822* 🌐 *www.cottamsskishops.com.*

Taos Mountain Outfitters. Stock up here on supplies for kayakers, skiers, climbers, and backpackers, as well as maps and books. The staff is happy to offer advice on where to pursue these activities, too. ✉ *114 S. Plaza* ☎ *575/758–9292* 🌐 *www.taosmountainoutfitters.com.*

SPORTS AND THE OUTDOORS

Whether you plan to cycle around town, jog along country lanes, or play a few rounds of golf, keep in mind that the altitude in Taos is higher than 7,000 feet. It's best to keep physical exertion to a minimum until your body becomes acclimated to the altitude—a full day to a few days, depending on your constitution.

BALLOONING

Hot-air ballooning has become nearly as popular in Taos as in Albuquerque, with a handful of outfitters offering rides, most starting at about $240 per person.

Eske's Paradise Balloons. This reliable company thrills participants with a "splash and dash" in the Rio Grande River as part of a silent journey through the 600-foot canyon walls of Rio Grande Gorge. ☎ *575/751–6098* 🌐 *www.taosballooning.com.*

Pueblo Balloon Company. This is one of the most popular outfitters in town for balloon rides over and into the Rio Grande Gorge. ☎ *575/751–9877* 🌐 *www.puebloballoon.com.*

BICYCLING

Taos-area roads are steep and hilly, and none have marked bicycle lanes, so be careful while cycling. The West Rim Trail offers a fairly flat but view-studded 9-mile ride that follows the Rio Grande canyon's west rim from the Rio Grande Gorge Bridge to near the Taos Junction Bridge.

Gearing Up Bicycle Shop. You can rent or buy bikes and equipment at this full-service bike shop. Staff can provide advice on the best routes and upcoming group rides. ✉ *129 Paseo del Pueblo Sur* ☎ *575/751–0365* 🌐 *www.gearingupbikes.com.*

FISHING

Carson National Forest has some of the best trout fishing in New Mexico. Its streams and lakes are home to rainbow, brown, and native Rio Grande cutthroat trout.

Blue Yonder Fly Fishing. Reasonably priced and with very knowledgeable guides, Blue Yonder can customize anything from a casual half-day outing for beginners to an extensive all-day adventure for experienced anglers—gear, instruction, and meals are included. ☎ *575/779–9002* 🌐 *www.blueyonderflyfishing.com.*

Taos Fly Shop & Streit Fly Fishing. Well-known area fishing guide Taylor Streit of the well-stocked Taos Fly Shop & Streit Fly Fishing takes individuals or small groups out for fishing and lessons. ✉ *308-C Paseo del Pueblo Sur* ☎ *575/751–1312* 🌐 *www.taosflyshop.com.*

GOLF

Taos Country Club. Views from the course at the Taos Country Club are some of the most dazzling in northern New Mexico. The layout is stunning and quite hilly, and water hazards are few. ✉ *54 Golf Course Dr., Carville Bourg* ☎ *575/758–7300* 🌐 *www.taoscountryclub.com* ⛳ *18 holes. 6123 yds. Par 72. Greens fee: $75* ☞ *Facilities: driving range, putting green, golf carts, pull carts, rental clubs, lessons, pro shop, restaurant, bar.*

HIKING

★ Fodor's Choice **Wheeler Peak.** Part of a designated wilderness area of Carson National Forest, travel to this iconic mountain summit—New Mexico's highest, at 13,161 feet—is by a rigorous hike or horseback ride. The most popular and accessible trail to the peak is the Williams Lake Trail, which is about 8 miles round-trip and begins in Taos Ski Valley just east of the Bavarian lodge and restaurant. Only experienced hikers should tackle this strenuous trail all the way to the top, as the 4,000-foot elevation gain is taxing, and the final mile or so to the peak is a steep scramble over loose scree. However, for a moderately challenging and still very rewarding hike, you take the trail to the halfway point, overlooking the shores of rippling Williams Lake. Numerous other rewarding hikes of varying degrees of ease and length climb up the many slopes that rise from the village of Taos Ski Valley—check with rangers or consult the Carson National Forest website for details. Trailheads are usually well signed. Dress warmly even in summer, take plenty of water and food, and pay attention to *all* warnings and instructions distributed by rangers. ✉ *Parking area for Williams Lake Trail is along Kachina Rd. by the Bavarian lodge and restaurant, Taos Ski Valley* ☎ *575/758–6200* 🌐 *www.fs.usda.gov/main/carson/home*.

LLAMA TREKKING

FAMILY **Wild Earth Llama Adventures.** Specializing in one of the more offbeat outdoor recreational activities in the area, this company offers a variety of llama treks, from one-day tours to excursions lasting several days in the Sangre de Cristo Mountains. Llamas are used as pack animals on these trips. Day hikes start at $99 and include gourmet lunches. Longer trips feature comfy overnight camping and delicious meals. ☎ *575/586–0174, 800/758–5262* 🌐 *www.llamaadventures.com*.

RIVER RAFTING

★ **Fodor's Choice** The Taos Box, at the bottom of the steep-walled canyon far below the Rio Grande Gorge Bridge, is the granddaddy of thrilling white water in New Mexico and is best attempted by experts only—or on a guided trip—but the river also offers more placid sections such as through the Orilla Verde Recreation Area (one of the two main parcels of newly christened Rio Grande Del Norte National Monument), just south of Taos in the village of Pilar (here you'll also find a small shop and café called the Pilar Yacht Club, which caters heavily to rafters and fishing enthusiasts), and the Rio Grande Gorge Visitor Center, a font of information on outdoor recreation in the region. Spring runoff is the busy season, from mid-April through June, but rafting companies conduct tours from March to as late as November. Shorter two-hour options usually cover the fairly tame section of the river.

Big River Raft Trips. In business since 1983, this respected outfitter offers dinner float trips as well as half- and full-day rapids runs (with picnic lunches included). ✉ *Pilar* ☎ *575/758–9711, 800/748–3746* 🌐 *www.bigriverrafts.com.*

Los Rios River Runners. The experienced guides here will take you to your choice of spots—the Rio Chama, the Lower Gorge, or the thrilling Taos Box. ☎ *575/776–8854, 800/544–1181* 🌐 *www.losriosriverrunners.com.*

Rio Grande Gorge Visitor Center. The Bureau of Land Management operates this visitor center in Pilar and can provide lists of registered river guides, information about running the river on your own, and plenty of other guidance on hiking and exploring the area. This is one of two visitor centers that make up the new Rio Grande Del Norte National Monument (the other is north of Taos, at the Wild Rivers Recreation Area). ✉ *NM 68, at Jct. of NM 570, Pilar* ☎ *575/751–4899* 🌐 *www.blm.gov/nm.*

SKIING

★ Fodor'sChoice **Taos Ski Valley.** With 113 runs—over half of them for experts—and an average of more than 300 inches of annual snowfall, Taos Ski Valley ranks among the country's most respected, and challenging, resorts. The slopes, which cover a 2,600-foot vertical gain of lift-served terrain and another 600 feet of hike-in skiing, tend to be narrow and demanding (note the ridge chutes, Al's Run, Inferno), but about a quarter of them (e.g., Honeysuckle) are for intermediate skiers, and another quarter are (e.g., Bambi, Porcupine) for beginners. Taos Ski Valley is justly famous for its outstanding ski schools, some of the best in the country. ✉ *End of NM 150, 20 miles north of Plaza, Taos Ski Valley* ☎ *575/776–2291, 866/968–7386* 🌐 *www.skitaos.org* 🎫 *Lift tickets $77* ⏲ *Late Nov.–early Apr.*

TRAVEL SMART SANTA FE

Visit Fodors.com for advice, updates, and bookings

GETTING HERE AND AROUND

A car is the best way to take in Santa Fe and the surrounding region. City buses and taxi service are available in Santa Fe and Albuquerque, but they're not very convenient for visitors. You can get around Santa Fe's Plaza area as well as some Taos and Albuquerque neighborhoods on foot, but a car is essential for roaming farther afield and visiting many of north-central New Mexico's most prominent attractions and scenic byways.

AIR TRAVEL

Most visitors to Santa Fe fly into Albuquerque, home of the region's main airport. From here, ground transportation is available to both Santa Fe (65 miles away) and Taos (130 miles), although most visitors rent a car.

Albuquerque's airport is served by all major U.S. airlines and has direct flights from most major West Coast and Midwest cities and a few cities on the East Coast (JFK in New York City on JetBlue, Atlanta on Delta, Washington Dulles on United, and Orlando and Baltimore-Washington on Southwest). However, Santa Fe's charmingly small and handily located airport has ramped up commercial service in recent years and now has direct flights on American Airlines from Dallas and Los Angeles, Great Lakes Airline from Denver and Phoenix, and United from Denver. Because there's less competition, flights into Santa Fe tend to cost a bit more than those to Albuquerque, but the convenience is well worth the extra expense for many travelers. If you're venturing north from Santa Fe up to Taos, you might also consider flying into Denver, which is an hour or two farther than Albuquerque (the drive is stunning) but offers a huge selection of direct domestic and international flights.

Flying time between Albuquerque and Dallas is 1 hour and 45 minutes; Los Angeles, 2 hours; Chicago, 2 hours and 45 minutes; New York, 4 to 4½ hours (direct, which is available only on JetBlue; factor in another hour if connecting).

TIP→ Long layovers don't have to be only about sitting around or shopping. These days they can be about burning off vacation calories. Check out *www.airportgyms.com* **for lists of health clubs that are in or near many U.S. and Canadian airports.**

Airport Information

Albuquerque International Sunport *505/244–7700* *www.cabq.gov/airport.* **Denver International Airport** *303/342–2000* *www.flydenver.com.* **Santa Fe Municipal Airport (SAF)** *505/955–2900* *www.santafenm.gov/?nid=171.*

GROUND TRANSPORTATION

From the terminal at Albuquerque's airport, Sandia Shuttle provides scheduled van service to hotels, B&Bs, and several other locations around Santa Fe; the cost per person is $28 one-way, $48 round-trip. RoadRunneR Shuttle & Charter offers airport shuttle van service as well as private rides from both the Albuquerque and Santa Fe airports to throughout Santa Fe and the surrounding area (including Albuquerque, Los Alamos, and Española)—for a price, you can charter a shuttle to just about any town in the state. RoadRunneR charges a bit more than Sandia from Albuquerque (about $40 one-way), but from Santa Fe's airport to local hotels, the cost is just $15 one-way and $27 round-trip.

Shuttle Contacts

RoadRunneR Shuttle & Charter ☎ *505/424–3367* 🌐 *www.rideroad-runner.com.* **Sandia Shuttle Express** ☎ *505/474–5696, 888/775–5696* 🌐 *www.sandiashuttle.com.*

BUS TRAVEL

There's no intercity bus service to Santa Fe, but you can get to Albuquerque from a number of cities throughout the Southwest and Rocky Mountain regions, and then catch a Rail Runner (see below) commuter train from Albuquerque's bus station to Santa Fe. This strategy really only makes sense if you're unable or unwilling to drive or fly; bus travel in this part of the world is relatively economical but quite time-consuming.

Bus Information

Greyhound ☎ *800/231–2222* 🌐 *www.greyhound.com.*

CAR TRAVEL

A car is a basic necessity in New Mexico, as even the few cities are challenging to get around solely using public transportation. Distances are considerable, but you can make excellent time on long stretches of interstate and other four-lane highways with speed limits of up to 75 mph. If you wander off major thoroughfares, slow down. Speed limits here generally are only 55 mph, and for good reason. Many such roadways have no shoulders; on many twisting and turning mountain roads speed limits dip to 25 mph. For the most part, the scenery on rural highways makes the drive a form of sightseeing in itself.

Interstate 25 runs north from the state line at El Paso through Albuquerque and Santa Fe, then angles northeast into Colorado and up to Denver. Interstate 40 crosses the state from Arizona to Texas, intersecting with Interstate 25 in Albuquerque, from which it's an hour's drive to Santa Fe. Although it's a long drive from big cities like Los Angeles, Dallas, and Chicago, a surprising number of visitors drive considerable distances to visit Santa Fe, which makes a great stop on a multiday road trip around the Four Corners region, or across the Southwest.

U.S. highways connect Santa Fe, Albuquerque, and Taos with a number of key towns elsewhere in New Mexico and in neighboring states. Many of these U.S. highways, including large stretches of U.S. 285 and U.S. 550, have four lanes and high speed limits. You can make nearly as good time on these roads as you can on interstates. Throughout the region, you're likely to encounter some unpaved surface streets. Santa Fe has a higher percentage of dirt roads than any other state capital in the nation.

Morning and evening rush-hour traffic is light in Santa Fe. It can get a bit heavy in Albuquerque. Keep in mind that there are only a couple of main routes from Santa Fe to Albuquerque, so if you encounter an accident or some other obstacle, you can expect significant delays. It's a big reason to leave early and give yourself extra time when driving to Albuquerque to catch a plane.

Parking is plentiful and either free or inexpensive in Santa Fe, Albuquerque, and Taos. During the busy summer weekends, parking in Santa Fe's most popular neighborhoods—the Plaza, Canyon Road, and the Railyard District—can be a bit more challenging. There are pay lots both downtown and in the Railyard District.

Here are some common distances and approximate travel times between Santa Fe and several popular destinations, assuming no lengthy stops and averaging the 65 to 75 mph speed limits: Albuquerque is 65 miles and about an hour; Taos is 70 miles and 90 minutes; Denver is 400 miles and 6 hours; Phoenix is 480 miles and 7 to 8 hours; Las Vegas is 630 miles and 9 to 10 hours; Dallas is 650 miles and 10 to 11 hours, and Los Angeles is 850 miles and 12 to 14 hours.

GASOLINE

Once you leave Santa Fe or other larger communities in the region, there's a lot of high, dry, lonesome country in New Mexico—it's possible to go 50 or 60 miles in some of the less-populated areas between gas stations. **For a safe trip, keep your gas tank full.** Self-service gas stations are the norm in New Mexico. The cost of unleaded gas in New Mexico is close to the U.S. average, but it's usually a bit higher in small out-of-the-way communities, and significantly cheaper on some Indian reservations—on the drive between Santa Fe and Albuquerque, the gas stations just off Interstate 25 at Santo Domingo Pueblo (exit 259), San Felipe Pueblo (exit 252), and Sandia Pueblo (234) all have very low-priced gas.

RENTAL CARS

All the major car-rental agencies are represented at Albuquerque's airport, and several of them have branches at Santa Fe airport (Avis and Hertz) or in downtown Santa Fe (Avis, Budget, Enterprise, Hertz).

Rates at the airports in Albuquerque and Santa Fe can vary greatly depending on the season (the highest rates are usually in summer) but typically begin at around $25 a day and $150 a week for an economy car with air-conditioning, automatic transmission, and unlimited mileage.

If you want to explore the backcountry, consider renting an SUV, which will cost you about $40 to $60 per day and $200 to $400 per week, depending on the size of the SUV and the time of year. You can save money by renting at a nonairport location, as you then are able to avoid the hefty (roughly) 10% in extra taxes charged at airports.

ROAD CONDITIONS

Arroyos (dry washes or gullies) are bridged on major roads, but lesser roads often dip down through them. These can be a hazard during the rainy season, late June to early September. Even if it looks shallow, don't try to cross an arroyo filled with water. Wait a little while, and it will drain off almost as quickly as it filled. If you stall in a flooded arroyo, get out of the car and onto high ground if possible. In the backcountry, never drive (or walk) in a dry arroyo bed if the sky is dark anywhere in the vicinity. A sudden thunderstorm 15 miles away can send a raging flash flood down a wash in a matter of minutes.

⚠ **Unless they are well graded and graveled, avoid unpaved roads in New Mexico when they are wet.** The soil contains a lot of caliche, or clay, which gets slick when mixed with water. During winter storms roads may be shut down entirely; check with the State Highway Department for road conditions.

At certain times in fall, winter, and spring, New Mexico winds can be vicious for large vehicles like RVs. Driving conditions can be particularly treacherous in passages through foothills or mountains where wind gusts and ice are concentrated.

New Mexico has a high incidence of drunk driving and uninsured motorists. Factor in the state's high speed limits, many winding and steep roads, and eye-popping scenery, and you can see how important it is to drive as alertly and defensively as possible.

Contact **New Mexico Department of Transportation Road Advisory Hotline** ☎ *800/432–4269* 🌐 *www.nmroads.com.*

ROADSIDE EMERGENCIES

In the event of a roadside emergency, call 911.

TRAIN TRAVEL

Amtrak's *Southwest Chief,* from Chicago to Los Angeles via Kansas City, stops in Las Vegas, Lamy (near Santa Fe), and Albuquerque.

The state's commuter train line, the *New Mexico Rail Runner Express,* runs from Santa Fe south through Bernalillo and into the city of Albuquerque, continuing south through Los Lunas to the suburb of Belén, covering a distance of about 100 miles and stopping at 13 stations. The Rail Runner offers a very inexpensive and scenic alternative to getting to and from the Albuquerque airport to Santa Fe (shuttle buses run from the airport to the

Rail Runner stop in downtown Albuquerque).

The *New Mexico Rail Runner Express* runs numerous times on weekdays from early morning until late evening, and less often on weekends. Tickets cost $2 to $10 one-way, depending on the distance traveled; day passes are available (and will save you money on round-trip journeys).

Contacts **Amtrak** ☎ *800/872–7245* 🌐 *www.amtrak.com.* **New Mexico Rail Runner Express** ☎ *866/795–7245* 🌐 *www.nmrailrunner.com.*

GETTING AROUND SANTA FE

BUS TRAVEL

The city's bus system, Santa Fe Trails, covers 10 major routes through town and is useful for getting from the Plaza to some of the outlying attractions. Route M is most useful for visitors, as it runs from Downtown to the museums on Old Santa Fe Trail south of town, and Route 2 is handy if you're staying at one of the motels out on Cerrillos Road and need to get into town (if time is a factor for your visit, a car is a much more practical way to get around). Individual rides cost $1, and a daily pass costs $2. Buses run about every 30 minutes on weekdays, every hour on weekends. Service begins at 6 am and continues until 10 pm on weekdays, 8 to 8 on Saturday, and 8:30 to 6:30 (limited routes) on Sunday.

Bus Contacts **Santa Fe Trails** ☎ *505/955–2001* 🌐 *santafenm.gov/index.aspx?nid=498.*

TAXI TRAVEL

Capital City Cab Company controls all the cabs in Santa Fe. The taxis aren't metered; you pay a flat fee based on how far you're going, usually $6 to $10 within the Downtown area. There are no cabstands; you must phone to arrange a ride.

Taxi Contact **Capital City Cab** ☎ *505/438–0000* 🌐 *www.capitalcitycab.com.* **Santa Fe Pedicabs.** Santa Fe Pedicabs offer a great alternative to getting around the heart of town, especially if your restaurant is a ways from your hotel. Friendly drivers can regale you with all sorts of information and trivia about Santa Fe as they whisk you along in bicycle carriages. Sit back and enjoy watching the crowds and the sights go by. You can nearly always hail a pedicab at the Plaza; from other locales, call to request a pickup. Cost is $1 per minute. ☎ *505/577–5056* 🌐 *www.santafepedicabs.com.*

TRAIN TRAVEL

Amtrak ☎ *800/872–7245* 🌐 *www.amtrak.com.*

GUIDED TOURS

Custom Tours by Clarice. These guided, 90-minute open-air tram excursions run four times a day from the corner of Lincoln Avenue and West Palace Avenue. Tours don't require reservations and offer a nice overview of Downtown. ☎ *505/438–7116* 🌐 *www.santafecustomtours.com.*

Great Southwest Adventures. Great Southwest Adventures conducts guided tours in 7- to 35-passenger van and bus excursions to

Bandelier, Tent Rocks National Monument, Taos (via the "Low Road" through the Gorge), O'Keeffe country, and elsewhere in the region. Guides are avid outdoors enthusiasts; in addition to their regular tour offerings, the company arranges single- and multiday custom trips throughout the region for groups of any size. ☎ *505/455–2700* 🌐 *www.swadventures.com.*

Rojo Tours. Established in 1986, this operator designs specialized trips—to view wildflowers, pueblo ruins and cliff dwellings, galleries and studios, Native American arts and crafts, and private homes—as well as adventure activity tours. ☎ *505/474–8333* 🌐 *www.rojotours.com.*

Santa Fe Detours. This reliable company offers daily walking tours (one in the morning and another in the afternoon) that depart from the Plaza; these last about 2½ hours. By reservation, you can also book several different guided auto tours, including both 75-minute and three-hour Santa Fe City excursions as well as longer trip to Taos (going up on the High Road, and then returning on the Low Road), Bandelier National Monument, the Puye Cliff Dwellings at Santa Clara Pueblo, and various venues for hiking and biking. Santa Fe Detours also offers full vacation planning and group tours throughout north-central New Mexico and the Four Corners region. ☎ *505/983–6565, 800/338–6877* 🌐 *www.sfdetours.com.*

Santa Fe Tour Guides. If you're trying to find an experienced local to lead you on a personal tour, call or visit the website of this member-based organization of more than 15 reliable and vetted independent tour guides. Guides are listed according to their areas of expertise (art, history, outdoor/recreation, and so on). ☎ *505/466–4877* 🌐 *www.santafeguides.org.*

ESSENTIALS

ACCOMMODATIONS

Although New Mexico itself has relatively affordable hotel prices, even in Albuquerque, tourist-driven Santa Fe (and to a slightly lesser extent Taos) can be fairly pricey, especially during high season, from spring through fall, with rates particularly dear during major Santa Fe festivals (such as the Indian and Spanish markets). Generally, you'll pay the most at hotels within walking distance of the Plaza and in some of the scenic and mountainous areas north and east of the city; B&Bs usually cost a bit less. The least expensive Santa Fe accommodations are south and west of town, particularly along drab and traffic-clogged Cerrillos Road, on the south side of town. Rates in Albuquerque, just an hour away, can be half as expensive (sometimes even less), exception during busy festivals, particularly the Balloon Fiesta in early October.

Check to make sure there's not a major event planned for the time you're headed to the area, and book well ahead if so.

If you book through an online travel agent (Expedia, Orbitz, etc.), discounter, or wholesaler, confirm your reservation with the hotel before leaving home—just to be sure everything was processed correctly.

Be sure you understand the hotel's cancellation policy. Some places allow you to cancel without any kind of penalty—even if you prepaid to secure a discounted rate—if you cancel at least 24 hours in advance. Others require you to cancel a week in advance or penalize you the cost of one night. Small inns and B&Bs are most likely to require you to cancel far in advance. Most hotels allow children under a certain age to stay in their parents' room at no extra charge, but others charge for them as extra adults; find out the cutoff age for discounts.

APARTMENT AND HOUSE RENTALS

Santa Fe (and Taos as well) is popular for short- and long-term vacation rentals. *See the book's individual chapters for rental agency listings in these locations.*

BED AND BREAKFASTS

B&Bs in these parts run the gamut from rooms in locals' homes to grandly restored adobe or Victorian homes. Rates in Santa Fe and Taos can be high, but there are several properties that offer excellent value for very comparable prices; they're a little lower in Albuquerque and rival those of chain motels in the outlying areas.

See the book's individual chapters for names of local reservation agencies.

Reservations **Bed & Breakfast.com** ☎ *512/322–2710, 800/462–2632* 🌐 *www.bedandbreakfast.com.* **Bed & Breakfast Inns Online** ☎ *800/215–7365* 🌐 *www.bbonline.com.* **BnB Finder.com** ☎ *888/469–6663* 🌐 *www.bnbfinder.com.* **New Mexico Bed and Breakfast Association** ☎ *800/661–6649* 🌐 *www.nmbba.org.*

HOME EXCHANGES

With a direct home exchange you stay in someone else's home while they stay in yours. Some outfits also deal with vacation homes, so you're not actually staying in someone's full-time residence, just their vacant weekend place.

Exchange Clubs **Home Exchange.com.** Home Exchange.com; $9.95 per month for a membership. ☎ *800/877–8723* 🌐 *www.homeexchange.com.* **HomeLink International.** HomeLink International ; $89 yearly for Web access and listing in the catalog. ☎ *800/638–3841* 🌐 *www.homelink.org.* **Intervac U.S.** Intervac U.S.; $99 for membership (includes Web access and a catalog). ☎ *800/756–4663* 🌐 *www.intervac-homeexchange.com.*

HOSTELS

Hostels offer bare-bones lodging at low, low prices—often in shared dorm rooms with shared baths—to people of all ages, though the primary market is young travelers, especially students. Most hostels serve breakfast; dinner and/or shared cooking facilities may also be available. In some hostels you aren't allowed to be in your room during the day, and there may be a curfew at night. Nevertheless, hostels provide a sense of community, with public rooms where travelers often gather to share stories. Many hostels are affiliated with Hostelling International (HI), an umbrella group of hostel associations with some 4,500 member properties in more than 70 countries. Other hostels are completely independent and may be nothing more than a really cheap hotel.

Membership in any HI association, open to travelers of all ages, allows you to stay in HI-affiliated hostels at member rates. One-year membership is about $28 for adults; hostels charge about $10 to $30 per night. Members have priority if the hostel is full; they're also eligible for discounts around the world, even on rail and bus travel in some countries.

Albuquerque, Cedar Crest (on the Turquoise Trail, near Albuquerque), Santa Fe, and Taos each have hostels.

Information **Hostelling International—USA** ☎ *240/495–1240* 🌐 *www.hiusa.org.*

EATING OUT

New Mexico is justly famous for its distinctive cuisine, which utilizes ingredients and recipes common to Mexico, the Rockies, the Southwest, and the West's Native American communities. Most longtime residents like their chile sauces and salsas with some fire—throughout north-central New Mexico chile is sometimes celebrated for its ability to set off smoke alarms. Most restaurants offer a choice of red or green chile with one type typically being milder than the other (ask your server, as this can vary considerably). If you want both kinds with your meal, when your server asks you if you'd like "red or green," reply "Christmas." If you're not used to spicy foods, you may find even the average chile served with chips to be quite a lot hotter than back home—so proceed with caution or ask for chile sauces on the side. Excellent barbecue and steaks also thrive throughout northern New Mexico, with other specialties being local game (especially elk and bison) and trout. Santa Fe, and increasingly Albuquerque and Taos, also abound with sophisticated restaurants specializing in farm-to-table contemporary regional cuisine, often with Mediterranean, Asian, and other global influences. It's also fairly easy to find extensive lists of interesting domestic and foreign wines, microbrew beers, and craft cocktails in this part of the state. The restaurants we list are the cream of the crop in each price category.

MEALS AND MEALTIMES

In cities like Santa Fe and Albuquerque, you'll find at least a few restaurants that serve food (sometimes from a bar menu) late, until 10 or 11, and sometimes a bit later on weekends. In smaller communities, including Taos, many kitchens stop serving around 8 pm. It's prudent to call first and confirm closing hours if you're looking forward to a leisurely or late dinner.

Unless otherwise noted, the restaurants listed in this guide are open daily for lunch and dinner.

PAYING

Credit cards are widely accepted at restaurants in major towns and cities and even most smaller communities, but in the latter places, you may occasionally encounter smaller, independent restaurants that are cash only. Many smaller establishments take MasterCard and Visa but not Discover and American Express.

For guidelines on tipping see Tipping below.

RESERVATIONS AND DRESS

In Santa Fe and Taos, it's a good idea to make a reservation if you can, especially at top restaurants during busy times. We only mention policies specifically when reservations are essential (there's no other way you'll ever get a table) or when they are not accepted. For the hottest restaurants in Santa Fe, especially in summer, book as far ahead as you can, and reconfirm as soon as you arrive. It's exceedingly unlikely you'll find a restaurant anywhere in New Mexico where men are expected to wear jackets or ties, but at upscale restaurants in Santa Fe, and to a lesser extent in Taos and Albuquerque, you may notice that the majority of diners dress in smartly casual attire—slacks, closed-toe shoes, dress shirts.

Online reservation services make it easy to book a table before you even leave home. You can use Open Table to reserve meals at any restaurants in Santa Fe, Albuquerque, and Taos.

Contacts **OpenTable** *www.opentable.com.*

HOURS OF OPERATION

Although hours differ little in New Mexico from other parts of the United States, some businesses do keep shorter hours here than in more densely populated parts of the country. Within the state, businesses in Santa Fe, Albuquerque, and Taos do tend to keep later hours than in rural areas. Hours of individual banks, post offices, and many other shops and services can vary greatly, so it's always wise to phone ahead before visiting.

Most major museums and attractions are open daily or six days a week (with Monday or Tuesday being the most likely day of closing). Hours are often shorter on Saturday and especially Sunday, and a handful of museums in the region stay open late one night a week, usually Friday. It's always a good idea to call ahead if you're planning to go out of your way to visit a museum, shop, or attraction in a smaller town.

In Santa Fe and Albuquerque, you can find some convenience stores and drugstores open 24 hours, and quite a few supermarkets open until 10 or 11 at night. Bars and discos stay open until 1 or 2 am.

MONEY

In New Mexico, Santa Fe is by far the priciest city: meals, gasoline, and accommodations all cost significantly higher in the state's capital. Overall travel costs in Santa Fe, including dining and lodging, typically run 30% to 50% higher than in Albuquerque and other communities in the state. Taos, too, can be a little expensive because it's such a popular tourist destination, but you have more choices for economizing there than in Santa Fe. As the state's largest metropolitan area, Albuquerque has a full range of price choices, and even high-end hotels and restaurants are quite a lot less expensive than in Santa Fe.

CREDIT CARDS

It's a good idea to inform your credit-card company before you travel, especially if you're going abroad and don't travel internationally very often. Otherwise, the credit-card company might put a hold on your card owing to unusual activity—not a good thing halfway through your trip. Record all your credit-card numbers—as well as the phone numbers to call if your cards are lost or stolen—in a safe place, so you're prepared should something go wrong. Both MasterCard and Visa have general numbers you can call (collect if you're abroad) if your card is lost, but you're better off calling the number of your issuing bank, since MasterCard and Visa usually just transfer you to your bank; your bank's number is usually printed on your card.

Reporting Lost Cards

American Express ☎ *800/992-3404 in U.S., 336/393-1111 collect from abroad* 🌐 *www.americanexpress.com.* **Discover** ☎ *800/347-2683 in U.S., 801/902-3100 collect from abroad* 🌐 *www.discovercard.com.* **MasterCard** ☎ *800/622-7747 in U.S., 636/722-7111 collect from abroad* 🌐 *www.mastercard.com.* **Visa** ☎ *800/847-2911 in U.S., 303/581-9994 collect from abroad* 🌐 *www.visa.com.*

PACKING

Typical of the Southwest and southern Rockies, temperatures can vary considerably in North-Central New Mexico from sunup to sundown. Generally, you should pack for warm days and chilly nights from late spring through early fall, and for genuinely cold days and freezing nights in winter if you're headed to Taos and Santa Fe (Albuquerque runs about 10 to 15 degrees warmer). Because temperatures vary greatly even within this relatively compact area, it's important to check local weather conditions before you leave home and pack accordingly. In April for instance, you may need to pack for nighttime lows in the 20s and daytime highs in the 60s in Taos, but daytime highs in the low 80s and nighttime lows in the 40s in Albuquerque. Any time of year pack at least a few warm outfits, gloves, a hat and a jacket; in winter pack very warm clothes—coats, parkas, and whatever else your body's thermostat and your ultimate destination dictate. Sweaters and jackets are also needed in summer at higher elevations, because though days are warm, nights can dip well below 50°F. And bring comfortable shoes; you're likely to be doing a lot of walking.

New Mexico is one of the most informal and laid-back areas of the country, which for many is part of its appeal. Probably no more than three or four restaurants in the entire state enforce a dress code, even for dinner, though men are likely to feel more comfortable wearing a jacket or at least a sport shirt in high-end restaurants in Santa Fe, especially during the summer opera season.

Bring skin moisturizer; even people who rarely need this elsewhere in the country can suffer from dry and itchy skin in New Mexico. Sunscreen is a necessity. And bring sunglasses to protect your eyes from the glare of lakes or ski slopes, not to mention the brightness present everywhere. High altitude can cause headaches and dizziness, so at a minimum drink at least half your body weight in ounces in water (150-pound person=75 ounces of water), and eat plenty of juicy fruit. When planning even a short day trip, especially if there's hiking or exercise involved, always pack a bottle or two of water—it's very easy to become dehydrated in New Mexico. Check with your doctor about medication to alleviate symptoms.

RESOURCES

ONLINE TRAVEL TOOLS

Check out the New Mexico Home page (*www.state.nm.us*) for information on state government, and for links to state agencies on doing business, working, learning, living, and visiting in the Land of Enchantment. Monthly *New Mexico Magazine* (*www.nmmagazine.com*) is a long-running publication with regular stories on culture and travel throughout the state. An excellent source of information on the state's recreation pursuits is the New Mexico Outdoor Sports Guide (*www.nmosg.com*). Check the site of the New Mexico Film Office (*www.nmfilm.com*) for a list of movies shot in New Mexico as well as links to downloadable clips of upcoming made-in-New Mexico movies. A wide range of reviews and links to dining, culture, and services in Santa Fe, Albuquerque, and Taos is available at *www.999dine.com*, a site that sells steeply discounted meal certificates to dozens of top restaurants in these cities. Visit *www.farmersmarketsnm.org* for information on the dozens of great farmers' markets around the state, *www.nmwine.com* for tours and details related to the region's fast-growing wine-making industry, and *www.nmbeer.org* for details on the North-central New Mexico's many craft breweries.

Safety **Transportation Security Administration** (*TSA*). Transportation Security Administration *www.tsa.gov*.

VISITOR INFORMATION

The New Mexico Department of Tourism can provide general information on the state, but you'll find more specific and useful information by consulting the local tourism offices and convention and visitors bureaus in Santa Fe, Taos, and Albuquerque.

Contacts **Indian Pueblo ultural Center** *505/843–7270, 866/855–7902 www.indianpueblo.org*. **New Mexico Tourism Department Visitor Center** *Lamy Building, 491 Old Santa Fe Trail, Old Santa Fe Trail and South Capitol, Santa Fe 505/827–7400 www.newmexico.org*. **Santa Fe Convention and Visitors Bureau** *201 W. Marcy St., The Plaza, Santa Fe 505/955–6200, 800/777–2489 www.santafe.org*. **USDA Forest Service, Southwestern Region** *505/842–3292, 877/864–6985 for fire restrictions and closures www.fs.fed.us/r3*.

TAXES

The standard state gross receipts tax rate is 5.125%, but municipalities and counties enact additional charges at varying rates. Sales tax in Santa Fe and Taos is just over 8%, and in Albuquerque it's 7%. If you're on a budget and plan on renting a car and/or staying in hotels, be sure to ask for the exact amount of your lodgers and rental car taxes, as they can be quite steep and can make a big dent in a tight budget.

TIME

New Mexico observes Mountain Standard Time, switching over with most of the rest of the country to daylight saving time in the spring through fall. In New Mexico, you'll be two hours behind New York and one hour ahead of Arizona (except during daylight saving time, which Arizona does not observe) and California.

TIPPING

The customary tipping rate for taxi drivers is 15% to 20%, with a minimum of $2; bellhops are usually given $2 per bag in luxury hotels, $1 per bag elsewhere. Hotel maids should be tipped $2 per day of your stay. A doorman who hails or helps you into a cab can be tipped $1 to $2. You should also tip your hotel concierge for services rendered; the size of the tip depends on the difficulty of your request, as well as the quality of the concierge's work. For an ordinary dinner reservation or tour arrangements, $3 to $5 should do; if the concierge scores seats at a popular restaurant or show or performs unusual services (getting your laptop repaired, finding a good pet-sitter, etc.), $10 or more is appropriate.

Waiters should be tipped 15% to 20%, though at higher-end restaurants, a solid 20% is more the norm. Many restaurants add a gratuity to the bill for parties of six or more. Ask what the percentage is if the menu or bill doesn't state it. Tip $1 per drink you order at the bar, though if at an upscale establishment, those $15 martinis might warrant a $2 tip.

INDEX

A

Abe's Cantina y Cocina ✕, *209*
Abiquiu, *134*
ABQ BioPark, *152*
Adobe & Pines Inn 🏨, *216*
Adobe Bar, *220*
Air travel, *230–231*
Albuquerque, 145
Santa Fe, 14, 15
Taos, 199
Albuquerque, *14–20, 141–194*
airport area, 144, 183
Barelas/South Valley, 143, 156–157, 170–171
climate, 145
dining, 157, 163–175
Downtown, 143, 156, 167, 170, 177, 180–181
East Side, 144, 162
exploring, 149–163
festivals and seasonal events, 17, 185
guided tours, 148–149
itineraries, 18–20, 147
lodging, 175–183
Los Ranchos/North Valley, 144, 159–160, 174–175, 181–182
nightlife and the arts, 183–187
Northeast Heights, 14, 160–161, 182
Old Town, 143, 149, 152–155, 164–167, 175–177
Old Town Plaza, 154
orientation and planning, 143–145, 149
price categories, 163, 175
shopping, 187–190
sports and the outdoors, 191–194
timing the visit, 145
transportation, 145–148
UNM/Nob Hill, 143–144, 157–159, 171–174
visitor information, 148
West Side, 145, 162–163
Albuquerque Aquarium, *152*
Albuquerque International Balloon Fiesta, *17*
Albuquerque Museum of Art and History, *152–153*
American International Rattlesnake Museum, *153*
Anderson-Abruzzo International Balloon Museum, *160*
Andiamo ✕, *59*
Andrew Smith Gallery, *97*
Antigua Inn 🏨, *75*
Antique shops, *101–102*
Antiquity ✕, *164–165*
Antonio's ✕, *209*
Apartment rentals, *236*
Aquariums, *152*
Architecture terms, *23–24*
Arroyo Seco Mercantile, *224*
Arroyo Vino 🏨, *62*
Art galleries and museums
Albuquerque, 152–153, 156, 158–159, 187–188
Ghost Ranch, 135
glossary of terms, 23–24
Los Alamos, 132
Santa Fe, 31, 32–33, 34, 38, 39, 40–41, 90–91, 96–101
Taos, 202, 203, 208, 222–223
Artichoke Café ✕, *167*
Aspen Vista, *119*
Atalaya Trail, *119*
Atrisco Café & Bar ✕, *62*

B

Back at the Ranch (shop), *104*
Ballet, *91*
Ballooning
Albuquerque, 191
Taos, 225
Bandelier National Monument, *131, 132–133*
Barelas Coffee House ✕, *164, 170–171*
Bars and lounges
Albuquerque, 183–184
Santa Fe, 88–90
Taos, 220–221
Bavarian, The ✕🏨, *215*
Bed and breakfasts, *236–237*
Bent Street Cafe & Deli ✕, *211*
Bert's Burger Bowl ✕, *62*
Best Western Rio Grande Inn 🏨, *175–176*
Bicycling and bike travel
Albuquerque, 191–192
Santa Fe, 117
Taos, 226
Bird-watching
Albuquerque, 192–193
Santa Fe, 117–118
Bishop's Lodge Resort and Spa 🏨, *84*
Bobcat Inn 🏨, *85*
Bookstores
Albuquerque, 189
Santa Fe, 103
Taos, 223
Böttger Mansion of Old Town 🏨, *177*
Boucher ✕, *62–63*

Bradbury Science Museum, *131*
Brewpubs, *184*
Buffalo Thunder Resort & Casino 🏨, *137*
Bumble Bee's Baja Grill ✕, *63*
Business hours, *239*
Bus travel, *231, 234*
Albuquerque, 145–146
Santa Fe, 14

C

Cafe Pasqual's ✕, *48–49*
Campanilla Compound 🏨, *75*
Camping
Santa Fe, 75
Car travel and rentals, *231–233*
Albuquerque, 146
roadside emergencies, 233
Santa Fe, 14
Taos, 200
Carson, Kit, *203, 205*
Casa Europa 🏨, *216*
Casas de Suenos 🏨, *177*
Casinos
Pojoaque Pueblo, 137
Cedar Crest, *126*
Chama, *135*
Chatter Sunday, *185–186*
Children's attractions
Albuquerque, 152, 153–155, 160, 161, 162, 163, 165–166, 172, 173, 180, 185
Bandelier National Monument, 132–133
Ghost Ranch, 135
Kasha-Katuwe Tent Rocks National Monument, 127
Los Alamos, 131
Sandia Park, 126
Santa Fe, 28–30, 40–41, 42, 57, 59, 60, 62, 63, 68–69, 75, 76, 77, 80, 81, 84, 85, 120
Taos, 203, 205, 206–207, 208, 212, 215, 219, 227
Valles Caldera National Preserve, 133–134
Chimayó, *137–138*
Chocolate Maven ✕, *65, 68*
Church of San Geronimo, *207*
Church Street Café ✕, *165*
Churches
Albuquerque, 155
Chimayó, 137–138
Ghost Ranch, 135
Santa Fe, 31, 36–38
Taos, 207
Cinnamon Morning B&B 🏨, *181*
Clafoutis ✕, *63*
Climate, *240*
Albuquerque, 145
Santa Fe, 14
Taos, 199
Clothing shops, *104–106, 189, 223–224*
Collected Works Book Store, *103*
Compound, *The* ✕, *58*
Concert venues, *91*
Cordova, *138*
Cottam's Ski & Outdoor (shop), *225*
Cottonwood Inn 🏨, *220*
Counter Culture ✕, *68*
Cowgirl BBQ ✕, *59*
Coyote Café ✕, *49, 51*
Crazy Fish ✕, *171*
Credit cards, *10, 239–240*
Cristo Rey Church, *37–38*
Cumbres & Toltec Scenic Railroad, *135*

D

Dining, *10, 237–238*
Albuquerque, 157, 163–175
best bets, 49, 164
menu guide, 21–23
price categories, 48, 163, 209
reservations and dress, 238
Santa Fe, 34, 39, 44, 47–72
symbols related to, 10
Taos, 209–215
tipping, 242
Dixon, *139–140*
Doc Martin's ✕, *211*
Dr. Field Goods Kitchen ✕, *68*
Don Gaspar Inn 🏨, *79*
Double Take at the Ranch (shop), *105*
Doubletree Hotel 🏨, *177*
Downtown Historic Bed & Breakfasts of Albuquerque 🏨, *180*
Downtown Subscription ✕, *39*
Dragonfly Café and Bakery ✕, *211*
Duran Central Pharmacy ✕, *165*

E

E.L. Blumenschein Home and Museum, *203*
Ecco Gelato (Santa Fe) ✕, *34*
El Farolito 🏨, *79*
El Mesón & Chispa Tapas Bar ✕, *51*
El Meze ✕, *213–214*
El Monte Sagrado 🏨, *216, 218*
El Museo Cultural de Santa Fe, *45*
El Pueblo Lodge 🏨, *218*
El Rancho de 🏨 **as Golondrinas,** *125*
El Rey Inn 🏨, *85*
El Santuario de Chimayó, *137–138*
El Tesoro ✕, *59–60*
El Zaguan, *38*

Eldorado Hotel & Spa 🏨, *75–76*
Embassy Suites Hotel Albuquerque 🏨, *180*
Emergencies, *233*
Estrella del Norte Vineyard, *136–137*
¡Explora!, *153*

F

Farina Pizzeria & Wine Bar ✕, *167*
Farm Shop at Los Poblanos, The, *189*
Festivals and seasonal events
Albuquerque, 185
Santa Fe, 42, 91–92
Taos, 221
Film, *91–92*
Fishing, *118, 226*
516 Arts, *156*
Five Star Burgers ✕, *212–213*
Flying Star Cafe ✕, *60, 171*
Food and cookery shops, *106–108*
Fort Marcy Suites 🏨, *75*
Fort Union National Historic Site, *130*
Fort Union Visitor Center, *130*
Four Seasons Resort Rancho Encantado Santa Fe 🏨, *84*
Fray Angélico Chávez Library, *28*
Frontier Restaurant ✕, *171–172*
Fuego ✕, *51*
Fuller Lodge Arts Center, *132*

G

Gabriel'sW, *64*
Galisteo Bistro ✕, *52*
Gardens, *15, 41–42, 152*
Garrett's Desert Inn 🏨, *79*
Gasoline, *232*
Georgia O'Keeffe Country, *134–135*
Georgia O'Keeffe Museum (Santa Fe), *28*
Gerald Peters Gallery, *38, 39, 98*
Geronimo ✕, *58*
Ghost Ranch, *135*
Gift shops
Albuquerque, 189
Taos, 224
¡Globalquerque!, *185*
Golden, *125–126*
Golden Crown Panaderia ✕, *165–166*
Golf
Albuquerque, 193
Sandia Park, 126
Santa Fe, 118
Taos, 226
Grove Cafe & Market ✕, *167, 170*
Gruet Winery, *161*
Gutiz ✕, *211–212*

H

Hacienda del Sol 🏨, *219*
Hacienda Nicholas 🏨, *80*
Harry's Roadhouse ✕, *68–69*
Harwood Museum, *202*
High Road to Taos, *17, 136–140*
Hiking
Albuquerque, 193
Santa Fe, 16–17, 118–120
Taos, 226–227
Hispanic cultural sites
Albuquerque, 157
Santa Fe, 45
Taos, 208
Hispanic imports, *190*
Historic Santa Fe Foundation (HSFF), *38*
Historic Taos Inn 🏨, *218*
Holiday Inn Hotel & Suites Albuquerque Airport 🏨, *183*
Home exchanges, *237*
Home furnishings shops, *101–102, 224*
Horseback riding, *120*
Horseman's Haven Cafe ✕, *69*
Hostels, *237*
Hotel Albuquerque at Old Town 🏨, *177*
Hotel Andaluz 🏨, *180*
Hotel Chimayó de Santa Fe 🏨, *76*
Hotel Parq Central 🏨, *180*
Hotel St. Francis 🏨, *76–77*
Hotel Santa Fe 🏨, *81*
Hotels, *10.* ⇨ *See also* Lodging
Hours of operation, *239*
House rentals, *236*
Houses of historic interest
Los Alamos, 132
Santa Fe, 38
Taos, 203, 205
Hyatt Regency Albuquerque 🏨, *181*
Hyatt Regency Tamaya 🏨, *182*

I

Il Piatto ✕, *52*
Indian Pueblo Cultural Center, *154–155*
Indian reservations. ⇨ *See* Native American sites
Inn and Spa at Loretto 🏨, *77*
Inn of the Anasazi ✕🏨, *52–53, 77*
Inn of the Five Graces 🏨, *79–80*
Inn of the Governors 🏨, *77*
Inn on La Loma Plaza 🏨, *218*
Inn on the Alameda 🏨, *80*

Inn on the Paseo 🏨, *77*
International Folk Art Market, *42*
Itineraries, *18–20*

J

Jackalope (shop), *102*
James Kelly Contemporary (gallery), *98*
Jennifer James 101 ✕, *172*
Jewelry shops, *108–109*

K

Kakawa ✕, *106*
Kasha-Katuwe Tent Rocks National Monument, *17, 127*
Kayaking, *194*
KiMo Theater, *156, 186*
Kit Carson Home and Museum, *203, 205*
KTAOS Solar Bar, *220–221*

L

La Boca & Taberna ✕, *53*
La Casa Sena ✕, *53*
La Chiripada Winery, *139*
La Choza ✕, *60*
La Crepe Michel ✕, *166*
La Cueva Cafe ✕, *212*
La Cumbre Brewing Co., *184*
La Dona Luz Inn 🏨, *218*
La Fonda 🏨, *32, 77, 79*
La Fonda de Taos 🏨, *218–219*
La Fonda del Bosque ✕, *157*
La Hacienda de los Martínez, *205*
La Luz Trail, *17*
La Posada de Santa Fe Resort and Spa 🏨, *80, 111–112*
La Posada de Taos 🏨, *219*
Las Vegas, *128, 130*
Las Vegas Chamber of Commerce Visitors Center, *130*
Libraries
Albuquerque, 157
Santa Fe, 28
Llama trekking, *227*
Lodge at Santa Fe 🏨, *84–85*
Lodging, *610, 236–237.* ⇨ *See also* Camping
Albuquerque, 175–183
best bets, 76, 176
Pojoaque Pueblo, 137
price categories, 74, 175, 216
rentals and rental agencies. 74
Santa Fe, 15, 73–86
symbols related to, 10
Taos, 216–220
tipping, 242
Loretto Chapel, *36–37*
Los Alamos, *131–132*
Los Alamos National Laboratory, *131*
Los Ojos, *135*
Los Poblanos Historic Inn & Organic Farm 🏨, *182*
Love Apple ✕, *214*
Low Road to Taos, *136*

M

Madeleine Inn 🏨, *80–81*
Madrid, *125–126*
Manitou Galleries, *99*
Man's Hat Shop, *The, 189*
Maria's New Mexican Kitchen ✕, *69*
Mariscos la Playa ✕, *57*
Markets, *45, 109*
Mauger Estate B&B Inn 🏨, *181*
Maxwell Museum of Anthropology, *158*
Mealtimes, *238*
Mellow Velo (shop), *117*
Michael's Kitchen ✕, *212*
Midtown Bistro ✕, *222*
Millicent Rogers Museum, *208*
Model Pharmacy ✕, *172*
Money matters, *239–240*
Monica's El Portal ✕, *166*
Mu Du Noodles ✕, *70–71*
Multipurpose sport center, *120*
Museum of Contemporary Native arts (MoCNA), *32–33*
Museum of Indian Arts and Culture, *39–40*
Museum of International Folk Art (MOIFA), *40–41*
Museum of New Mexico Press, *28*
Museum of Spanish Colonial Art, *41*
Museums. ⇨ *See also* Art galleries and museums
in Albuquerque, 152–155, 157, 158, 159, 160, 162
anthropology, 158
architecture, 38
ballooning, 80
children's, 42
Georgia O'Keeffe, 28
Ghost Ranch, 135
Hispanic culture, 157
history, 28–30, 152–153, 162, 205
Kit Carson, 203, 205
Los Alamos, 131
miniatures, 126
Native American culture, 32–33, 34, 39–40, 41, 42–43, 45, 154–155, 208
natural history, 153–154
nuclear science, 162
rattlesnakes, 153
Sandia Park, 126
in Santa Fe, 28–30, 31, 32–33, 34, 39–41, 42–43, 45

science, 35, 37, 174
in Taos, 202, 203, 205, 208
Music
Albuquerque, 185–186
Santa Fe, 92–93
Taos, 221

N

Nambé Pueblo, *136–137*
Nathalie (shop), *105*
National Hispanic Cultural Center, *157*
National Museum of Nuclear Science & History, *162*
Native American arts and crafts shops
Albuquerque, 190
Santa Fe, 109–110
Taos, 225
Native American sites
Albuquerque, 154–155, 163
Nambé Pueblo, 136–137
Pojoaque Pueblo, 136
Santa Fe, 25–30, 39–40
Taos, 206–207
Nativo Lodge Hotel 🏨, *182*
Nedra Matteucci Galleries, *99*
New Mexico Culture Pass, *30*
New Mexico History Museum, *28–30*
New Mexico Museum of Art, *31*
New Mexico Museum of Natural History and Science, *153–154*
New Mexico Railrunner Express, *14, 233–234*
New Mexico State Capitol, *36*
Nob Hill Bar and Grill ✕, *172–173*

O

O'Farrell Hats (shop), *105*
O'Keeffe, Georgia, *28*
Old Martina's Hall ✕, *213*
Old Santa Fe Inn 🏨, *81*
Old Taos Guesthouse B&B 🏨, *219*
Online travel tools, *241*
Open Space Visitor Center, *192*
Opera, *93*
Orlando's ✕, *214*
Outdoor activities and sports. ⇨ *See specific areas*
Overland Sheepskin Company (shop), *224*

P

Paa-Ko Ridge Golf Course, *126*
Pablita Velarde Museum of Indian Women in the Arts, *34*
Packing for the trip, *240*
Palace of the Governors, *16, 28*
Palacio de Marquesa 🏨, *219*
Pantry, The ✕, *71*
Parks and forests
Albuquerque, 152, 160
Bandelier National Monument, 132–133
Kasha–Katuwe Tent Rocks National Monument, 127
Pecos National Historic Park, 128
Sandia Park, 126
Valles Caldera National Preserve, 133–134
Parks Gallery, *222*
Patina (shop), *108*
Pecos National Historic Park, *128*
Peñasco, *139*
Performing Arts Center, *186*
Petroglyph National Monument, *163*
Photo Archives, *28*
Photo-eye Bookstore and Gallery, *103*
Plaza Café ✕, *54*
Pojoaque Pueblo, *136*
Price categories, *10*
Albuquerqe, 163, 175
dining, 48, 163, 209
lodging, 74, 175, 216
Santa Fe, 48, 74
Taos, 209, 216
Pueblo Bonito B&B Inn 🏨, *80*
Pueblos. ⇨ *See* Native American sites

R

Raaga ✕, *60–61*
Railroads, *14, 147–148, 233–234.* ⇨ *See also* Train travel
Ranch House ✕, *71*
Rancher's Club ✕, *173*
Ranchos de Taos, *206*
Randall Davey Audubon Center, *117*
Range Cafe & Bakery ✕, *173*
Residence Inn 🏨, *85*
Restaurant Martin ✕, *57*
Rio Grande Botanic Garden, *152*
Rio Grande Gorge Bridge, *17, 208*
Rio Grande Nature Center State Park, *160*
Rio Grande Zoo, *152*
River rafting
Santa Fe, 120–121
Taos, 227–228
Road conditions, *233*
Robert L. Parsons Fine Art, *222–223*
Robert Nichols Gallery, *110*
Rooftop Pizzeria ✕, *54*

S

Sabroso ✕, *215*
St. Francis Cathedral Basilica, *31–32*
Salinas Pueblo Missions National Monument, *155*

San Miguel Mission, *16, 36*
Sandia Park, *126*
Sandia Peak Aerial Tramway, *161*
Sandia Ranger Station, *88*
Sangre de Cristo Mountain Works (shop), *106*
Santa Fe, *11–140*
climate, 14
dining, 34, 39, 44, 47–72
East Side and Canyon Road, 12, 37–39, 58–59, 80–81
exploring, 25–46
festivals and seasonal events, 42, 91–92
guided tours, 117–118
itineraries, 20, 33, 38, 40, 45
lodging, 15, 73–86, 137
Museum Hill, 12, 39–43
nightlife and the arts, 87–94
North Side, 12, 46, 64–65, 84–85
Old Santa Fe Trail and South Capitol, 12, 34, 36–37, 56–57, 79–80
price categories, 48, 74
Railyard District, 12, 43–44, 45, 59–61, 81
Santa Fe Plaza, 12, 28–34, 48–49, 51–56, 75–77, 79
Sena Plaza, 34
shopping, 95–114
side trips, 123–140
South Side, 12, 46, 65, 68–72, 85–86
spas, 110–114
sports and the outdoors, 16–17, 115–122
timing the visit, 14
transportation and services, 14
visitor information, 116
west of the Plaza, 12, 44, 62–64, 81, 84
Santa Fe Bite ✕, *57*
Santa Fe Botanical Garden, *15, 41–42*
Santa Fe Children's Museum, *42*
Santa Fe Courtyard by Marriott 🏨, *85–86*
Santa Fe Dry Goods (shop), *106*
Santa Fe Farmers Market, *45, 109*
Santa Fe Opera, *93*
Santa Fe Sage Inn 🏨, *81*
Santa Fe School of Cooking, *70*
Santa Fe Spirits (shop), *107*
Santa Fe Trail, *127–130*
Santacafé ✕, *55*
Santuario de Guadalupe, *44, 45*
Seasons Rotisserie & Grill ✕, *166*
Secreto Lounge, *90*
Shed, The ✕, *55*
Sheraton Albuquerque Airport Hotel 🏨, *183*
Shidoni Foundry and Galleries, *100*
Shiprock Santa Fe (shop), *110*
Shohko ✕, *55*
Shopping
Albuquerque, 187–190
Santa Fe, 95–114
Taos, 222–225
Silver Saddle Motel 🏨, *86*
SITE Santa Fe, *45*
Skiing
Santa Fe, 121–122
Taos Ski Valley, 228
Slate Street Cafe ✕, *170*
Sophia's Place ✕, *174–175*
Spa at Four Seasons Rancho Encantado, *112–113*
Spas, *110–114*
Sporting goods shops, *225*
Standard Diner ✕, *170*
Symbols, *10*

T

Tamarind Institute, *158–159*
Taos, *195–228*
Arroyo Seco, 199, 208–209, 215, 220
climate, 199
dining, 209–215
El Prado, 198, 213–214, 219
exploring, 201–209
festivals and seasonal events, 221
itineraries, 203
lodging, 216–220
nightlife and the arts, 220–221
orientation and planning, 197–199, 201
price categories, 209, 216
shopping, 222–225
South Side, 198, 205–206, 212–213, 219
sports and the outdoors, 225–228
Taos Plaza and vicinity, 197, 202–203, 205–206, 209, 211–212, 216, 218–219
Taos Pueblo, 198, 206–207
Taos Ski Valley, 215
timing the visit, 199
transportation, 199–201
visitor information, 201
West Side, 198–199, 208
Taos Art Museum at the Fechin House, *202*
Taos Box, *227*
Taos Cow Cafe ✕, *209, 215*
Taos Pizza Out Back ✕, *214*
Taos Pueblo, *16, 198, 206–207*
Taos School of Music Program and Festival, *221*
Taos Ski Valley, *228*
Taos Solar Music Festival, *221*

Taxes, *241*
Taxis
Albuquerque, 147
Santa Fe, 234
Taos, 201
Teahouse ✕, *58–59*
Tecolate Cafe ✕, *71*
Ten Thousand Waves 🏨, *85, 113*
Terra ✕, *64–65*
Terra Cotta Wine Bistro ✕, *55–56*
Tesuque Village Market ✕, *65*
Theater
Albuquerque, 186–187
Santa Fe, 94
315 Restaurant & Wine Bar ✕, *56*
Tia Sophia's ✕, *56*
Time, *242*
Timing the visit, *14*
Tinkertown Museum, *126*
Tipping, *242*
Todos Santos (shop), *107–108*
Total Arts Gallery, *223*
Tours, *234–235*
Albuquerque, 148–149
High Road to Taos, 136
Santa Fe, 117–118
Trading Post Cafe ✕, *213*
Train travel, *233–234*
Albuquerque, 147–148
Santa Fe, 14, 234
Tramway rides, *161*
Transportation, *14, 230–235*
Truchas, *138–139*
Tune Up Cafe ✕, *72*
Turquoise Trail, *124–126*

U

University of New Mexico, *158, 159*
UNM Art Museum, *159*

V

Valles Caldera National Preserve, *133–134*
Vanessie ✕, *64*
Viet Taste ✕, *173*
Vinaigrette ✕, *61, 166–167*
Visitor information, *241*
Albuquerque, 148, 192
Bandelier National Monument, 133
Fort Union, 130
Las Vegas, 130
Santa Fe, 116
Taos, 201
Vivac Winery, *140*

W

Water Street Inn 🏨, *84*
Waxlander Gallery, *100*
Weather information, *240*
Websites, *241*
Wheeler Peak, *17, 226–227*
Wheelwright Museum of the American Indian, *42–43*
When to go, *14*
White Rock Visitor Center, *133*
Whoo's Donuts ✕, *44*
Wo' P'in Spa at Buffalo Thunder Resort, *114*
Wineries, *136–137, 139, 140, 161*

Y

Yanni's Mediterranean Grill ✕, *173–174*

Z

Zacatecas ✕, *174*
Zia Diner ✕, *61*
Zinc Wine Bar and Bistro ✕, *174*
Zoos, *152*

Photo Credits

Front cover: Ron Crabtree/ Photographer's Choice RF/Getty Images. [Description: Santa Fe]. 1, kman59//iStockphoto. 2, Chris Corrie/Santa Fe Tourism. 3 (top), Doug Merriam/Santa Fe Tourism. 3 (bottom), Ron Watts / age fotostock. 4 (top left), Richard Susanto/Shutterstock. 4 (top right), Robert Reck/Santa Fe Tourism. 4 (bottom), Stephen Husbands. 5 (top), © Ffooter | Dreamstime.com. 5 (bottom), Donald Riddle Images. 6 (top), Georgia O'Keeffe Museum. 6 (bottom), SumikoPhoto/iStockphoto. 7, Ian Cook / age fotostock. 8 (top left), Sumikophoto/Shutterstock. 8 (top right), Douglas Merriam/Santa Fe Tourism. 8 (bottom), Seth Roffman/Santa Fe Tourism. Chapter 1: Experience Santa Fe: 11, Jeffrey M. Frank/Shutterstock. Chapter 2: Exploring Santa Fe: 25, MarkKane.net/Santa Fe Tourism. Chapter 3: Where to Eat: 47, Douglas Merriam/Santa Fe Tourism. Chapter 4: Where to Stay: 73, Donald Riddle/Rosewood Inn of the Anasazi. Chapter 5: Nightlife and the Arts: 87, sutsaiy/Shutterstock. Chapter 6: Shops, Galleries, and Spas: 95, © Bambi L. Dingman | Dreamstime.com. Chapter 7: Sports and the Outdoors: 115, Corrie Photography/Santa Fe Tourism. Chapter 8: Day Trips from Santa Fe: 123, © Gloria P. Meyerle | Dreamstime.com. Chapter 9: Albuquerque: 141, sjlayne/iStockphoto. Chapter 10: Taos: 195, Russ Bishop / age fotostock. Spine: Henryk Sadura/Shutterstock.

NOTES

NOTES

NOTES

NOTES

Fodor's InFocus SANTA FE 2014

Publisher: Amanda D'Acierno, *Senior Vice President*

Editorial: Arabella Bowen, *Editor in Chief*; Linda Cabasin, *Editorial Director*

Design: Fabrizio La Rocca, *Vice President, Creative Director*; Tina Malaney, *Associate Art Director*; Chie Ushio, *Senior Designer*; Ann McBride, *Production Designer*

Photography: Melanie Marin, *Associate Director of Photography*; Jessica Parkhill and Jennifer Romains, *Researchers*

Maps: Rebecca Baer, *Senior Map Editor*; David Lindroth; *Cartographer*

Production: Linda Schmidt, *Managing Editor*; Evangelos Vasilakis, *Associate Managing Editor*; Angela L. McLean, *Senior Production Manager*

Sales: Jacqueline Lebow, *Sales Director*

Marketing & Publicity: Heather Dalton, *Marketing Director*; Katherine Fleming, *Senior Publicist*

Business & Operations: Susan Livingston, *Vice President, Strategic Business Planning*; Sue Daulton, *Vice President, Operations*

Fodors.com: Megan Bell, *Executive Director, Revenue & Business Development*; Yasmin Marinaro, *Senior Director, Marketing & Partnerships*

Editors: Eric B. Wechter, Perrie Hartz

Writers: Lynne Arany, Andrew Collins

Production Editor: Elyse Rozelle

1st Edition

ISBN 978-0-8041-4206-9

ISSN 2333–7958

SPECIAL SALES

This book is available at special discounts for bulk purchases for sales promotions or premiums. For more information, e-mail specialmarkets@randomhouse.com

PRINTED IN THE UNITED STATES OF AMERICA

10 9 8 7 6 5 4 3 2 1

ABOUT OUR WRITERS

Its complex cultural heritage first lured **Lynne Arany** to New Mexico for an archaeology career, which set her firmly in thrall to both this stunning state and its Mexico neighbor. Now a full-timer after a stint in her native New York, she has written often for *Fodor's New York City* and *Fodor's New Mexico*. Other credits include the much-lauded *New Mexico: A Guide for the Eyes* (consulting editor) and *Little Museums* (co-author); she has also written for the *New York Times* and *New Mexico* magazine. While interests and digressions center on traditional arts and vernacular architecture—whether in Budapest, Glasgow, or Tamazulapan—she is always up for a rambling trip along New Mexico's byways.

Former Fodor's staff editor **Andrew Collins** lives in Portland Oregon, but resided in New Mexico for many years and still visits often (usually stuffing his carry-on bag with fresh green chiles). A longtime contributor to this guide, he's also the author of Fodor's *Gay Guide to the USA* and has written or contributed to dozens of other guidebooks. He's the expert "guide" on gay travel for About.com, and he writes for a variety of publications (including *Travel + Leisure, New Mexico Journey, Sunset, Out Traveler,* and *New Mexico Magazine*).